£ 32-50

2814

c

D. H. Lawrence is often seen either as an artist whose novels are spoiled by the intrusion of ideas or as a philosopher whose ideas happen to be expressed in fiction; neither of these perspectives does justice to the unity and complexity of Lawrence's vision. In *The visionary D. H. Lawrence: Beyond philosophy and art* Robert E. Montgomery places Lawrence in the tradition both of great Romantic poet–philosophers, including Blake, Wordsworth, Coleridge, Shelley, Carlyle, and Emerson, and of the visionary thinkers Nietzsche, Heraclitus, and Jacob Boehme. Dr. Montgomery reveals a context which illuminates Lawrence's fiction and nonfiction, discusses his work in depth, and shows how Lawrence's place in the prophetic–poetic tradition compares to that of his contemporaries Eliot and Yeats. The result is an exploration of the vision that informs and unifies Lawrence's work.

THE VISIONARY D. H. LAWRENCE

THE VISIONARY
D. H. LAWRENCE

Beyond philosophy and art

ROBERT E. MONTGOMERY

CAMBRIDGE
UNIVERSITY PRESS

Published by the Press Syndicate of the University of Cambridge
The Pitt Building, Trumpington Street, Cambridge, CB2 1RP
40 West 20th Street, New York, NY 10011-4211, USA
10 Stamford Road, Oakleigh, Melbourne 3166, Australia

First published 1994

Printed in Great Britain at the University Press, Cambridge

A catalogue record for this book is available from the British Library

Library of Congress cataloguing in publication data

Montgomery, Robert E. (Robert Eugene)
The visionary D. H. Lawrence: beyond philosophy and art/Robert E.
Montgomery.
p.   cm.
Includes bibliographical references and index.
ISBN 0 521 45213 9 (hardback)
1. Lawrence, D. H. (David Herbert), 1885–1930 – Criticism and interpretation. 2.
Prophecies in literature. 3. Visions in literature. 1. Title.
PR6023.A93Z68149   1994
823'.912—DC20   93-5303CIP

ISBN 0 521 45213 9 hardback

UP

Contents

Acknowledgments

Many people have helped me along the way. Mark Schorer's enthusiasm for the first expression of my ideas gave me the courage to proceed. John Paterson read early drafts and consistently responded with patience and tact to the excesses of my ego. Owen Barfield's writings were a continuous source of inspiration, as was a memorable afternoon tea at his home in Kent, England. Lenora DeSio's love of language, intuitive teaching, and critical intelligence helped me see new possibilities in my writing. Melvene Dyer-Bennet, a guiding and sustaining presence in my life for many years, helped me understand why I needed to complete the book. William Park gave generously of his valuable time to read each chapter and to engage with the ideas. Michael Black of Cambridge University Press made invaluable suggestions for revision. Kevin Taylor, my editor at the Press, was consistently efficient, supportive, and helpful.

My greatest debt is to my wife Jill, who has been a true intellectual companion. She read every word of every draft, understood what I was trying to say, and told me when I had failed to say it. Her enthusiasm and belief in me never wavered, and for that I am profoundly grateful.

Introduction

THE IMAGINATION

Lawrence criticism from the start has been polarized around two conflicting, mutually exclusive views of his life and work. One view sees him as an artist whose ideas are relevant only insofar as they are embodied in a concrete work of art; the other sees him as a prophet whose real importance is his life and message. The two most influential early critics epitomize this polarity. For Middleton Murry, the essential Lawrence is not an artist at all: "At bottom he was not concerned with art." He was rather "the great life-adventurer of modern times," the author of a "gospel" transcending art (153–55). In rejoinder, F. R. Leavis insisted that Lawrence is above all an artist, "a great novelist, one of the very greatest, and it is as one of the major novelists of the English tradition that he will, above all, live" (*D. H. Lawrence* 4). Beyond their common estimate of Lawrence's greatness, there is no point of contact between these two distinguished critics. Leavis emphasizes Lawrence's "transcendent intelligence" and champions him as a positive moral force, but his interest is in exploring the aesthetic "resources of organization in the whole" (19), and his ideal is the "wholly impersonal" (177) work of art that has been fully rounded off and separated from its creator. For Murry, the tracts and the novels alike are interesting only as evidence of the thoughts and inner life of their creator. Leavis considers *Aaron's Rod* one of Lawrence's worst novels, ruined by "the direct presence of Lawrence's preaching" (29), whereas for Murry it is Lawrence's greatest novel because "there is more of

the essential Lawrence in this than in any other of his novels"
(200).

Neither of these positions is finally satisfactory, each leaving
us with only half of Lawrence. Leavis obscures one of the most
salient facts about Lawrence – that he devoted more of his
creative life to expository works setting forth a philosophy than
any other novelist, major or minor, who comes to mind. Murry
does not do justice to the fact that Lawrence was above all an
artist. Leavis rightly quotes Lawrence's own dictum as a
rejoinder to Murry: "Art speech is the only speech" (176).
Lawrence, however, was a certain kind of artist, whose aims and
achievement were fundamentally different from the novelists
with whom Leavis groups him. To compare Lawrence with
Jane Austen and Henry James is to miss Lawrence's essential
quality, the quality that made E. M. Forster place him in a
special category with Dostoevsky and Melville as a "prophetic"
novelist. According to Forster's *Aspects of the Novel*, we find in
Lawrence "colour, gesture and outline in people and things, the
usual stock-in-trade of the novelist, but evolved by such a
different process that they belong to a new world" (144). We
realize that "he is not looking at the tables and chairs at all"
(127); his vision "reaches back" to the "infinity [that] attends
them" (132). Lawrence wanted to lead us into deeper levels of
awareness, to move towards the cosmic, towards, in other
words, the religious dimension that Murry emphasizes. It was
Lawrence after all who said, "I always feel as if I stood naked
for the fire of Almighty God to go through me – and it's rather
an awful feeling. One has to be so terribly religious, to be an
artist" (*Letters* 1 : 519).

Succeeding critics have taken up positions on either side
of the Leavis-Murry divide. Eliseo Vivas finds that there are
"two Lawrences," the pure artist and the impure prophet.
When the artist is in the ascendancy, in the novels from *Sons and
Lovers* to *Women in Love*, the novels are "triumphs"; when the
prophet takes over, from *Aaron's Rod* on, they are "failures."
Vivas does not believe it possible for the artist and prophet to
coexist in the same work: "to find an 'ethic' in a poet is to turn
the poet into a moralist and to deny him his role as poet" (293).

William York Tindall, on the other hand, agrees with Murry: "Mr. Murry is correct in considering Lawrence a prophet rather than an artist." Tindall views Lawrence as a poor artist, a "disappointed saviour" whose "novels became the only outlet for his zeal ... But literature's loss was philosophy's gain" (24–28).

This divergence of critical opinion is so extreme that it raises the question whether our critical categories are adequate to deal with a phenomenon like Lawrence. We can either treat him as an artist or as a philosopher, it seems, but there is no term for a third possibility which is both artist and philosopher at once. Yet an integrated view of Lawrence will have to embrace both the poet and the prophet, in the belief that, in Mary Freeman's words, "the rigorous dichotomizing of the artist from the prophet destroys the basic unity of his work" (10). A truly unified view will have to penetrate to the ground of unity between the fiction and philosophy, to see them as twin products of the same consciousness. To do this, we will have to understand not only the ways in which the fiction is prophetic but also the ways in which the philosophy is poetic. We will have to recognize, with Mark Spilka, that "the custom to divide D. H. Lawrence into aesthetic and prophetic halves" prevents us from seeing that his creative work is "as prophetic and didactic, in its own way, as his sermons and pronouncements" (11). We will also have to recognize that his didactic and expository works are products of the same creative imagination and that they exploit the imaginative resources of language to communicate to the feelings as well as to the intellect.

Lawrence himself leaves no doubt that his own goal is the union of fiction and philosophy. He says in his essay on "The Future of the Novel":

Plato's Dialogues, too, are queer little novels. It seems to me it was the greatest pity in the world, when philosophy and fiction got split. They used to be one, right from the days of myth. Then they went and parted, like a nagging married couple, with Aristotle and Thomas Aquinas and that beastly Kant. So the novel went sloppy, and philosophy went abstract-dry. The two should come together again, in the novel. (155)

Despite Lawrence's casualness of tone, this is a deeply considered statement and tells us something essential, at least about his intentions if not his achievement. Philosophy and fiction used to be one. He is thinking not only of Plato but of ancient myth, which, in the words of the Frankforts in their *Before Philosophy*, "is a form of poetry which transcends poetry in that it proclaims a truth; a form of reasoning which transcends reasoning in that it wants to bring about the truth it proclaims" (3). Myth provides a story, a narrative, that is not just an imitation of a piece of life but that is also truth, a true explanation of the "why" of things, and a motive to action. This synthesis Lawrence wants to recapture in the modern art-form of the novel.

But it is also essential to realize that the ancient union of art and philosophy means as well that the philosophy was artistic. Lawrence is thinking of the pre-Socratic philosophers as well as of Plato, Greek tragedy, and myth. We cannot grasp the nature of his philosophical writings without realizing that for him, as he says in *Apocalypse*, the "pagan thinkers were necessarily poets" (96). It was "the greatest pity in the world" when philosophy "went abstract-dry." By excluding Aristotle and Aquinas and Kant, Lawrence makes it clear that by "philosophy" he means something very different from what we ordinarily think of as philosophy. His philosophy is not abstract or logical, not an attempt to arrive at a systematically rational understanding of the world. Philosophy for Lawrence is what he found in the thought of the ancients, "a great and intricately developed sensual awareness, or sense-awareness, and sense-knowledge": "It was a great depth of knowledge arrived at direct, by instinct and intuition, as we say, not by reason. It was a knowledge based not on words but on images. The abstraction was not into generalisations or into qualities, but into symbols. And the connection was not logical but emotional" (*Apocalypse* 91).

In Lawrence's view, however, the modern mind, after more than two thousand years of abstract conceptualizing, simply cannot conceive the synthesis that he has in mind. To the modern mind, art and philosophy, image and concept, feeling and reason, action and truth, are distinct and separate. In order to understand Lawrence, we must thus transcend our normal categories. This requires an extraordinary effort of thought, but without it we cannot grasp Lawrence in his wholeness. Without a fundamental reconceptualizing of art and philosophy we will be left with a false dichotomy and a false choice between the prophet and the poet.

Interestingly, it is F. R. Leavis who has come the closest to overcoming the split. In his *Thought, Words and Creativity: Art and Thought in Lawrence*, published twenty years after his first book on Lawrence, Leavis stresses that Lawrence "demanded that one should transcend – transcend so impossibly – the common-sense, the whole cultural ethos, in which one had been brought up, and in terms of which one did one's thinking" (48–49). "Our civilization desperately lacks the thought it has lost the power even to recognize *as* thought – the thought that entails the creative writer's kind of creativity" (93). *Thought, Words and Creativity* is the fruit of a major critic's lifelong engagement with Lawrence and achieves a balance missing from his earlier work. He insists throughout on the essential identity between the "art-which-is-thought" of the novels and the art-thought of the essays. There can be "no originative priority as thought ascribable either to *Women in Love* on the one hand or to *Psychoanalysis and the Unconscious* on the other – they derive in perfect directness from the one vital intelligence and the one achieved wholeness of individual being…" (22).

Leavis's sustained and brilliant meditation needs to be read in its own right, but two essential points emerge as starting points for further discussion. The first point is Leavis's emphasis on the *imagination* as the source of Lawrence's thought. "The live, the *living* nature of Lawrence's thought" (94), its essential creativity in both its expository and fictional modes, is due to its origin in the imagination. Leavis quotes the following passage from Lawrence's "Introduction to These Paintings":

Any creative act occupies the whole consciousness of a man. This is true of the great discoveries of science as well as art. The truly great discoveries of science and real works of art are made by the whole consciousness of man working together in unison and oneness: instinct, intuition, mind, intellect all fused into one complete consciousness, and grasping what we may call a complete truth, or a complete vision, a complete revelation in sound. A discovery, artistic or otherwise, may be more or less intuitional, more or less mental; but intuition will have entered into it and mind will have entered too. The whole consciousness is concerned in every case. And a painting requires the activity of the whole imagination, for it is made of imagery, and the imagination is that form of the complete consciousness in which predominated the intuitive awareness of forms, images, the *physical* awareness. (573–74)

There is no better statement in Lawrence of his fundamental awareness that in the "whole consciousness," which is the "whole imagination," the instinctual, the intellectual, the intuitional and the physical are all present at once.

Leavis's second essential point, closely related to the first, is that Lawrence's

approach to his theme, and his mode of developing his thought, are nowhere a philosopher's, and his aphorism, "Art-speech is the only speech," bears not only on those imaginative creations of his that are in the full sense creative works, but on his discursive writings too; it is a conclusion ... of the most important kind about the nature of thought. (40–41)

Leavis insists with Lawrence that real thinking, that is, thinking concerned with life, does not start "from a mathematico-logical assumption about the criteria of valid thought" (23), which is why Lawrence's thinking has nothing in common with Aristotle, Aquinas, or "that beastly Kant," and even less in common with what Bertrand Russell or A. J. Ayer call thinking. This is so because, in Lawrence's words, "Logic is far too coarse to make the subtle distinctions life demands" (23).

We need not go as far back as the Greeks to find examples of the union of art and philosophy. There are numerous examples among the Romantics, who are Lawrence's closest predecessors. As Ernst Cassirer says in his *Essay on Man*, "the highest aim of all the romantic thinkers" was "to poeticize philosophy and to philosophize poetry" (199). Coleridge for instance says in the *Biographia Literaria* that "no man was ever yet a great poet, without being at the same time a profound philosopher" (2: 25–26). Plato wrote "poetry of the highest kind" (2: 27) and

Shakespeare "gave proof of a most profound, energetic & philosophical mind" (*Notebooks* 3: 3290). Shelley echoed Coleridge in proclaiming in *A Defense of Poetry* that Shakespeare and Dante were "philosophers of the very loftiest power" and that Plato and Bacon were "poets" (421–22). Everywhere we turn among the great English Romantics, we find this insistence on the unity of the poetic and the philosophical and the prophetic, whether it is in Keats's belief in "the truth of Imagination" (37) or Blake's affirmation of the unity of the "Poetic" and "Prophetic" characters (2) or in Wordsworth's vision of "Poets, even as Prophets, each with each / Connected in a mighty scheme of truth" (*Prelude* 226).

The primary consideration for the Romantics is the greatness or spiritual stature of a man, and this greatness can manifest in any number of ways. As Shelley has it, "Poets, according to the circumstances of the age and nation in which they appeared, were called, in the earlier epochs of the world legislators, or prophets" (19). Carlyle's heroes have in common the possession of "intellect," "vision," or "power of insight," but may be anything from a poet to a founder of a new religion to a general. Sometimes the hero will be a "Poet in word; or failing that, perhaps still better, a Poet in act. Whether he write at all; and if so, whether in prose or in verse, will depend on accidents" (*Heroes* 337). In his refusal to separate life, art, and thought, Lawrence is thus a pure Romantic, perhaps the last.

Lawrence also shares with the "Visionary Company" of the great Romantics an apocalyptic intention. He wants nothing less than a new revelation or vision that will renew the world. The visionary's is a mode of total knowledge, preceding and transcending the split between art and philosophy, which is itself a symptom of man's postlapsarian state. Lawrence believed that the restoration of man to wholeness of being will occur when "the unison between art and philosophy is complete, then knowledge will be in full, not always in part, as it is now" (*Symbolic* 138). We are reminded of St. Paul, as well as Blake's "Endeavor to Restore what the Ancients called the Golden Age" (545) or Wordsworth's questioning why "Paradise, and groves Elysian" should be "A history only of departed

things" (*Poetical* 590). Lawrence's agenda is the agenda of the
Carlylean hero and the Shelleyan visionary poet. The "seeing
eye" of Carlyle's hero enables him to penetrate the mystery of
the universe and to bring us a new vision: "That always is his
message; he is to reveal that to us – that sacred mystery which
he more than others lives ever present with" (314). For Shelley,
the visionary "creates anew the universe" by "purging from
our inward sight the film of familiarity which obscures from us
the wonder of our being." True poetry unifies our being, "It
compels us to feel that which we know" (445).

It is the imagination that is explicitly identified by Blake,
Wordsworth, Shelley, and Carlyle as the faculty of apocalypse
and vision, and to understand this central Romantic concept we
need to turn to Coleridge, whose famous definition in *Biographia
Literaria* is at once the most influential and the most comprehensive:

The IMAGINATION then I consider either as primary, or secondary. The
primary IMAGINATION I hold to be the living Power and prime Agent
of all human Perception, and as a repetition in the finite mind of the
eternal act of creation in the infinite I AM. The secondary I consider as
an echo of the former, co-existing with the conscious will, yet still as
identical with the primary in the *kind* of its agency, and differing only
in *degree*, and in the *mode* of its operation. (1 : 304)

The primary imagination is associated with the divine "act of
creation" of the universe itself, which is repeated in the act of
perception of the individual or finite mind. The secondary
imagination is identical in kind with the primary, yet differs in
its operation. By asserting a radical identity in "*kind*" between
the individual mind and the mind of God, Coleridge establishes
the basis for his belief in a fundamental union between the self
and nature – and therefore in the capacity of the imagination to
know and communicate reality. The secondary imagination is
the "unifying" or "reconciling" power that produces poetry,
but it has other equally important aspects. According to the
editors of the Bollingen edition of the *Biographia*, the imagination
works on three different but analogous levels. These three
reconciliations are represented by perception, art, and phil-

osophy. Each involves a mingling or union of "the individual I am" with the created universe, the work of "the infinite I AM.' The imagination thus performs three syntheses that are the same in *kind* but that differ in *degree*" (lxxxii). There is a "philosophic imagination" as well as a poetic. Just as the philosophic imagination seizes the central phenomenon in nature and renders it translucent by revealing the laws that created it, so the poetic imagination creates the relevant symbol that reconciles "the general, with the concrete; the idea, with the image" (2: 17). Without pursuing the complexities of Coleridge's theory of the imagination, it is only necessary to emphasize here Coleridge's insistence on the oneness of the imagination, whether in its poetic or philosophic aspect, whether in the "visions" of the Hebrew poet-prophets or in the intellectual "intuitions" of Plotinus.

We can scarcely exaggerate the status of the imagination in Romantic thought. It is associated with the divine itself; it is the organ of revelation. Coleridge calls it a "sacred power" (*Biographia* 1: 241) and Wordsworth calls it "the vision and the faculty divine" (*Poetical* 592). For Coleridge, imagination has the power to awaken "the mind's attention from the lethargy of custom, and direct it to the loveliness and the wonders of the world before us; an inexhaustible treasure, but for which in consequence of the film of familiarity and selfish solicitude we have eyes, yet see not, ears that hear not, and hearts that neither feel nor understand" (*Biographia* 2: 7). The imagination for Wordsworth reveals "a new world" in the midst of "life's everyday appearances" (*Prelude* 228). Coleridge's Biblical language and Wordsworth's allusions to Christ's promise of a "new world" and to the promise in *Revelation* of a "new heaven and earth" point to the ultimately religious function of imagination.

Wordsworth and Coleridge are engaged in what M. H. Abrams in his *Natural Supernaturalism* calls the "Romantic enterprise" – "to save the overview of human history and destiny, the experiential paradigms, and the cardinal virtues of their religious heritage, by reconstituting them in a way that would make them intellectually acceptable, as well as emotionally pertinent, for the time being" (66). Redemption is still the goal, but the imagination replaces Christ and the Holy Ghost as its agent, and the earth replaces Heaven as its place, the earth that Wordsworth called "the world / Of all of us, the place in which, in the end, / We find our happiness, or not at all" (*Prelude* 197). The enlightened rationalism of the seventeenth and eighteenth centuries had done its demolition work. The Romantic must now, like Keats, seek "a system of Salvation which does not affront our reason and humanity," that is free of "dogmas and superstitions" (250). The Romantic is essentially religious – whether a believing Christian like Coleridge and Wordsworth or an anti- or non-Christian like Shelley and Keats – whose task is to find a place for the concerns and values of religion in an increasingly non-religious world.

This paradigm fits Lawrence closely and gives us a model for understanding his career. The son of a staunch Congregationalist, Lawrence was a very religious young man who described himself in a letter written to the family minister as "emotional, perhaps mystical," and as having been "brought up to believe in the absolute necessity for a sudden spiritual conversion; I believed for many years that the Holy Ghost descended and took conscious possession of the "elect" – the converted one; I thought all conversions were, to a greater or less degree, like that of Paul's. Naturally I yearned for the same" (*Letters* 1: 39). The crisis in Lawrence's religious faith occurred when "I couldn't get the religious conversion that I longed for" (1: 49). In 1907, at the age of twenty-two, he told the Reverend Reid, "I do not, cannot believe in the divinity of Jesus" (1: 40) and expressed similar doubts "on the subjects of the Miracles, Virgin Birth, [and] the Atonement" (1: 37). Jessie Chambers describes herself and Lawrence talking out such dogmatic articles of faith "as the Virgin Birth, the Atonement, and the Miracles," which they "discarded as irrelevant to the real matter of religion" (1: 84). In the very act of rejecting the central doctrines of his church, Lawrence is thus engaged in the quintessential Romantic task as described by Abrams: "to give up what one was convinced one had to give up of the dogmatic understructure of Christianity, yet to save what one could save of its experiential relevance and values"

(68). Within five months of the letter to Reverend Reid, Lawrence is asking a correspondent, "Do you think the idea of the mystic oneness of three is empty and barren? It is not" (*Letters* 1: 52). He is already rethinking his religion, in the Romantic conviction that each man must create his own – "I have my own religion, which is to me the truth" (1: 215). This religion preserves a belief in what he called "the living soul which is the essence of mankind" (1: 30) and in God: "There still remains a God, but not a personal God: a vast, shimmering impulse which wavers onwards towards some end, I don't know what" (1: 256). He no longer talks in terms of a transcendent personal God or an afterlife, but in terms of "life," a central Romantic term: "I believe in life" (1: 72). "All mysteries and possibilities lie in things and happenings" (1: 107).

Faced with the loss of the Christian faith that had oriented and sustained him, Lawrence in the spring of 1906 began reading with a "seriousness that was at times almost frightening in its intensity" (Chambers 102). He read Emerson's *Essays* and a great deal of Carlyle, including the *French Revolution, Heroes and Hero Worship*, and *Sartor Resartus* (101–2). He described himself as "suffering acutely from Carlylophobia, which you will understand if that rabid philosopher has ever bitten you" (1: 49) and proclaimed to Jessie "weightily, 'I feel I have something to say,' and again, 'I think it will be didactic'" (102). I believe that this is an extremely important moment in Lawrence's development, for he found in Carlyle and Emerson a way out of his crisis of faith and a way of being "didactic," poetic, and religious at once.

Carlyle too had lost his faith in Christianity but had nevertheless experienced a religious conversion described in *Sartor Resartus* in which he "awoke to a new Heaven and a new Earth" (186). He also forged a powerful identity for himself as sage and prophet and a style that combined with startling originality the poetic and the philosophic. Carlyle proclaimed that man had simply outgrown Christianity: "the Mythus of the Christian Religion looks not in the eighteenth century as it did in the eighth" (194). The "dead letter" of custom has quenched "the living Spirit of Religion" (114), which in every era needs a new expression. There is a "perennial continuance of inspiration" and prophecy; "there are true Priests ... in our own day" (193). These contemporary priests possess "Imagination," which is "Priest and Prophet to lead us heavenward" (222). It is in "this immeasurable froth-ocean we name LITERATURE" that fragments of the new religion can be found, in writers like Goethe and Wordsworth. "Highest of all Symbols are those wherein the Artist or Poet has risen into Prophet, and all men can recognise a present God, and worship the same: I mean religious Symbols" (224). Here in brief compass and intoxicating rhetoric are the essential elements of Romanticism that became essential elements of Lawrence's creative identity.

Emerson simply reinforced in his own highly original manner Carlyle's message. In his "Divinity School Address," he observed that "Nations and races flit by on the sea of time" (253); religion succeeds religion, prophet succeeds prophet. The Christian creed too is "passing away, and none arises in its room" (252). But that does not mean that there is no possibility of a new revelation. The spirit is eternal. "Men have come to speak of the revelation as somewhat long ago given and done, as if God were dead" (248), but any man may become "a new-born bard of the Holy Ghost" (254). Emerson turns to the "Poet" for the new revelation, but as his list of the great "poets" of the past indicates, they include what we normally call prophets and philosophers as well: "Orpheus, Empedocles, Heraclitus, Plato, Plutarch, Dante, Swedenborg" (307). "For it is not metres, but a metre-making argument, that makes a poem" (310). The poet possesses a power of insight, "an ulterior intellectual perception" (315) which Emerson calls "Imagination" – "a very high sort of seeing" (318). This power enables men to "found within their world another world" (320) and to achieve thereby their liberation. "The religions of the world are the ejaculations of a few imaginative men" (322).

In Carlyle and Emerson Lawrence found a view of life that was religious without being Christian. They reconciled him to the loss of his Christianity and showed him an alternative in what could be called the religion of Romanticism. We are to hear Emerson and Carlyle – as well as Blake and Shelley and Wordsworth and Coleridge – behind the following words from the "Foreword" to *Fantasia of the Unconscious*, one of Lawrence's most important statements of his program:

> Men live and see according to some gradually developing and gradually withering vision. This vision exists also as a dynamic idea or metaphysic – exists first as such. Then it is unfolded into life and art. Our vision, our belief, our metaphysic is wearing woefully thin, and the art is wearing absolutely threadbare. We have no future; neither for our hopes nor our aims nor our art. It has all gone gray and opaque.
>
> We've got to rip the old veil of a vision across, and find what the heart really believes in, after all: and what the heart really wants, for the next future. And we've got to put it down in terms of belief and of knowledge. And then go forward again, to the fulfillment in life and art. (57)

POLARITY

Graham Hough, whose early attempt in *The Dark Sun* to describe Lawrence's vision remains one of the best, describes it as "radically dualistic. Reality exists only as a pair of opposites" (224). This is certainly true of all Lawrence's writings, whether fiction or philosophy or travel book. As a tourist observing an old Italian woman in *Twilight in Italy*, or a critic discussing Renaissance painting in the *Study of Thomas Hardy*, or a novelist analyzing the relationships between two couples in *Women in Love*, Lawrence is singularly – obsessively – preoccupied with the opposites into which human experience always seems to resolve. Anything to which he turns his attention sooner or later reveals their presence. Hough (224) provides a convenient table of some of the most important of the opposites with which Lawrence is obsessed:

Light	Dark
Sun	Moon
Intellect	Blood
Will	Flesh
Male	Female
Love	Law

Spirit	Soul
Mind	Senses
Consciousness	Feelings
Moon	Sun
Knowledge	Nature
Motion	Inertia
The Son	The Father

Sometimes the opposites remain implicit in experience, sometimes they are embodied in a symbol, sometimes they reach expression in a doctrinal formulation. Henry Miller observes that Lawrence's most important symbols, "Phoenix, Crown, Rainbow, Plumed Serpent, all ... center about the same obsessive idea" (qtd. in Daleski 10), which is the idea of the opposites and their relation. One can turn virtually anywhere in Lawrence's expository writings for explicit statements of the idea:

Everything that exists, even a stone, has two sides to its nature. ("Love," 343)

I know I am compounded of two waves ... I am framed in the struggle and embrace of the two opposite waves of darkness and of light. ("Crown," 265)

Every new thing is born from the consummation of the two halves of the universe ... the dynamic elements of material existence are dual ... ("Two," 230–31)

Lawrence, however, is not content with mere recognition of the existence of the opposites. For him the great problem of both life and knowledge always was to grasp the relation between the opposites in such a way that one could see them as aspects of a whole and thereby avoid falling into a dualism that sundered the unity of life. Hough correctly stresses that the "integration or balance" of the opposite forces is for Lawrence "the key to the whole vital process," and that "the proper relation between the opposites is ... described by Lawrence as polarity – a word that obsesses him, both in fiction and expository writing" (227). Again, instances of this idea of polarity can be found throughout Lawrence:

The two exist by virtue of juxtaposition in pure polarity... the primary law of all the universe is a law of dual attraction and repulsion, a law of polarity. ("Reality," 693)

All force, spiritual or physical, has its polarity, its positive and its negative. ("Love," 151)

It is this idea of polarity that is "the dynamic idea or metaphysic" at the heart of Lawrence's vision. The opposites which seem to sunder life into an irreconcilable dualism are in fact *polar* opposites, the two forces of a *single* power, like the positive and negative poles of a magnet. The opposing forces are seen in their essential unity, a unity that yet allows each to retain its own distinct identity. The two are one, the one is two. Lawrence is always aware of the encompassing unity that is the source out of which the opposites emerge and which persists through all their interactions.

Since terminological consistency is always a problem in philosophy, let me be clear at the outset that "polarity" as I use it is the exact opposite of "dualism." I thus disagree with H. M. Daleski, whose *The Forked Flame* is the most extensive treatment of this aspect of Lawrence's thought, when he says that "the most striking feature of Lawrence's *Weltanschauung* is its dualism" (13). Donald Gutierrez in his *Subject-Object Relations in Wordsworth and Lawrence* rightly characterizes Lawrence as a "monist" as opposed to a dualist, although I avoid the term "monism" because of its associations with Spinoza and later thinkers like Haeckel from whom Lawrence must be distinguished. When Gutierrez, however, refers to "Lawrence's dualistic predilection for polarities" (62), he is collapsing terms which I insist on distinguishing. When we speak of philosophical dualism we must mean something like Descartes's position, and, as will become abundantly apparent, the essence of Lawrence's philosophical position, embodied in the idea of polarity, is its opposition to Cartesianism.

Lawrence is of course not alone in his central concern. The idea of polarity is closely related to ideas widespread in Western thought. It runs through the Neoplatonic tradition from the *concordia discors* of Plotinus, to the triads of John Scotus Erigena, to the *coincidentia oppositorum* of Nicholas of Cusa, to the dialectic of Giordano Bruno. It is prominent in the various occult streams that run underground through the entire history of Western thought, including Gnosticism, the Kabbalah, and Hermetism. Graham Hough points out parallels with Jung's concept of integration, and George H. Ford in *Double Measure* cites Paracelsus, Schelling, and Madame Blavatsky as parts of "a long tradition" from which Lawrence's thought derives (37). Nor is the idea limited to Western thought. Two comparative religionists, Mircea Eliade in *The Two and the One* and Alan Watts in *The Two Hands of God*, have discussed the idea's appearance in virtually every culture and tradition. The Yin and Yang of Taoism and the Shiva and Shakti of Tantric yoga should be mentioned as particularly close parallels to Lawrence.

The most important influence on Lawrence's thinking, however, in this area as in so many others, is Christianity. To say that Lawrence lost his faith in Christianity is not to say that he ever left it behind. Lawrence criticism too often makes the mistake, whether out of ignorance or prejudice, of overlooking the religion in which Lawrence was born and raised and which had such a pervasive impact on him. The Old and New Testaments are always subliminally if not explicitly present in Lawrence's language, and his ideas always directly or indirectly refer to Christianity. The Trinity is Lawrence's most frequent example of polarity, Father and Son representing the universal primordial opposites and the Holy Ghost representing their union. God the Father in the initial act of polarization projects the Son out of Himself, thus creating the original opposition. While the Father must be thought of logically and temporally as preceding the Son, yet the Son paradoxically is coeternal with the Father. Michael Black in his important recent study, *D. H. Lawrence: The Early Philosophical Works*, distinguishes two uses of the Trinity in Lawrence. Sometimes Lawrence sees the Trinity as "a purely temporal or evolutionary ... sequence, in which Son succeeded Father and Holy Ghost succeeded Son"; sometimes "Father and Son are perpetually counterposed, while the Holy Ghost is perpetually hovering above that opposition [in] an eternal polarity which is not so much succeeded or transcended as expressed or defined by the eternally co-present third term" (464). The difference between these two schemes should not be overemphasized, however, since they are two ways of attempting to express the same thing. The difficulty is in the inability of the human intellect and of language to grasp a relation in which the three are one, the one is three. The mind inevitably modulates an ontological relationship into a temporal one. The emphasis swings irresistibly from one aspect to its counterpart, from the union to the separateness, from the eternal to the temporal, and back again, never able except at moments to hold the two in balance.

Given the universality of the idea of polarity and the wealth of possible sources and parallels, we can most profitably turn again to the Romantics, with whom Lawrence has so many affinities. M. H. Abrams's monumental *Natural Supernaturalism* surveys the "interrelated concepts and images" (255) that constitute the "high Romantic argument" (217) of that truly remarkable group of "philosopher-seers" and "poet-prophets" (12) who created the "decisive turn in Western culture" known as Romanticism. These include Fichte, Schelling, Hegel, Novalis, and Holderlin in Germany and Blake, Wordsworth, Coleridge, and Carlyle in England. Abrams demonstrates abundantly and brilliantly that at the center of the vision shared by these thinkers is the idea of polarity. He finds the essence of Romantic philosophy as the interplay between two "prime agencies," "man and the world, mind and nature, the ego and the non-ego, the self and the not-self, spirit and the other, or (in the favorite antithesis of post-Kantian philosophers) subject and object." Romantic philosophy begins "with an undifferentiated principle which at once manifests itself in the dual mode of subject and object, whose interactions (in and through individual human selves) bring into being the phenomenal world and constitute all individual experience, as well as all the history of mankind" (91). "The nisus which drives the universe [is] the energy inherent in polarities – conceived as antitheses, contraries, contradictions – which manifests itself as a tension of repulsion and attraction, of centrifugal and centripetal forces" (173). This "dynamism of opposing forces … not only sustains [the universe's] present existence but also keeps it moving along the way" toward the conclusion in which the "original unity is restored at a higher level" (171). "Romantic philosophy is thus primarily a metaphysics of integration, of which the key principle is that of the "reconciliation," or synthesis, of whatever is divided, opposed, and conflicting" (182).

As we have seen, Abrams defines the central quest of Romanticism as "radically to recast" the Christian myth and religion "into terms appropriate to the historical and intellectual circumstances of their own age" (29). The Romantic philosophers "explicitly undertook to translate religious doctrine into their conceptual philosophy" (33). They hoped "to reconstitute the grounds of hope" by the "assimilation and reinterpretation of religious ideas, as constitutive elements in a world view founded on secular premises" (12–13). Thus "the personal God the Father tends to become an impersonal first principle, or absolute" (151), and the traditional scheme based on the relation of the Father to his Creation is reformulated "within the prevailing two-term system of subject and object" (12–13). Abrams's paradigm is extraordinarily fruitful in discussing Lawrence because it places so precisely Lawrence's own effort to translate the traditional Trinity into the language of polarity and helps us see how Lawrence carries on the central quest of Romanticism.

There are many possible routes by which the idea of polarity could have reached Lawrence. Joseph Sigman has shown the centrality of "The Imagery of Polarity in *Sartor Resartus*" and other writings of Carlyle. Emerson devoted an entire essay, "Compensation," to polarity and his writings are sprinkled with references to it, such as the following from "The American Scholar":

That great principle of Undulation in nature, that shows itself in the inspiring and expiring of the breath; in desire and satiety; in the ebb and flow of the sea; in day and night; in heat and cold; and as yet more deeply ingrained in every atom and every fluid, is known to us under the name of Polarity … (*Writings* 232)

We know that as a young man Lawrence was "fascinated" (Worthen 121) by Blake, whose doctrine of Contraries is close to Lawrence's philosophy of polarity. John Colmer points out that Lawrence's philosophy of "polarity" as embodied in "The Two Principles" "brings together in a single developing argument the main substance of Blake's personal system" (13). In *Twilight in Italy* Lawrence includes Blake's Tiger and Lamb, which are examples of the "contraries" underlying all human existence, in a list of his familiar polarities: "The Infinite is twofold, the Father and the Son, the Dark and the Light, the Senses and the Mind, the Soul and the Spirit, the self and the not-self, the Tiger and the Lamb" (58). Lawrence shares not only Blake's perception of the opposites but also his horror of merging opposites in a union that destroys their individual identities.

Among the English Romantics, however, it is Samuel Taylor Coleridge who is the closest parallel to Lawrence. Polarity is at the center of Coleridge's thought in much the same way it is in Lawrence's, and Coleridge spent the last decades of his life trying to explain it to his contemporaries. Scattered through his many philosophical writings is an exposition of unparalleled complexity and depth combined with clarity and rigor that enables us to grasp the different aspects of Lawrence's very similar vision in its manifold interrelatedness. I do not think of Coleridge as a direct influence – there is no evidence that Lawrence read any of his philosophical works – although his amazingly seminal mind seems to permeate the entire Romantic movement, and the essence of Coleridge's thought could easily have reached Lawrence through Emerson and Carlyle, who were both heavily indebted to him. Coleridge has been called Carlyle's "truest precursor" (Bloom, *Carlyle* 1), and Emerson's essays, when read with a knowledge of Coleridge, reveal themselves as constructed on a framework of Coleridgean ideas.

Coleridge alone among the major English Romantics was a true philosopher in the sense of one who spent years of arduous discipline mastering the logic and the systems of the great philosophers, and in the following chapters I use his ideas to make explicit the logic and system that remain implicit in Lawrence. We do not find in Lawrence a philosophy in the sense of a structure of logically related propositions built up out of abstract concepts. He was hesitant to use the word philosophy, referring to his work in one letter as "philosophy – or whatever it is" (3: 24) and calling it "philosophicalish." He uses the terms "philosophy," "metaphysic," "thought," "Weltan-schauung," and "vision" loosely and interchangeably, but he would have accepted the distinction Graham Hough makes when he says that "Lawrence is not a philosopher. What he offers is a Weltanschauung, his own vision of life" (217–18). While Lawrence's vision is never systematically elaborated, it is nevertheless a complexly integrated whole, "a whole Weltanschauung," as he described it in a letter to his publisher (3: 400), and reveals an internal self-consistency and interrelatedness. As Michael Black says, "After seventy years of writing about [Lawrence] ... he is taking shape, and the shape is surprisingly consonant with the idea of system," an organic system "where the whole both supports and demands each part" (*Early Fiction* 15–16).

The relation of the Romantic philosopher-poet to philo-sophical systems is uneasy if not hostile. Wordsworth is typical: "Kant, Schelling, Fichte; Fichte, Schelling, Kant: all this is dreary work and does not denote progress" (qtd. in Hirsch 3). Carlyle mocked Coleridge's need for "formidable apparatus, logical swim-bladders, transcendental life-preservers and other precautionary and vehiculatory gear, for setting out" on the sea of conversation (*Life* 55). Emerson "disparaged all system, all elaborate chains of reasoning, and the whole method of discursive philosophy" (Wellek, "Emerson" 187). And we have seen Lawrence's opinion of "that beastly Kant." Yet each drank deeply at philosophy's fountain, and the vision of each is informed by philosophic ideas and has a logic of its own. Emerson speaks for the other poet-philosophers: "We want in every man a logic; we cannot pardon the absence of it, but it must not be spoken. Logic is the procession or proportionate unfolding of the intuition; but its virtue is as silent method; the moment it would appear as propositions and have a separate value, it is worthless" (qtd. in Dewey 24). The poet's desire for silent logic is balanced by what John Dewey in his essay on

Emerson calls "the desire for an articulate ... logic [which] is intrinsic with philosophy" (25). I assume that the logic that is present but silent in Lawrence's writings is articulate and audible in Coleridge. I assume that, as A. C. Bradley said of Wordsworth and Hegel, we find "the same mind" in Lawrence and Coleridge ("Wordsworth" 129).

In the next pages I attempt to present in as brief a space as possible Coleridge's central ideas as preparation for all that will follow. My understanding of Coleridge is heavily indebted to Owen Barfield, whom Harold Bloom describes as "among all living critics [the] closest in spirit to Coleridge" (*Coleridge* vii). Barfield's brilliant and authoritative treatment of *What Coleridge Thought* is the first to succeed in presenting Coleridge's thought in its entirety as a comprehensive and self-consistent system. He succeeds in reconstructing what existed in Coleridge's mind but remains fragmentarily expounded in the major philosophical works – the *Biographia Literaria*, *The Friend*, the *Theory of Life*, *Aids to Reflection*, *The Statesman's Manual*, and the *Philosophical Lectures*.

Barfield does this by focusing on the idea of polarity, a term that came into widespread currency in the late eighteenth and early nineteenth centuries as a result of exciting advances in the study of magnetism and electricity. Philosophical scientists like Schelling, Oken, and Goethe found in the natural phenomena of magnetism and electricity a striking manifestation of a universal law, contemplating, in Coleridge's words, "in the phaenomena of electricity the operation of a law which reigns through all nature, the law of POLARITY, or the manifestation of one power by opposite forces" (*Friend* 1 : 479). The poles of the magnet are by definition fundamentally opposed to each other; each is the negation of the other, their very existence making them mutually exclusive. The power of the magnet is the result of their opposition; the greater the opposition, the greater the power. Yet the opposite poles are necessary to each other, and neither can exist alone, each defining and constituting itself in relation only to its opposite. Despite their antithetical nature, each yet paradoxically exists only in and by and through the other. We can distinguish them but we cannot divide them.

Cutting the magnet at any point simply creates a new magnet, with the same power now manifesting through a new negative and positive pole. This phenomenon points us to the essential fact – and this is critical – that they are the "two forces of one Power."

Polarity, however, is not a material phenomenon in the sense that a specific magnet is a material object. Magnetism and electricity are manifestations of a higher power. Coleridge describes polarity as a "law" that is productive of phenomena and that must therefore be "pre-" or "super-" phenomenal. To invoke a Scholastic distinction used often by Coleridge, polarity belongs to *natura naturans* not *natura naturata*. Magnetism and electricity are simply "the most obvious and striking of its innumerable forms" (*Friend* 479) or, as Barfield puts it, "*natura naturata* masquerading as *natura naturans*" (37).

Polarity has certain advantages over other closely related ideas, such as the reconciliation of opposites. For one thing, it is easier, through the concrete examples of electricity and magnetism, to grasp. It is also less subject to abstraction and to purely logical treatment. Barfield emphasizes that the essential characteristics of polarity are twofold: (1) it is real not abstract, and (2) it is dynamic not static:

Polarity is, according to Coleridge, a "law": it is a law which reigns through all Nature; the duality of the "opposite forces" is the *manifestation* of a prior unity; and that unity is a "power." It is not, that is to say, any abstract "principle of unity" or of identity – a point which it is hardly possible to over-emphasise ... Polarity is dynamic, not abstract. It is not "a mere balance or compromise," but "a living and generative interpenetration." Where logical opposites are contradictory, polar opposites are generative of each other – and together generative of new product. Polar opposites exist by virtue of each other *as well as* at the expense of each other; "each is that which it is called, relatively, by predominance of the one character or quality, not by the absolute exclusion of the other." Moreover each quality or character is present *in* the other. We can and must distinguish, but there is no possibility of *dividing* them. (36)

Coleridge thus distinguishes logical opposites from real or polar opposites: opposites "are of two kinds, either logical, that is, such as are absolutely incompatible; or real, without being contradictory" (*Biographia* 1 : 259). Matter itself is a product of polar opposites, "the resulting Phenomenon of the equilibrium of the two antagonist Forces, Attraction and Repulsion, *that* the Negative and *this* the Positive Pole" (*Philosophical* 434). The relationship between opposite poles is dynamic because it is antagonistic. The opposites are locked in fierce, unremitting struggle with each other, and there is always in Coleridge a strong sense of strife, of the fierce oppugnancy between hostile opposites. As Barfield says, "each force – from its own point of view, so to speak – *is* literally *striving* for total ascendancy over the other – in blind ignorance, or ruthless disregard, of the inevitable consequence: that, if it 'had its way,' polarity, and with it life itself, would cease" (89).

Two of the many examples offered by Coleridge may help. The first is from the world of nature:

There is a sort of *minim immortal* among the animalcula infusoria which has not naturally either birth, or death, absolute beginning, or absolute end: for at a certain period a small point appears on its back, which deepens and lengthens till the creature divides into two, and the same process recommences in each of the halves now become integral. (*Biographia* 1 : 83)

The second example is Coleridge's explanation of the origin of meter:

This I would trace to the balance in the mind effected by that spontaneous effort which strives to hold in check the workings of passion. It might be easily explained likewise in what manner this salutary antagonism is assisted by the very state, which it counteracts; and how this balance of antagonists became organized into *metre* ... Now these two conditions must be reconciled and co-present. There must be not only a partnership, but a union; an interpenetration of passion and of will, of *spontaneous* impulse and of *voluntary* purpose. (*Biographia* 2: 64–65)

Not only is polarity a law of nature, manifest at every level from "inanimate" matter to man, it is also "an idea of the pure intellect" (*Friend* 1 : 463). Coleridge discovers "this one power with its two inherent indestructible yet counteracting forces" in nature and in the mind, "in the living principle and in the process of our own self-consciousness" (*Biographia* i : 299). Just as every *thing* is polaric (because of "the very definition of a THING as the synthesis of opposing energies" [*Formation* 590]), so is every *thought* (because of "the *polarizing* property of all finite mind, for which Unity is manifested only by correspondent opposites" [*Friend* i : 515]). Reality is a "Unity" but it is only manifest to the "finite mind" as a duality or opposition. To understand this essential point, we must invoke Coleridge's "momentous distinction" (*Aids* xvii) between understanding and reason.

It is only reason, as opposed to the understanding, that is capable of "intuitively contemplating" polarity. The "polar logic" of reason is distinguished from the logic of dichotomy of the understanding. For the understanding, Aristotle's two laws of logic are incontrovertible: the law of contradiction states that A cannot be both B and not-B at the same time; the law of excluded middle states the converse of this – A must be either B or not-B, there being no third possibility. For the "higher logic" of reason, however, A can be both B and not-B at the same time. It is reason alone that can reconcile the seemingly irreconcilable dichotomies of the understanding. In fact, it is a "test and sign" of any truth of reason that "it can come forth out of the moulds of the understanding only in the disguise of two contradictory conceptions" (*Aids* 171). Coleridge cites the following as examples of truths that are inconceivable to the understanding: "Before Abraham *was*, I *am* – God is a Circle, the centre of which is everywhere, and circumference nowhere. The soul is all in every part" (*Aids* 154). Reason sees deeper than the understanding; it sees the producer not the product, *natura naturans* not *natura naturata*. In Barfield's words, "only that which itself transcends two contradictories can have produced them ... The first step towards apprehending reason, as active, is thus the apprehension of polarity" (111). Reason intuitively contemplates and is one with the living whole, whereas the understanding contemplates the negations of reality. The understanding transfers reality to abstractions and to separate, external objects, which cannot be brought into a living relationship with each other.

This hasty excursion through Coleridge will have at least partially prepared us for Coleridge's most difficult and most important assertion: "the productive power, which is in nature as nature, is essentially one (i.e. of one kind) with the intelligence, which is in the human mind above nature" (*Friend* 1: 497–98). Or, as Barfield puts it, "in speaking on the one hand of nature and on the other of what he terms the 'act of consciousness,' he is not depicting process B in terms of process A, but is describing one single homogeneous process" (59). Nature and mind are polar opposites, twin manifestations of a single power. To make such an assertion is of course to flatly contradict the dualism of Descartes, which insists on an absolute separation between mind and nature, and Coleridge makes it clear throughout *Biographia Literaria* that the primary importance to him of the idea of polarity is that it enables him to fulfill the Romantic agenda of overcoming the dualism that has fastened itself upon the Western mind since Descartes.

Coleridge describes Descartes as "the first philosopher, who introduced the absolute and essential heterogeneity of the soul as intelligence, and the body as matter" (*Biographia* 1: 129). In his *Discourses on Method* Descartes concludes that he is a mind, "of which the whole essence or nature consists in thinking," and that his mind is "entirely distinct from the body" (54). Mind and body have nothing in common – one is wholly spiritual (living, immortal, and free); the other is wholly corporeal (a mechanism composed of lifeless particles, mortal, and determined). In a marginal note to a volume of Descartes, Coleridge calls this insistence on the "absolute and essential heterogeneity of the soul ... and the body" the original sin of Descartes, from which philosophy ever since has been trying to recover:

This utter disanimation of Body and its *not* opposition but contrariety ... to Soul, as the assumed Basis of Thought and Will; this substitution, I say, of a merely logical *negatio alterius omnino et singulo*, for a philosophic antithesis necessary to the manifestation of the identity of both – 2 = 1, as the only form in which the human understanding can represent to itself the 1 = 2; is the *peccatum originale* of the Cartesian system. (Qtd. in Barfield 228)

Descartes confuses logical with real opposites. His system is a product of the understanding, which can only conceive body and soul as negations of one another, rather than the reason, which alone can grasp their relation as polar opposites.

The distinction between reason and understanding parallels Coleridge's distinction between imagination and fancy. Fancy, like the understanding, has "no other counters to play with but fixities and definites" and is confined to externals, to abstractions, and to objects which (as objects) are essentially fixed and dead" (*Biographia* 1 : 304). Imagination, however, like reason, is "essentially vital" and is capable of apprehending reality as a living unity manifesting through polar opposites. There is thus no essential difference between reason and imagination. In Barfield's words, "between the act of thinking ... and the act of imagination no very sharp distinction transpires" (76). "The apprehension of polarity is itself *the basic act of imagination,*" as it is of reason (36).

Sharing reason's power of direct insight into reality, imagination's most important function is to communicate this reality to the understanding and the senses in the form of symbols. The imagination is the "intermediate faculty" (*Biographia* 2 : 175) and is essential because "an IDEA, in the highest sense of that word, cannot but be conveyed by a *symbol*" (*Biographia* 1 : 100). The imagination is "that reconciling and mediatory power, which incorporates the reason in images of the sense, and organizing (as it were) the flux of the senses by the permanent and self-circling energies of the reason, gives birth to a system of symbols, harmonious in themselves, and consubstantial with the truths of which they are the conductors" (*Statesman's* 29).

Such stunning passages are the reward for reading Coleridge. This one will frame our consideration of Lawrence. Drawing on Coleridge's explanations of polarity as an idea of the reason communicable only by the imagination, we will find in Lawrence a system of symbols organized by the "self-circling energies of the reason." It is a system of symbols, images of the senses that are yet consubstantial with the truths of reason. Such consubstantiality is an impossibility, a contradiction, to the understanding, but "all symbols of necessity involve a contradiction" (*Biographia* 1 : 156). The image and idea united in the symbol are polar opposites which we can distinguish but which we can no more separate than we can separate that other pair of polar opposites, art and philosophy.

In 1907 or 1908, while a student at University College, Nottingham, Lawrence read William James's *Pragmatism*. Jessie Chambers reports that the book "especially appealed to him" (113). The appeal is not hard to understand, since James's first chapter "The Present Dilemma in Philosophy" describes precisely the dilemma in which Lawrence himself was caught. Surveying the contemporary philosophical landscape, James finds that he and his contemporaries are faced with an unhappy choice between "an empirical philosophy that is not religious enough, and a religious philosophy that is not empirical enough" (24).

You want a system that will combine both things, the scientific loyalty to facts and willingness to take account of them, the spirit of adaptation and accommodation, in short, but also the old confidence in human values and the resultant spontaneity, whether of the religious or of the romantic type. And this is then your dilemma : you find the two parts of your *quaesitum* hopelessly separated. You find empiricism with inhumanism and irreligion ; or else you find a rationalistic philosophy that indeed may call itself religious, but that keeps out of all definite touch with concrete facts and joys and sorrows. (26–27)

James describes the entire history of philosophy as the clash between two temperaments, the "tender-minded" and the "tough-minded," or as he also calls them the "rationalist" and the "empiricist," the "idealist" and the "realist" (21). The former tends to be "religious" and the latter "irreligious." The contemporary versions of these eternal opposites are, on the one hand, the transcendental idealists, who are allied with the "traditional theism of protestantism at large," and, on the other hand, the materialistic monists like Haeckel, with "his ether-god and his jest at your God as a "gaseous vertebrate," and Spencer, "treating the world's history as a redistribution of matter and motion solely, and bowing religion politely out the front door" (24–25).

The idealists and theists are fighting a rearguard action, while the materialist monists are carrying the day under the banner of Darwin: "Never were as many men of a decidedly empiricist proclivity in existence as there are at the present day" (23).

> For a hundred and fifty years past the progress of science has seemed to mean the enlargement of the material universe and the diminution of man's importance. The result is what one may call the growth of naturalistic or positivistic feeling ... The romantic spontaneity and courage are gone, the vision is materialistic and depressing. Ideals appear as inert by-products of physiology; what is higher is explained by what is lower and treated forever as a case of "nothing but" – nothing but something else of a quite inferior sort. You get, in short, a materialistic universe, in which only the tough-minded find themselves congenially at home. (24–25)

Lawrence read Haeckel and Spencer, as well as Darwin and Huxley, and Jessie Chambers reports that "This rationalist teaching impressed Lawrence deeply. He came upon it at a time of spiritual fog, when the lights of orthodox religion and morality were proving wholly inadequate ... My feeling was that he tried to fill up a spiritual vacuum by swallowing materialism at a gulp" (112). His "coming up against the materialist attitude to life seared his youthful freshness" (83), and he lost his "spontaneous gaiety" (86). Jessie creates a moving portrait of Lawrence bravely espousing the modern attitude, "although it made him miserable" (86).

In the letter to the family minister that we have already quoted, Lawrence mentions Spencer and Darwin in the course of challenging some of the central tenets of his religion. He also criticizes J. R. Campbell's *New Theology*, whose views Reid espoused: "A glance through [the book] convinced me that his position was untenable, indeed almost incomprehensible to an ordinary mind that cannot sustain a rationalist attitude in a nebulous atmosphere of religious yearning" (1: 37). This materialist attitude, however, in Jessie's words, "did not carry him far" (112). While he knew that the Chapel religion in which he had been raised could not withstand the assaults of scientific materialism, he also knew that, as he declared in a letter to Reverend Reid written two months later, "I cannot be a materialist."

He describes himself as "by nature ... emotional, perhaps mystical," and the letter expresses the anguish of a tender-minded soul in a tough-minded world: "I cannot be a materialist – but Oh, how is it possible that a God who speaks to all hearts can let Belgravia go laughing to a vicious luxury, and Whitechapel cursing to a filthy debauchery – such suffering, such dreadful suffering – and shall the short years of Christ's mission atone for it all?" (1 : 40). "Belief in a hypothesis that cannot be proved" is no answer to "this enormity, this horror" of a world, in which "Men – some – seem to be born and ruthlessly destroyed," and "the bacteria are created and nurtured on Man, to his horrible suffering" (1 : 40–41).

While Lawrence undoubtedly read and was affected by the materialists, there has been a tendency among some critics to greatly exaggerate their importance. Roger Ebbatson calls Haeckel's *The Riddle of the Universe* a book "pregnant with import to the young Lawrence," one that "radically extended" his concept of Nature; he similarly finds that Spencer's *First Principles* was "of great import to the young Lawrence," who "goes on to advance ideas which are pure Spencerean doctrine" (*Lawrence* 38, 34, 40). Daniel J. Schneider also finds that Lawrence's "intellectual awakening began," and his "basic principles ... were shaped by his reading of materialists" like Spencer and Haeckel (*D. H. Lawrence* 8, 12). Spencer and Haeckel were indeed valuable sources of scientific ideas and formulations (*The Riddle of the Universe* and *First Principles* are virtual primers of the explosive growth of science in the nineteenth century), but they were of little use to Lawrence *philosophically*. Insofar as they were materialists, they existed for him largely as something to be overcome, in the same way that Coleridge had to overcome the rationalism and scientific materialism of Descartes, Locke, and Hartley. Interestingly, both Ebbatson (32) and Schneider (9) quote Jessie Chambers's

remarks that materialism "impressed Lawrence deeply" and
that he tried "swallowing materialism at a gulp," but neither
quotes the sentence immediately following: "But it did not
carry him far" (112). "I am not a materialist," he said at the
very time he was reading the materialists. Neither Ebbatson
nor Schneider suggests that Lawrence actually became a
materialist, but each fails to see how fundamentally antipathetic
materialism *per se* was to him and each fails to observe that
Haeckel and Spencer are embodiments of the positivist temper
at its most superficial. Haeckel is an extremely naive philosopher, and Spencer's shortcomings, "his fearful array of
insufficiencies," are nicely described by James: "His dry
schoolmaster temperament, the hurdy-gurdy monotony of him,
his preference for cheap makeshifts in argument, his lack of
education even in mechanical principles, and in general the
vagueness of all his fundamental ideas, his whole system
wooden, as if knocked together out of cracked hemlock boards"
(37). The inadequacies of Haeckel and Spencer could not have
escaped Lawrence, and it is impossible to think that either man
exerted a vital or lasting influence on a mind like his. The
quality of the mind surely has something to do with the nature
and extent of the influence.

If we are searching for influences, we would do better to turn
to figures like Emerson and Carlyle, in whom Lawrence found
all the essentials of his own philosophical position. Carlyle in
Sartor Resartus and Emerson in *Nature* can both be called
Idealists. The soul, which is directly linked to God, precedes
and produces nature. As Carlyle expresses it, "this so solid-
seeming World, after all, were but an air-image, our ME the only
reality: and Nature, with its thousandfold production and
destruction, but the reflex of our own inward Force, the
'phantasy of our Dream'" (*Sartor* 55). Emerson's "Idealism"
"fastens the attention upon immortal necessary uncreated
natures, that is, upon Ideas; and in their beautiful and majestic
presence, we feel that our outward being is a dream and a
shade" (70). There is no separate, self-subsistent realm of
matter; "matter is a phenomenon, not a substance" (*Nature*
77–78).

This "idealism," however, is just as much a realism, this "Transcendentalism" just as much a "Descendentalism" (*Sartor* 65). The outer world of physical objects is not degraded or diminished. On the contrary, "rightly viewed no meanest object is insignificant; all objects are as windows, through which the philosophic eye looks into Infinitude itself" (*Sartor* 72). "Idealism sees the world in God" (*Nature* 74). There is a continuity of essence between soul and world, which are organically one, nature being the efflux of the divine. Life is the "bodying forth" of the invisible (*Sartor* 218), the manifestation in material form of the spirit. "The visible creation is the terminus or the circumference of the invisible world" (*Nature* 44).

Carlyle and Emerson passionately counter the tendency of the last few centuries, which have witnessed, as James said, "the enlargement of the material universe and the diminution of man's importance" (24). Teufelsdrockh's unhappiness and crisis of faith came of overestimating his insignificance in the physical universe, and his rebirth into a new heaven and earth is a result of realizing his spiritual infinitude. For Emerson likewise, man is "placed in the centre of beings, and a ray of relation passes from every other being to him" (*Selected* 35). Carlyle and Emerson remove man from the periphery where he has mistakenly placed himself to the center where he rightfully belongs. "That spirit, that is, the Supreme Being, does not build up nature around us, but puts it forth through us, as the life of the tree puts forth new branches and leaves through the pores of the old" (*Nature* 79).

Coming in the midst of intense intellectual struggles and doubts, James must have appeared to Lawrence at first as a breath of fresh air. Not only was James's philosophical mind greatly superior to Haeckel's or Spencer's, but he also seemed to be in the same spiritual place at the same time as Lawrence. James too described contemporary Christianity as being "out of all definite touch with concrete facts and joys and sorrows" (27), too refined, "airy and shallow" (31) to justify God's horrors to man. And James offered a brash and breezy criticism of Haeckel's "unintelligible pantheistic monster" that, in John

Worthen's view (179), helped steer Lawrence away from materialism.

Not only did James describe precisely the dilemma of minds caught between science and religion, he also offered a way out. Pragmatism is a way of being at once idealistic and realistic, rationalist and empiricist, tender and tough. Pragmatism is "the mediating way" (37) that "can remain religious like the rationalisms, but at the same time, like the empiricisms, it can preserve the richest intimacy with facts" (33). Pragmatism does this precisely by giving up the claim to truth and concerning itself only with the practical consequences – the "cash-value" (46) – of ideas: "The pragmatic method is primarily a method of settling metaphysical disputes that otherwise might be interminable. Is the world one or many? – fated or free? – material or spiritual? … Disputes over such notions are un-ending. The pragmatic method in such cases is to try to interpret each notion by tracing its respective practical conse-quences" (42). James's is an "instrumental view of truth," in which "ideas (which themselves are but parts of our experience) become true just in so far as they help us to get into satisfactory relations with other parts of our experience" (49). Pragmatism remains open to any ideas – scientific, mystical, or theological – and gives its allegiance to whatever idea seems to work best at the moment: "The whole function of philosophy ought to be to find out what definite difference it will make to you and me, at definite instants of our life, if this world-formula or that world-formula be the true one" (45).

As immediately attractive as James was to Lawrence, his influence did not last. In a letter dated December 1909 to his former college Botany professor Ernest Smith, who introduced him to James, Lawrence wrote: "You were my first live teacher of philosophy: you showed me the way out of a torturing crude Monism, past Pragmatism, into a sort of crude but appeasing Pluralism" (1 : 147). This implies that by the time he left college in 1908 he was no longer a Pragmatist and within another year had moved past Pluralism. Pragmatism could not for long satisfy Lawrence's philosophical appetite. Instead of truly mediating between idealism and realism, instead of accommodating both the spiritual and the physical, Pragmatism, it could be argued, gives us neither, and in fact gives up philosophy altogether – it certainly gives up the possibility of ideas with truth-value instead of cash-value. It is probably this aspect of James's thought that Lawrence came to view as "crude."

Lawrence himself had an absolute passion for ideas, an imperative need for a philosophy that is true, which means a philosophy that is more than the set of largely unconscious assumptions that most of us live by and more than a set of makeshift instruments to satisfy the need of the moment. He read voraciously and widely, and, as Jessie Chambers observes, the reading was out of a deep personal need, a "groping for something that he could lay hold of as a guiding principle in his own life" (113). There is no mistaking the urgency in his letters when speaking of his philosophy: "it is absolutely necessary to get it out, fix it, and have a definite foothold, to be *sure*" (3: 224). At times he preferred philosophy to fiction, saying, "One is happy in the thoughts only that transcend humanity" (3: 127). His hunger was for ideas that were true, that had a metaphysical reach, and that were systematic and comprehensive. He spoke specifically of the need for a philosophy that was "constructive, synthetic, metaphysical" (*Letters* 2: 448). This is not the kind of person who will be satisfied with Pragmatism, with its casual attitude towards "world-formulae" and its easy accommodation of more than one ultimate principle.

From this point on, however, Lawrence's philosophical agenda is clear and can be expressed in Jamesian terms: he must find a philosophy that will preserve a place for the romantic and the religious but that will also come to terms adequately with the real world, that will be religious without being Christian, scientific without being materialistic. His break with formal Christianity was decisive. He was convinced that Christianity could no longer serve man's deepest needs. A new vision was needed.

Many people at the time were convinced that that vision had already been revealed in the writings of the next thinker to enter Lawrence's life. Jessie Chambers reports that in 1908–9 in the library at Croydon "Lawrence found Nietzsche. He never mentioned him directly to me, nor suggested that I should read him, but I began to hear about the 'Will to Power,' and perceived that he had come upon something new and engrossing" (120). Lawrence's early philosophical development is a history of rapidly absorbing many disparate influences and then moving beyond them, but Nietzsche remained an abiding presence and an influence second to none in Lawrence's philosophical development. He found in Nietzsche "the Antichrist" a great thinker and artist living in a post-Darwinian world and articulating a new, non-Christian myth or vision intended to fulfill both man's scientific and religious needs. In a book review written in 1913, Lawrence credited Nietzsche with demolishing "the Christian religion as it stood" (*Phoenix* 304), underscoring the immediate basis of Nietzsche's appeal. Nietzsche's brilliant psychological diagnosis of Christianity provided the basis for Lawrence's own views as expressed in works from *The Rainbow* through *Apocalypse*. Lawrence also found in Nietzsche an exposition of the relation between the opposites in terms of Apollo and Dionysus that influenced his own thinking about polarity.

Nietzsche was critically important to Lawrence in working out his own philosophy, and with Nietzsche Lawrence moves from his early groping development into his full maturity. By 1912–13 Lawrence had arrived at his own position. From this point on, he rewrote his philosophy again and again, but it was essentially the same philosophy. He was no longer as easily influenced as he had been as a young man and no longer showed the same excitement at new discoveries. There are, however, two important exceptions, two points at which he shows real enthusiasm for something he has just read, and one has the feeling that here is a significant new philosophical influence, that Lawrence's mind has been enlarged and altered. One of these new influences is the pre-Socratic philosophers, the other is Theosophy.

After reading John Burnet's *Early Greek Philosophy* in 1915, he exclaimed in a letter to Bertrand Russell that "I have been wrong, much too Christian, in my philosophy. These early

Greeks have clarified my soul. I must drop all about God " (2 : 364). And to Lady Ottoline Morrell he declared, "I shall write all my philosophy again. Last time I came out of the Christian camp. This time I must come out of these early Greek philosophers" (2: 367). In the early Greeks Lawrence discovered a way of thinking that was at once scientific and religious and that existed long before Christianity. The early Greeks aided him immeasurably in the continuing process of weaning himself from Christianity and Christian patterns of thought.

The same can be said for Theosophy. After reading Madame Blavatsky, Lawrence exclaimed that her ideas were "marvelously illuminating" (*Letters* 3: 143) "One can glean a marvelous lot from [her writings], enlarge the understanding immensely" (3: 150). The subtitle of Blavatsky's *The Secret Doctrine* is "The Synthesis of Science, Religion, and Philosophy," and, like Nietzsche and the pre-Socratics, she offered Lawrence a way of being religious and scientific at the same time. Blavatsky's anti-Christian animus, her adoption of modern scientific theories, and her heavy borrowings from many different religions, all appealed immensely to Lawrence. If the pre-Socratics opened up vistas into the time before Christianity, Theosophy opened Lawrence to contemporaneous ways of being religious outside the orbit of Christianity.

From among the pre-Socratics and from within the theosophical tradition, there are two thinkers who express a philosophy of polarity virtually identical to Lawrence's. They are Heraclitus and Jacob Boehme. As George A. Panichas observes, it is clearly Heraclitus of all the Greeks who is "closest in spirit to Lawrence" (341) and who made by far the greatest impression. "I shall write out Herakleitos on tablets of bronze," he declared to Bertrand Russell (*Letters* 2: 364). In the case of Theosophy, it was the ideas contained in Madame Blavatsky's encyclopedic writings that Lawrence found so exciting, not Blavatsky herself, whose writings were "not *very* much good" (3: 299), "in many ways a bore, and not quite real" (3: 150). Boehme, of whom Lawrence was aware (4: 460), is perhaps the greatest of all theosophers, as well as the source of many of

Blavatsky's ideas, and it is to Boehme that we must turn for the closest and most instructive parallel to Lawrence.

The inclusion of Heraclitus and Boehme is confirmed by Coleridge, for they were the two historical predecessors in whom he found most fully embodied his own philosophy of polarity. Coleridge credited Heraclitus with being the "first promulgator" of the "universal law of Polarity" (*Friend* 1 : 94). Boehme's importance not only to Coleridge but to the whole tradition of polaric thought can scarcely be overestimated. He could justly be called the founder of German Romantic philosophy. Hegel credited him with the creation of "Modern Philosophy in Its First Statement" and Schelling called him "a miraculous phenomenon in the history of mankind ... As popular mythologies and theogonies preceded science, so did J. Boehme, in the birth of God, as he describes it for us, precede all the scientific systems of modern philosophy" (qtd. in Abrams, *Natural* 170). Through the German Romantics and through Schopenhauer, who venerated Boehme, his influence flows into Nietzsche.

Like James, Coleridge sees the history of Western philosophy as a struggle between two parties, the idealists and the realists, although unlike James he also sees a third possibility:

There are therefore essentially but three kinds of philosophers and more are not possible: the one is those who give the whole to the subject and make the object a mere result involved in it; secondly those who give the whole to the object and make the subject, that is the reflecting and contemplating, feeling part, the mere result of that; and lastly those who, in very different ways, have attempted to reconcile these two opposites and bring them into one. (*Philosophical* 116)

Materialist philosophies begin with a material substrate and must account for the supervention to it, or the evolution out of it, of the mental or spiritual. But this is impossible as long as one starts, as Descartes and his successors start, with the complete separation, "the absolute and essential heterogeneity" (*Biographia* 1 : 129), of material and mental. To Coleridge it is self-evident that "things utterly heterogeneous can have no intercommunion" (*Friend* 511). "The law of causality holds only between homogeneous things, i.e. things having some common property; and cannot extend from one world into another, its opposite" (*Biographia* 1: 130): "For, grant that an object from without could act upon the conscious *self*, as on a consubstantial object; yet such an affection could only engender something homogeneous with itself. Motion could only propagate motion. Matter has no *Inward*. We remove one surface, but to meet with another" (*Biographia* 1: 133).

Materialism is both cause and effect of "the despotism of the eye," which "attempts to render *that* an object of the sight which has no relation to sight": "[W]e are restless because invisible things are not the objects of vision; and metaphysical systems, for the most part, become popular, not for their truth, but in proportion as they attribute to causes a susceptibility of being *seen*, if only our visual organs were sufficiently powerful" (*Biographia* 1: 106–7). In its effort to close the gap between mind and matter, materialism resorts to chimerical entities – Coleridge calls them "fanciful hypotheses" – such as Descartes's "material ideas" or Hartley's "vibratiuncles" (*Biographia* 1: 98, 106). Haeckel for instance attempts to derive "all psychic activity" from the "material basis" of protoplasm by postulating the existence of what he calls "psychoplasm" (90–91). This perfectly exemplifies Barfield's point that "the system of materialism or mechanical causality ... is in fact only maintainable by the surreptitious smuggling in of unreduced 'immaterial influences.' This is usually done by impounding them semantically in some particular word or words" (205). The procedure becomes almost comic in Haeckel as he goes on to create "soul-cells," "will-cells," and "sexual cell-love" (115, 137).

Materialism asserts that what we perceive is not real; our perceptions are images created by our minds as the result of particles impinging on our sense organs. In contrast, Coleridge insists that "in our immediate perception, it is... the object itself, which is immediately present." Materialism "is as thorough idealism as Berkeley's, inasmuch as it equally (perhaps, in a more perfect degree) removes all reality and immediateness of perception, and places us in a dream-world of phantoms and spectres" (*Biographia* 1: 137). Unlike Locke and

Hartley, Coleridge does not think of the object as "really"
composed of lifeless, quality-less particles; unlike Berkeley,
Coleridge does not dissolve the reality of the object before us
into an idea that exists only in God's consciousness; unlike
Kant, he does not point beyond the appearance of the object to
a more real although unknowable "thing-in-itself."

If it be said that this is Idealism, let it be remembered that it is only so
far idealism, as it is at the same time, and on that very account, the
truest and most binding realism. For wherein does the realism of
mankind properly consist? In the assertion that there exists a
something without them, what, or how, or where they know not,
which occasions the objects of their perception? Oh no! This is neither
connatural or universal. It is what a few have taught and learnt in the
schools, and which the many repeat without asking themselves
concerning their own meaning. The realism common to all mankind
is far elder and lies infinitely deeper than this explanation skimmed
from the mere surface of mechanical philosophy. It is the table itself,
which the man of common sense believes himself to see, not the
phantom of a table, from which he may argumentatively deduce the
reality of a table, which he does not see. If to destroy the reality of all,
that we actually behold, be idealism, what can be more egregiously so,
than the system of modern metaphysics, which banishes us to a land of
shadows, surrounds us with apparitions, and distinguishes truth from
illusion only by the majority of those who dream the same dream?
(*Biographia* 1 : 261–62)

This "true and original realism" (262) Coleridge calls "ideal
Realism" (*Biographia* 1 : 303).

   The paradoxical quality of "ideal Realism" or "natural
supernaturalism" is echoed by Aldous Huxley, who calls
Lawrence a "mystical materialist." In one of the best essays
ever written about Lawrence, Huxley describes him as "a
subjectivist as well as a materialist," whose "dislike of abstract
knowledge and pure spirituality" was equaled only by his
dislike of the "stony cold world" of mechanistic materialism.
"Matter must be intrinsically as lively as the mind which
perceives it and is moved by the perception" (122–23). Unlike
the materialist who "excludes all modes of existence which [he]
cannot in imagination, at least, *finger* and *peep* at" (Coleridge,
Theory 575), Lawrence "had eyes that could see, beyond the

walls of light, far into the darkness" (118), to the necessarily invisible sources of our being: "Lawrence's special and characteristic gift was an extraordinary sensitiveness to ... the dark presence of the otherness that lies beyond the boundaries of man's conscious mind ... Paradoxically, this something not ourselves is yet a something lodged within us; this quintessence of otherness is yet the quintessence of our proper being" (117).

Coleridge points out that "the system of idealism may be traced to sources equally remote with ... materialism" (*Biographia* 1: 90). Both philosophical positions began with the Eleatics, who were the first who "reject[ed] all that was objective as real, and affirmed that the whole existed only in the mind" (*Philosophical* 120). Parmenides was the first thinker who decisively sundered the relation between the mind and the senses, an act that led to the postulation of a non-sensuous realm, called Spirit by the idealists and the atom by the materialists. John Burnet makes the same point – in fact it is his "main thesis" (vi) – in his *Early Greek Philosophy*, the book that had such a great impact on Lawrence. Burnet paradoxically calls Parmenides, the first idealist, "the father of Materialism." As we have seen, Coleridge traces his own ancestry to Heraclitus, whose philosophy predates the Parmenidean split between ideal and real. Each of the thinkers with whom we are concerned here shares an identity with Heraclitus. Nicolas Berdyaev said of Boehme that "the only thinker to whom he is close is Heraclitus" (xxxvii). Coleridge called himself "*Heraclitus redivivus*" (*Letters* 4: 775). Nietzsche has been called "the modern Heraclitus" (Ghose 57). And Lawrence set himself the task of "writ[ing] out Herakleitos, on tablets of bronze."

There is clear evidence that Lawrence knew Nietzsche and Heraclitus and knew *of* Boehme, and I trace their influence, both direct and indirect, where it appears in Lawrence's work. Yet this is not a study in influence. There are too many difficulties in the way of demonstrating direct and causal influence. Most of the ideas discussed here could have come from numerous sources, and the strands making up the web of Lawrence's thought are hopelessly tangled. Moreover, Lawrence may have been greatly influenced by someone whose

name never appears in the letters, writings, or memoirs, as
Emile Delavenay maintains in the case of Edward Carpenter.
There is also the striking fact that even in the cases of the
greatest influence, like Nietzsche's, Lawrence's essential thought
remains always distinctly his own. As Michael Bell says in his
fine study of Lawrence, "the vision is clearly *sui generis* and not
dependent on the reading" (6). Nietzsche, Heraclitus, and
Boehme are treated here as what Bell calls "explicatory
parallels" that help to "bring out the internal complexity and
cogency of his conception" (3–4).

I use Coleridge in the following chapters as a kind of *lingua
franca* into which the other thinkers are translated. The
philosophical position or vision shared by these thinkers is
presented in terms defined by Coleridge – "polarity," "life,"
"will," "subject," "object," "ideal realism," "imagination,"
"reason," and "understanding." The danger, however, in
translating the poetic vision into philosophical terms is not only
that they may be incompatible idioms but that the very life of
the poetry is in its concrete, non-abstract specificity – in its very
own language – and that we will murder the body to dissect the
bones beneath the skin. Some of the best recent studies of
Lawrence – Michael Black's two books, Michael Bell's *D. H.
Lawrence: Language and Being*, and Michael Ragussis's *The
Subterfuge of Art* – attempt to avoid this danger by remaining at
the level of Lawrence's largely metaphoric language and
exploring its implications in its own terms. I am nevertheless
encouraged in my own procedure by critics like A. C. Bradley
and E. D. Hirsch. Bradley in his essay on "English Poetry and
German Philosophy in the Age of Wordsworth" apologizes for
"spoiling" the poetry "in order to show the skeleton of ideas in
it" (123), and Hirsch in his *Wordsworth and Schelling* notes that
"poetry cannot justly be translated into philosophy. Each
discipline follows its own special laws and conventions" (6).
Despite these reservations, Bradley and Hirsch succeed brilliantly in illuminating the poetry of Wordsworth in terms of
Hegel's and Schelling's philosophical systems. As Hirsch
reminds us, "it may also be said that poetry and philosophy are
separate only as disciplines. Both may spring from an identical

Weltanschauung. The same person, for example, might be both philosopher and poet" (6–7). Coleridge was such a person, whose systematic philosophy and whose poetry both remained true to the same vision.

Lawrence's tradition is not, it is worth repeating, a novelistic one at all. It is a "visionary" tradition, and the fact that Lawrence chose to cast his vision primarily in the form of the novel is not of the essence. The link between a modern novelist, a pre-Socratic Greek philosopher, a seventeenth-century Christian theosophist, and a post-Darwinian "atheist" is the vision they share, a vision that can also be described as a philosophical position, ideal realism. They think in widely variant historical circumstances, vocabularies, and genres, but the thought is the same, whether it is expressed in terms of the Heraclitean opposition between fire and water, Boehme's sulphur and mercury, Nietzsche's will to power, or Lawrence's polarity.

The works of each of these figures are products of the imagination as Coleridge defines it, the imagination that is indistinguishable from reason and is alone able to apprehend and communicate the idea of polarity. In none of these figures can we separate the philosopher from the poet. For instance, the key to Boehme's importance, the reason he is able to make us "*feel*" the presence of the two forces of one power, is that he is an imaginative writer. His works have been called "metaphysical novels" by one of his best commentators (Koyre 27). The quasi-mythic entities and living powers that inhabit his pages are alive with the life of the imagination. It is for this reason that Coleridge credited Boehme with helping him "to keep alive the *heart* in the *head*" (*Biographia* 1: 184).

Their works are "systems of symbols ... consubstantial with the truths of which they are the conductors." Their imaginative universes are completely animate, alive with the life of the "essentially vital" imagination; dead matter and lifeless abstractions are equally alien to their visions. They all hearken back to what Lawrence called "the days of myth" before "fiction and philosophy got split." Heraclitus in fact – and this was a large part of his importance to Lawrence – hovers on the historical border between myth and philosophy. He lived and wrote before the abstract concept had even been evolved as a tool of thought, a process that we can see developing in Plato and culminating in Aristotle, who accused Heraclitus of violating the law of contradiction. But, as Coleridge says, "all symbols of necessity involve a contradiction" to the Aristotelean understanding. Heraclitus' "fire," for instance, is such a symbol or image-idea; it is at one and the same time Zeus's thunderbolt, the logos or "intelligence by which all things are steered through all things" (Wheelwright 102), and the familiar physical element that crackles and burns.

Again, however, it must be emphasized that it is not a system of abstract ideas that these thinkers share, it is an imaginative vision expressed primarily as symbol and myth. Boehme's "sulphur" and "Sophia," Nietzsche's Zarathustra and Dionysus, Lawrence's "Crown" and Don Ramon, like Heraclitus' fire, are consubstantial with the eternal principles of which they are the symbolic, mythic embodiments.

CHAPTER 2

Flesh, Word, and Holy Ghost:
Lawrence and Schopenhauer

WILL AND IDEA

Jessie Chambers says that Lawrence "seemed to read everything" (123). In addition to an impressive array of major and
minor novelists, poets, playwrights, and essayists, he educated
himself in philosophy. Not only did he make himself truly
contemporary with the latest philosophical thought in the form
of figures like James, Haeckel, Spencer, and Huxley, but he also
read a number of other philosophers like Locke, Berkeley, and
Mill (Chambers 112). There may well have been others. Jessie
points out that her "account of Lawrence's reading makes no
claim to be exhaustive ... He certainly read much more than is
indicated here" (123). Her account makes clear, however, that
there was one philosopher in particular who had a singular
impact on Lawrence:

It was during his second year in College that Lawrence began to read
philosophy. I cannot be sure whether he read Kant during this period,
but he advised one of my brothers to give me Schopenhauer's *Essays*
for my birthday, and read *The Metaphysics of Love* aloud to us. He
translated the Latin quotations in pencil in the margin ... This essay
made a deep impression upon him ... He followed the reasoning
closely, as always applying it to himself, and his own case ...
Schopenhauer seemed to fit in with his mood. He thought he found
there an explanation of his own divided attitude and he remained
under the influence of this line of reasoning for some time. (111–12)

The impact of Schopenhauer was apparent to other observers
like Jessie's sister: "Bert began to change and I asked him if

College was doing it, or was it Schopenhauer? 'Life,' he said, 'and it gives me spiritual dyspepsia'" (Nehls 3: 609).

The White Peacock, the novel on which Lawrence was working during this period, shows Cyril, the Lawrence figure, expounding his "rudimentary metaphysics" and enthusiastically explaining Schopenhauer's ideas to George, who was modeled on Jessie's brother (66). *The White Peacock* parades Lawrence's wide reading on almost every page, to the extent that the reviewers found the characters "insufferably cultured" and the novel "overcharged intellectually" (Draper 37, 40). Amid all the allusions, ranging from Horace to Tristram Shandy to Aubrey Beardsley, those to Schopenhauer predominate and are clearly most central to the novel's themes.

It is thus easy to establish a direct connection and to make a case for the influence of the great German pessimist on the young Englishman from the Midlands, and several critics, including Daniel J. Schneider, Allan R. Zoll, Mitzi M. Brunsdale, and Eleanor H. Green, have explored the indebtedness of Lawrence to Schopenhauer. My approach, while intent on exploring the *relation* between Lawrence and Schopenhauer, differs from these others in that it is emphatically not a study in influence. I treat Schopenhauer not as a source of certain ideas that appear in Lawrence but rather as an "explicatory parallel" (Michael Bell). For instance, Lawrence's first philosophical essay, the "Foreword" to *Sons and Lovers*, proposes two terms, Flesh and Word, that are strikingly close to Schopenhauer's will and idea. I use Schopenhauer's principal work *The World as Will and Idea* to explore the meaning of Lawrence's terms. Schopenhauer's work is a philosophically systematic, reticulated version of ideas that remain more implicit in Lawrence's more condensed and metaphoric style. I also use Schopenhauer to highlight and to throw into greater relief philosophical issues raised in Lawrence's writings. Schopenhauer's attempt to overcome Cartesian dualism sheds light on Lawrence's own attempt. In addition, Schopenhauer is Lawrence's first contact with a vitalist philosophical tradition in German thought extending from Boehme through the Romantics to Nietzsche.

I do not use *The World as Will and Idea* as a source or influence because there is no evidence, direct or indirect, that Lawrence actually read part or all of the book. In order to establish influence, the critic must first prove that A actually read certain works by B; he then must resist the powerful temptation to find evidence of B's influence where it does not exist; he must also not ascribe to B ideas and formulations that could just as well have come from C or D or any number of others, not to mention the possibility that A may have had an idea of his own. Daniel J. Schneider, for instance, says in *D. H. Lawrence: The Artist as Psychologist* that "a major part of Lawrence's art can be regarded as a development from the Schopenhauerian antithesis between *will* and *idea*" (29). Schneider quotes freely from *The World as Will and Idea*, clearly assuming that Lawrence read and studied it. Zoll and Brunsdale make the same assumption. These critics may be relying on Rose Marie Burwell's "A Catalogue of D. H. Lawrence's Reading from Early Childhood," which lists *The World as Will and Idea* (210) as well as the translation of the *Essays* by Mrs. Rudolf Dircks. Burwell's source for citing *The World as Will and Idea* is Harry T. Moore's *The Intelligent Heart*, which states that Lawrence read aloud to Jessie and her brother "The Metaphysics of Love" chapter from *The World as Will and Idea*" (68). But "The Metaphysics of Love" is not a chapter of *The World as Will and Idea*, although it is published in some editions as a Supplement. Even if it were a chapter of the larger work, Lawrence encountered it in Dircks's *Essays*, and there is no evidence that he ever held in his hands *The World as Will and Idea*. Burwell seems to have realized Moore's mistake because a later version of her "Checklist" printed in Keith Sagar's *A D. H. Lawrence Handbook* omits the citation of *The World as Will and Idea*, leaving the *Essays* as the only work by Schopenhauer that Lawrence definitely read.

Emile Delavenay published the annotations to "The Metaphysics of Love" that Lawrence wrote in the margins of Jessie's copy, providing further evidence that Lawrence read at least that essay. Again, however, there is no evidence that Lawrence even read any of the other essays, despite Eleanor H. Green's assumption that "It is unlikely that Lawrence did not read and reflect at length on the entire volume before asking Jessie to read it" (330). Mitzi M. Brunsdale shares this assumption (74), in spite of having quoted (49) Lawrence's own vehement statement: "Systematic reading be damned!... I find that by reading what I feel I want to read, I get the most benefit" (*Letters* 1: 59). It is entirely conceivable that Lawrence only read the one essay that discussed the topic of most burning concern to him – sexual love. All of the references to Schopenhauer in *The White Peacock* are to this essay, and there is nowhere in Lawrence's writings evidence that he read anything else of Schopenhauer's. I am not saying that Lawrence did not read the other essays or even *The World as Will and Idea*; I am saying that there is no evidence that he did, and we cannot assume any but the briefest familiarity with Schopenhauer's system. "The Metaphysics of Love" merely glances in passing at the concepts of will and idea, nowhere explaining them in any detail, and Lawrence never uses the terms "will" and "idea" in a specifically Schopenhauerian sense. Moreover, Lawrence seems to have been most taken with some of Schopenhauer's less rational, more bizarre ideas. According to Jessie, Lawrence "was vehemently of Schopenhauer's opinion that a white skin is not natural to man, and had a fierce argument with my brother who disputed the statement that 'fair hair and blue eyes are a deviation from type'" (111).

In addition to lacking sufficient evidence for direct influence, Schneider and Zoll in particular ascribe a role to Schopenhauer in Lawrence's intellectual development out of all proportion to its reality. Schneider goes so far as to assert that Lawrence read Schopenhauer as Thomas Mann read him: "as one reads only once in a life-time" (*Consciousness* 49). Allan R. Zoll in his essay on "Vitalism and the Metaphysics of Love: D. H. Lawrence and Schopenhauer" similarly assumes Lawrence's extensive familiarity with Schopenhauer's ideas and overstates his importance: "the fundamental metaphysics of being described by Schopenhauer remains basic to and a constant in his thinking; indeed Lawrence's works can be taken as a progression of working out the implication of Schopenhauer's ideas" (19). In addition to exaggerating Schopenhauer's importance, Zoll's

statement obscures the fact that, after a period of youthful
enthusiasm, Lawrence decisively departed from Schopenhauer's philosophical position.

It is nevertheless easy to understand Schneider and Zoll
because the similarities between Lawrence and Schopenhauer
are so striking and extensive. Schopenhauer is undeniably
important to an understanding of Lawrence. For one thing,
Schopenhauer is a convenient summary and representative of
much that was "in the air" and that could have, and did, come
to Lawrence from any number of other sources. Lawrence
himself has helped place Schopenhauer's importance in a list of
his early reading in a short story called "A Modern Lover":

There, by that hearth, they had threshed the harvest of their youth's
experience, gradually burning the chaff of sentimentality and false
romance that covered the real grain of life. How infinitely far away
now, seemed *Jane Eyre* and George Eliot. These had marked the
beginning. He smiled as he traced the graph onwards, plotting the
points with Carlyle and Ruskin, Schopenhauer and Darwin and
Huxley, Omar Khayyam, the Russians, Ibsen and Balzac; then Guy
de Maupassant and *Madame Bovary*. They had parted in the midst of
Madame Bovary. Since then had come only Nietzsche and William
James. They had not done so badly, he thought. (6)

This passage nicely traces the curve from the Victorians to the
moderns and shows that Schopenhauer's was but one of a
chorus of voices all contributing to the same result. The benign
and retrospectively assured tone, however, belies the dev-
astating impact of these thinkers, not only on Lawrence but on
his entire generation. As John Lester's convincing and well-
documented *Journey Through Despair* 1880–1914 reminds us, this
period was one of widespread pessimism and hopelessness.
Among the intelligentsia at least, there was a sense that man
had lost his place in the universe and, with that, his sense of the
meaning of life. According to Lester, as a result of this "major
transformation taking place in man's imaginative orientation to
the world," "two axioms which had long been assumed to be
vital if existence was to have any significance" were struck
down: "The first axiom held that somewhere within or behind
or beyond the world of observable experience there was an

eternal and credible truth, a truth accordant to, or at least consistent with, the human spirit and its aspirations. The second axiom held that man possessed a faculty capable of at least dimly perceiving that truth" (20–21).

The challenge to these axioms came primarily from Darwin, who seemed to have proven scientifically that man is not a special creation of a conscious Creator. Darwin extended the scientific way of thinking from the sphere of inanimate matter described once and for all by Newton to the biological sphere. There, too, blind matter and brute force are the only ultimate realities. There is no inherent purpose or meaning in creation; consciousness, will, reason are mere epiphenomena. To the empty infinity of space that so terrified Pascal was added an infinity of time. Darwin opened up a temporal perspective that further dwarfed man and displaced him from the center of the universe, a perspective that moreover revealed countless eons of time before man, the accidental product of natural selection, even existed.

The major movements of thought of the age – from the materialism of Huxley and Haeckel, to the realism of Ibsen and Maupassant, to the perspectivism of Nietzsche and the pragmatism of James – can all be seen as responses to Darwinism. For the realists and naturalists, man is henceforth to be seen as what he actually is, an animal struggling for survival who deludes himself with false ideas and metaphysical fantasies. For Huxley, drawing out the implications Darwin himself was reluctant to face, "life" is nothing more than the combination of oxygen, hydrogen, nitrogen, and carbon. "Man has no spirit or soul independent of the body, but only a brain in which molecular changes, determined by external stimuli, give automatic rise to all his thoughts and all his actions" (70). Nietzsche – at least one side of him – has much in common with James's Pragmatism; his slashing attacks on logic and reason place human thought in an evolutionary perspective in which "truth" is constantly changing and ideas are to be judged only by their adequacy in furthering life.

Depression and pessimism need not be the inevitable result of these ideas, but they certainly were in the case of many sensitive souls besides Lawrence, especially when these ideas were combined with those of Schopenhauer, the other great influence on the pessimism of the time. *The World as Will and Idea* first appeared much earlier, in 1819, but it was only in the latter part of the century that his ideas took hold and he became the most famous Continental philosopher after Kant. John Lester calls "the powerful appeal of Schopenhauer's entire despairing view of the world to a generation sixty years after his first major pronouncement ... the most striking instance of prophecy ... in the cultural life of the nineteenth century" (65). It was only after the shock of Darwin had been absorbed that Schopenhauer's views could be widely entertained, and the fact that Schopenhauer's will bore such striking similarities to Darwin's nature gave the earlier thinker an almost prophetic status. Darwin and Schopenhauer became associated in men's minds (the passage from "A Modern Lover" quoted above shows that for Lawrence the two names were linked). That Schopenhauer was neither an evolutionist nor a philosophical materialist posed few problems, as the case of Thomas Hardy shows. Already a confirmed Darwinian by the time he read Schopenhauer, Hardy easily incorporated the German's thought and became a Schopenhauerian as well.

A good deal of Schopenhauer's immense appeal to artists like Hardy, Wagner, and Thomas Mann lies in his style, second among German philosophers only to his disciple Nietzsche in its clarity and wit. Even at his most technical, he is never as abstruse as his master Kant or his hated enemy Hegel. His system as presented in *The World as Will and Idea* has a grand bipartite symmetry, built around a single overarching division – between the world as idea (or representation) and the world as will. The world as idea is the outer world of objects perceived by our senses and reflected upon by our thought processes. Like Kant's phenomenal world, the world as idea is illusory and unreal. We cannot know it as it exists in itself, apart from the forms and categories imposed upon it by our minds. The will, by contrast, is real and partakes of the noumenal reality of the *ding an sich*.

For Kant the *ding an sich* is unknowable, but Schopenhauer

asserts that man can know the inner reality of the will through
the body, which alone of all objects is given to us in two ways,
as an external object perceived by our senses and as an inner,
immediate experience. This inner sense of ourselves as an
individual – that in us which feels, desires, suffers, that which
affirms "I am" – is the will. Schopenhauer says that a "single
thought" sums up his entire philosophy : "My body and my will
are one" (119). It is through the body, not the mind, through
feeling not reason, that man experiences the reality not only of
himself but of nature, for all objects, from atoms to minerals to
plants to animals to humans, comprise an ascending series of
objectifications of one and the same will. This thought marks a
major shift in the traditional hierarchies of Western thought
and is Schopenhauer's most important legacy to his successors.
Nietzsche, Freud, and James all begin with the body, and
psychology gradually displaces idealist metaphysics as the
queen of the sciences. Henceforth we must learn to read the
body, for the body is the "will become visible," and its language
is a "paraphrase" of the will. "Every true act of his will is also
and without exception a movement of his body": "As the
human form generally corresponds to the human will generally,
so the individual bodily structure corresponds to the indi-
vidually modified will, the character of the individual, and
therefore it is throughout and in all its parts characteristic and
full of expression" (124–25). Lawrence's presentation of the
body marks him as a Schopenhauerian novelist, for, as W. H.
Auden says, "When we try to read a person's character, not
from his words, not even from his face, but from the shape and
movement of his body, we are doing something Lawrence
taught us to do" (482).

   The good news, then, would seem to be that through the body
Schopenhauer has found a way out of Kantian agnosticism.
Man can indeed know the eternal truth "within or behind or
beyond the world of observable experience" (Lester 21). The
bad news, however, is the nature of the will. Far from being
"accordant to, at least consistent with, the human spirit and its
aspirations" (Lester 21), the will is directly inimical to them.
The will is not rational or beautiful or good; it is irrational,

blind, terrible. The will is simply a will to live. Like Darwin's nature, the will has no end or purpose beyond sheer perpetuation of itself. It cares nothing for the transitory individual in which it is momentarily objectified. Just as any single organism is dwarfed and lost in the face of nature's prodigality and immensity, so the phenomenal world of forms is devoured by the insatiable will. In a passage typical of many, Schopenhauer strikes this Darwinian note:

> For it is not the individual, but only the species that Nature cares for, and for the preservation of which she so earnestly strives, providing for it with the utmost prodigality through the vast surplus of the seed and the great strength of the fructifying impulse ... Therefore she is always ready to let the individual fall, and hence it is not only exposed to destruction in a thousand ways by the most insignificant accident, but originally destined for it, and conducted towards it by Nature herself. (288)

In one respect at least, Darwin takes this disheartening vision a step further, for where Schopenhauer assumes the constancy of species – man, if not individual men, will survive – Darwin opens up an evolutionary perspective in which countless species have become extinct, a fate from which man himself is not logically exempt.

Schopenhauer's will is every bit as red in tooth and claw as Darwin's nature. The will is eternally "hungry," and since "there exists nothing beside it," the will must live on itself. "Everywhere in nature we see strife, conflict, and alternation of victory": "This universal conflict becomes most distinctly visible in the animal kingdom ... for each animal can only maintain its existence by the constant destruction of some other. Thus the will to live everywhere preys on itself ... till finally the human race ... reveals in itself with most terrible distinctness this conflict ... and we find *homo homini lupus*" (162–63). The will can never be satisfied – a satisfied will is a contradiction in terms. There is only a "constant transition from desire to satisfaction, and from satisfaction to a new desire." There is only constant suffering, since "All willing arises from want, therefore from deficiency, and therefore from suffering" (209).

Schopenhauer's powerful message can be summarized in the simple proposition that life is endless pain and suffering without meaning or purpose.

Jessie Chambers tells us that Lawrence "felt compelled to accept" this view of life "for lack of an alternative": "He would tell me with such vehemence that nature is red in tooth and claw, with the implication that 'nature' included human nature. Yet when he heard the cry of a rabbit tracked by a weasel he would shiver in pain. His dominant feeling seemed to be a sense of hopelessness" (117). *The White Peacock* dwells obsessively on the bloody and cruel aspect of nature. The atmosphere around Nethermere is repeatedly shattered by the screams of the maimed and dying. We hear "the scream of a rabbit caught by a weasel" (27), "the cruel pitiful crying of a hedgehog caught in a gin...baited with the guts of a killed rabbit" (50), "a thin, wailing cry" from some wild animal in the woods, and "the cruel yelling" of pigs being slaughtered. Nature produces far more than she can support, necessitating the early death of most of her progeny. Even mothers are heedless of the welfare of their offspring: a sow eats part of her own litter; a baby chick abandoned by its mother is put on the stove to warm and falls into the red-hot coals. Nature's swarming fecundity is evoked in scenes of casual mass destruction. A little family of mice is uncovered in the grass and destroyed. George carelessly "put his hand to the bottom of the trough, bringing out a handful of silt, with the grey shrimps twisting in it. He flung the mud on the floor where the poor grey creatures writhed" (253). And it is George again who desultorily pokes at a bee's nest, trapping one of the agitated creatures and pulling its wings off, then tearing the nest apart to examine the eggs; "When he had finished he flung the clustered eggs into the water" (4).

Lawrence's sensitive characters, Lettie, Emily, and Cyril, repeatedly shudder with horror at the fact that, as Lettie exclaims, "If we move the blood rises in our heel-prints" (17). One is reminded of Hardy, in whom, as John Lester says, "sympathy for animals in pain becomes an indication" of any character's "moral worth" (18). Lester notes an increased sympathy with animals as a phenomenon of the times, the explanation of which may also lie in Darwinism. If man is no longer different in some crucial way from the animals, if both are strictly natural phenomena subject alike to unrelieved suffering and pain, then our sympathy for ourselves is easily extended to other species which share our fate.

In *The White Peacock*, however, even the sensitive are guilty of participating in the round of carnage. The thin veneer of civilization is quickly stripped away as Leslie, the cultured mine-owner's son, almost pulls the head off a rabbit "in his excitement to kill it." Emily – diffident, tender, soft-hearted – gets caught up in the lust to kill as she joins in the chase for one of the sheep-killing dogs and catches it:

There, in the mouth of one of the kilns, Emily was kneeling on the dog, her hands buried in the hair of its throat, pushing back its head. The little jerks of the brute's body were the spasms of death; already the eyes were turning inward, and the upper lip was drawn back from the teeth by pain ... She shuddered violently, and seemed to feel a horror of herself... looking at herself with blood all on her skirt, where she had knelt on the wound ... and pressed the broken rib into the chest. There was a trickle of blood on her arm. (75–76)

That Lawrence felt compelled to create such an implausible scene is a telling indication of the depth of his preoccupation with this theme.

What arguments can be brought to bear in opposition to Schopenhauer's view of things? A rejoinder might run as follows: Granted that man is a physical animal born to suffer and die and that the will is cruel and unheeding – but what about the culture that man has created in opposition to nature? Culture transcends nature; through art, philosophy, and religion, man gains access to a higher realm. Beauty, reason, and love lead us beyond the merely natural. Schopenhauer has anticipated this rejoinder and will have none of it. Love is an illusion. In his essay on "The Metaphysics of the Love of the Sexes," which Lawrence read with intense fascination, Schopenhauer describes all love, "however ethereal," as rooted in the "incredible strength" of the sexual impulse, which is

merely the will's way of insuring the propagation of the species
(335). There is no Platonic ladder reaching from sexual to
divine love. There is only the will's overmastering need to live,
against which the higher aspirations of the individual count for
nothing. A man who thinks he is in love with a beautiful woman
is "the dupe of the species" (346). Beauty too is an illusion,
whose only purpose is to draw the man to the woman and hold
him to her long enough to reproduce. "Just as the female ant
loses its wings after mating, since they are then superfluous,
indeed harmful to the purpose of raising the family, so the
woman usually loses her beauty after one or two childbeds"
(363).

Schopenhauer's notorious misogyny comes out in such
statements as the following: "Only a male intellect clouded by
the sexual drive could call the stunted, narrow-shouldered,
broad-hipped and short-legged sex the fair sex; for it is with this
drive that all beauty is bound up" (344). His dislike of woman
stems from, among other things, the fact that she is an
accomplice of the will. "Women exist solely for the propagation
of the race." They are incapable of anything else, lacking
reasoning power, having no feeling for the arts, and being
unfitted for physical labor. Marriage to such a creature spells
disaster for the man, whose potential for higher things is
sacrificed on the marital altar (Hardy's Jude and Arabella are
the classic Schopenhauerian couple):

But so much more powerful is the will of the species than that of the
individual that the lover shuts his eyes to all those qualities which are
repellent to him, overlooks all, ignores all, and blinds himself forever
to the object of his passion – so entirely is he blinded by that illusion,
which vanishes as soon as the will of the species is satisfied, and leaves
behind a detested companion for life. Only from this can it be
explained that we often see very reasonable and excellent men bound
to termagants and she-devils, and cannot conceive how they could
have made such a choice. (364)

Lawrence underlined this passage from "The Metaphysics of
the Love of the Sexes" in his copy of Schopenhauer's *Essays* and
doubly underlined the description of marriage as most often "a
howling discord" (Delavenay 236). Obviously thinking of his

own parents, Lawrence was obsessed by the idea of the sacrifice of the individual in the marriage trap. Lettie mockingly says to George, "You, for instance – fancy *your* sacrificing yourself – for the next generation – that reminds you of Schopenhauer, doesn't it? – for the next generation, or love, or anything!" (230). Of course this is precisely the fate of George and of Lettie herself, as well as of every other character in the novel except Cyril.

Lawrence differs from Schopenhauer in that his sympathy is extended as much to the woman as to the man, and Lettie's beauty and intelligence make her something quite different from Schopenhauer's breeding ninnies. But she is not exempted from the Schopenhauerian fate. Married to Leslie, with whom she is quickly disillusioned, she gradually loses the spark of life that made her the most captivating character in the novel. "A subtle observer might have noticed a little hardness about her mouth, and disillusion hanging slightly on her eyes." She seeks relief in children: "I hope I shall have another child next spring, there is only that to take away the misery of this torpor. I seem full of passion and energy, and it all fizzles out in day to day domestics." Most of "the things in life seemed worthless and insipid" to her, and she "determined to put up with it, to ignore her own self, to empty her own potentialities into the vessel of another or others, and to live her life at second-hand … to abandon the charge of herself to serve her children" (309–11).

While Lawrence identifies and sympathizes with the woman, he also has a fear of the female that exceeds even Schopenhauer's. Lawrence's natural analogue is the black widow spider or the praying mantis rather than the flying ant. In *The White Peacock*, the female, once fertilized, turns on the male and kills him. She turns all her love and care towards the child, excluding the man, who is "put away, quite alone, neglected, forgotten, outside the glow which surrounded the woman and her baby" (303). George comes to realize that "marriage is more of a duel than a duet" and that the woman wins because "she has the children on her side" (329–30). Cyril sees this clearly as he contemplates Meg with one of her children:

The mother's dark eyes, and the baby's large, hazel eyes looked at me serenely. The two were very calm, very complete and triumphant together. In their completeness was a security which made me feel alone and ineffectual. A woman who has her child in her arms is a tower of strength, a beautiful, unassailable tower of strength that may in its turn stand quietly dealing death. (320)

So much for love. What then of man's capacity for rational thought, traditionally believed to give him access to an eternally true realm of ideas? For Schopenhauer, thought is a pale reflection of the will, a secondary phenomenon belonging to the world as idea or representation. Thought cannot lead us beyond the body and the senses. On the contrary, "Abstract knowledge . . . always merely approximates to ... sensuous knowledge" (75). Rational knowledge merely reproduces in concepts what has already become known through the body, and this knowledge is "one-sided" and narrow, the "direct opposite" of the "immeasurably wide" world of feeling (68). Schopenhauer even suggests that man would be better off without reason:

As from the direct light of the sun to the borrowed light of the moon, we pass from the immediate idea of perception ... to reflection, to the abstract, discursive concepts of the reason ... As long as we continue simply to perceive, all is clear, firm, and certain. There are neither questions nor doubts nor errors; we desire to go no further, can go no further; we find rest in perceiving, and satisfaction in the present ... But with abstract knowledge, with reason, doubt and error appear in the theoretical, care and sorrow in the practical. (50)

Doubt and sorrow attend the birth of rational consciousness. This was Lawrence's own experience, recreated in the histories of George and Lettie. Before he begins to think, George is a happy, healthy animal living in harmony with his bucolic surroundings. The modern ideas to which Cyril and Lettie introduce him merely baffle him, check his free-flowing life. "There was a painful perplexity in his brow, such as I often pictured afterwards, a sense of something hurting, something he could not understand" (35). He adopts socialist ideas, but they only increase his misery, exemplifying Schopenhauer's view that abstract thoughts "inflict torments in comparison with

which all the sufferings of the animal world are very small"
(311). At an impasse, incapable of moving further into thought
or of forgetting what he has learned, he begins to wither and
shrink. Thought ravages his body as much as alcohol, until by
the end his once-magnificent physique is a decayed wreck.
Thought, says Schopenhauer, can "wear out the body oftener
and more than physical hardships" (311).

Thought is also partially responsible for destroying Lettie's
vitality. The virus of modern ideas – "the torture of strange,
complex modern life" – enters her system, causing her to
become feverish and fretful. "She, who had always been so
rippling in thoughtless life, sat down at the window sill to think,
and her strong teeth bit at her handkerchief till it was torn in
holes. She would say nothing to me; she read all things that
dealt with modern woman" (83). And Cyril, the most intelligent character in the novel, seems merely paralyzed,
suspended, by his greater awareness. He "burns his body in his
head" (105) and is unable to find release from his painful self-
consciousness even in drink. Only Emily's husband Tom is
happy, precisely because he does not think: "He was ex-
ceedingly manly: that is to say he did not dream of questioning
or analysing anything. All that came his way was ready labelled
nice or nasty, good or bad. He did not imagine that anything
could be other than just what it appeared to be: – and with this
appearance, he was quite content" (38).

Trapped between nature and culture, Lawrence's characters
can find fulfillment in neither. Every important male figure
comes to a bad end, with the possible exception of Cyril, who is
present through the last part of the novel only as an observing
intelligence necessitated by the first-person narrative, and about
whom we know little except that he is living abroad. Rejected
by their mother years ago, Cyril's and Lettie's father dies a
pathetic alcoholic, alone, "worn with sickness and dissipation,"
and tortured by bad dreams. George reaches a similar end,
rotten clear through, "like a tree that is falling, going soft and
pale and rotten, clammy with small fungi" (354). And Annable
the gamekeeper is crushed to death in the quarry. Nor do the
women fare much better. Lettie's attainment of a higher social

status, complete with cultured evenings with cultured guests, is no more of a real solution for her than are her children. Emily attains a measure of contentment with the stolid Tom but shirks her further development by retreating from her melancholy awareness of life's pain into a falsely cheery, willed domesticity.

Annable, introduced into the novel late in its writing, is a desperate attempt on the part of Lawrence's imagination to find an alternative, a resolution of the conflict between nature and culture, body and mind. Annable has been to Cambridge and was once a parson married to a lady. Now, however, he has turned his back on civilization, which he considers nothing but "the painted fungus of rottenness," and taken to the woods, where he busies himself with purely physical tasks. His "magnificent physique, great vigour and vitality" embody primal natural energy, like "Pan" or "a devil of the woods." A "thorough materialist," his motto is "Be a good animal, true to your animal instinct." He takes pride in his large brood of children, "natural as weasels ... bred up like a bunch o' young hares, to run as they would" (143–44).

Cyril is strongly attracted to Annable, who at first seems to hold out the possibility of a return to nature, of a life in accord with the will. The unhappy truth, however, is that Annable is gloomy, miserable, and bitter. His wife is "dragged to bits" trying to care for his eight children and one on the way. The family's life is a squalid horror, with dirty screaming children fighting over their few possessions and his wife flying into rages and beating them. After Annable's death, as much a suicidal act as an "accident," the family descends even further, forced to move into slums in town and steal food for dinner. Cyril, who had looked upon Annable as a substitute father, is forced to conclude, "I suppose he did not know what he was doing, any more than the rest of us" (203).

There are scattered hints of a way out of the Schopenhauerian dilemma. Early in the novel, Lettie says to George:

"You never grow up, like bulbs which spend all summer getting fat and fleshy, but never wakening the germ of a flower. As for me, the flower is born in me, but it wants bringing forth. Things don't flower if they're overfed. You have to suffer before you blossom in this life.

When death is just touching a plant, it forces it into a passion of flowering." (33)

There is an implicit rejection here of the fatalistic view of man as a helpless victim of the will of the species. "The Metaphysics of Love" maintains that man is helpless because the will is "the immortal part" of him. Lawrence wrote two exclamation marks opposite this phrase and asked the question, "Is the 'will to live' the only immortal part?" (Delavenay 237). Is there not something in the individual as immortal as the species? The Lawrence who asked this question is the same Lawrence who believes that George's fate could have been otherwise. George has free will but shirks the responsibility to himself to take the terrifying leap into greater being, to burst the fleshy rind. Yes, life is suffering, but suffering, if embraced and not evaded, can eventuate in a joyous creativity, a "passion of flowering." Blossoming is more than a mere metaphor; it points to a communion of substance between flower and man. Both are products of nature, life forms through which the same force flows. Just as the flower is latent in the seed, so for Lettie "the flower is born in me, but it wants bringing forth." The question then becomes, What is *human* flowering? It must involve the integration of the physical and the mental, for man is inescapably both. Committed to a Schopenhauerian view of the mental, however, Lawrence cannot conceptualize its role in this integration, and his characters all wither in the bud.

Despite such hints, and despite moments of gaiety and lyrical celebration of nature as a source of beauty and solace, the bright notes consistently give way to horror and a sense of failure and frustration. What one chapter heading calls "the dominant motif of suffering" prevails. Lawrence himself described *The White Peacock* as "a decorated idyll running to seed in realism." The idyll he apparently intended becomes, under the pressure of his personal and philosophical concerns, an elegiac lament for a lost world (one hears "Nevermore" in "Nethermere"). Gone is the vitality of former times when Robin Hood roamed the local woods and monks prayed in the now-ruined monastery. Modern civilization is vitiated and rotten; it has torn apart the fabric of the once-pastoral Midlands, just as modern thought fractures and cripples those exposed to it. Here again Schopenhauer has the last word. He describes the idyll as an attempt to portray "a genuine enduring happiness," but the attempt must fail: "all happiness is only of a negative not a positive nature," and "just on this account it cannot be lasting satisfaction and gratification" (331).

BLOOD AND INTELLECT

Lancelot Law Whyte's *The Unconscious Before Freud* shows that, far from being Freud's discovery, the unconscious as a concept already had a long history before Freud began to write and that most of Freud's ideas had been anticipated by thinkers like Schopenhauer and Nietzsche. Whyte's brilliant historical sketch helps us to grasp Schopenhauer's historical importance and to identify a distinct intellectual tradition to which he and Lawrence both belong. The tradition begins as a reaction to Descartes, "the first thinker to assert a sharp division of mind from matter" (23). Descartes postulates two completely separate realms of being, one of which is characterized exclusively by awareness. "For those who were loyal to Descartes, all that was not conscious in man was material and physiological, and therefore not mental" (55). Whyte feels that this separation "may prove one of the fundamental blunders made by the human mind" and takes as his theme "the development of the conception of 'unconscious mental processes' as a first correction of that Cartesian blunder" (23–24).

Until an attempt had been made (with apparent success) to choose *awareness* as the defining characteristic of an independent mode of being called mind, there was no occasion to invent the idea of *unconscious* mind as a provisional correction of that choice. It is only after Descartes that we find, first the idea and then the term, "unconscious mind" entering European thought. (25)

In opposition to Descartes, the thinkers who assert the existence of unconscious mind "say, in effect, either: 'If there are two realms, physical and mental, awareness cannot be taken as the criterion of mentality,' or, going further: 'The assumption of two separate realms is untenable, for the unity displayed in their interactions is more important than their separation'" (24).

Despite its immense success and consequent prestige, Cartesianism is a blunder, according to Whyte, because consciousness is "secondary" not "primary." Consciousness arises as the result of a clash between man and his environment. "Thus *self-awareness is basically self-eliminating*; its biological function is apparently to catalyze processes which tend to remove its cause, in each situation. Consciousness is like a fever which, if not excessive, hastens curative processes and so eliminates its source. Hence its transitory, wandering, and often strangely unreasonable character" (30).

After Descartes, a new character type appears, "*self-conscious man*, as the individual who is excessively self-aware, does not understand the etiology or limitations of this condition, and treats self-awareness not as a sequence of self-eliminating moments of fever, but as primary in theory, in value, or in action" (30). Self-conscious man cannot be "whole-natured" and is "doomed to misery," his consciousness being preoccupied with "pain and conflict" (30–31). Moreover,

valid rational understanding of man and nature cannot be reached by treating as primary what is self-eliminating and therefore normally transient. It is philosophically inconceivable that so slippery a feature as consciousness could hold the clue to an ordering of anything. . . man's self-awareness is not itself an independent controlling organ. It is one differentiated aspect only of the total organ of mind, important for the identification and ordering of contrasts, yet never the ultimate determinant of any ordering process, in thought or behavior. The decisive factors, the primary decisions, are unconscious. (32–33)

At first, this awareness of unconscious mind appeared in scattered thinkers like Paracelsus, Montaigne, Shakespeare, Boehme, whose "importance cannot be measured" (76), Shaftesbury, and Leibniz. Then, after 1750, what Whyte calls "the great transformation" (44) occurred – a profound shift in Western thought whose most important representatives are "a sequence of German philosophers: Schelling, Hegel, Schopenhauer, and Nietzsche, who developed the conception of the unconscious mind as a dynamic principle underlying conscious reason" (112). Schopenhauer's central place in this tradition is a result of his making "the idea of an unconscious will in nature and man the center of his thought... He touched on most aspects of the unconscious as we think of it today" (132). Schopenhauer's prescience and influence are truly remarkable – again and again he formulates ideas that could have been written by Freud – and can be seen in the Schopenhauerian cast of Whyte's own description of consciousness. The compelling description of the vastly superior strength of the unconscious will in comparison to conscious choice, the identification of the will with the body, the conception of the unconscious as man's link with the organic and the powers of nature, the view of consciousness as secondary and epiphenomenal, the association of consciousness with misery, the awareness of the limitations of "self-conscious man" – all these are essential features of a world-view first articulated in all its aspects by Schopenhauer and shared by Lawrence.

This Schopenhauerian legacy remained a constant in Lawrence's thought. We see it clearly in an important, oft-quoted letter to Ernest Collings written in January 1913, six or seven years after he first read Schopenhauer:

My great religion is a belief in the blood, the flesh, as being wiser than the intellect. We can go wrong in our minds. But what our blood feels and believes and says, is always true. The intellect is only a bit and a bridle. What do I care about knowledge. All I want is to answer to my blood, direct, without fribbling intervention of mind, or moral, or what not. I conceive a man's body as a kind of flame, like a candle flame forever upright and yet flowing: and the intellect is just the light that is shed onto the things around. And I am not so much concerned with the things around; – which is really mind: – but with the mystery of the flame forever flowing ... (*Letters* 1: 503)

It is the blood, which is the unconscious, that links man with reality, not the mind, which is secondary and hopelessly mistaken in its conclusions.

For Schopenhauer this reversal of the traditional Western hierarchies has important ethical consequences. He notes that the traditional idea of the freedom of the will from Plato on places the inner nature of man in a *soul*, which is originally a *knowing*, and indeed really an abstract *thinking* nature, and only in consequence of this a *willing* nature – a doctrine which thus regards the will as of a secondary or derivative nature, instead of knowledge which is really so. The will indeed came to be regarded as an act of thought, and to be identified with the judgment, especially by Descartes and Spinoza. According to this doctrine every man ... must first know a thing to be *good*, and in consequence of this will it, instead of first *willing* it, and in consequence of this calling it *good*. According to my fundamental point of view, all this is a reversal of the true relation. Will is first and original; knowledge is merely added to it as an instrument belonging to the phenomenon of will. (304)

Lawrence is thus a complete Schopenhauerian when he continues in the letter to Collings:

The real way of living is to answer to one's wants. Not "I want to light up with my intelligence as many things as possible" – but "For the living of my full flame – I want that liberty, I want that woman, I want that pound of peaches, I want to go to sleep, I want to go to the pub, and have a good time, I want to look a beastly swell today, I want to kiss that girl, I want to insult that man." – Instead of that, all these wants, which are there whether-or-not, are utterly ignored, and we talk about some sort of ideas. (504)

The month in which this letter was written, January 1913, is an important one in Lawrence's life because it also saw the writing of his first extended philosophical essay. Lawrence was residing at Lago di Garda, having won and carried off the woman who would become his wife and having written *Sons and Lovers*, a novel that he knew was "a great book" (*Letters* 1 : 477). Riding a crest of success and confidence, Lawrence for the first time comes fully into his prophetic vocation and speaks with a new authority.

The essay, intended to be a "foreword" to *Sons and Lovers*, extends the basic opposition between "blood" and "intellect" into the opposition between Flesh and Word. The first of a life-long series of attempts to formulate a coherent Weltshan-schauung, the essay is a remarkable document, containing in germ all of Lawrence's later thought and demonstrating its essential characteristics. Lawrence characteristically seeks to overturn the traditional hierarchy: "John, the beloved disciple, says, 'The Word was made Flesh.' But why should he turn things round? The women simply go on bearing talkative sons, as an answer. 'The Flesh was made Word'" (467). Lawrence's counter-testament rejects the spirituality of Christianity, insisting that it is as absurd to say that the Word created the Flesh as it is to say that the son creates the father. Christ was a man, a living body of flesh, and "flesh cometh only out of flesh" (467).

To reinforce his point, Lawrence – again characteristically – embarks upon an extended metaphor. In the case of an apple, it is a mistake to focus on the apple itself or the blossom as primary and to regard the seed as "mere secondary produce." The seed is the essential apple: "The little pip that one spits out has in it all the blossom and apple ... in its bit of white flesh ... " We look at the showy apparition of the blossom and think, "'This is the Utmost!'" but the blossom is only the "begetting stuff" of the dark source, the seed, beaten out "thin, thin, thin, till it is a pink or a purple petal, or a thought, or a Word" (470). The Flesh (the Father, the Seed) has a clear priority – temporally, causally, and ontologically – over the Word (the Son, the apple). Lawrence's choice of terminology is unfortunate, because we naturally associate the Flesh with the apple itself, but his point and his preoccupation are clear.

The essay is largely concerned to make the case that Christianity's reversal of the true order of things has created the predicament in which modern man finds himself. "The Son has usurped the Father. And so, the Father, which is the Flesh, withdraws from us ... " (468). Christianity has created in us an over-balance of spirituality. We have bound up our passions and constrained our desires in a net of words. We deny our desires and sacrifice ourselves for our neighbor, whereas the Flesh asserts its desires "and suffereth not from the hunger of the neighbour, but only from its own hunger" (468).

It should not be necessary at this point to underscore the parallels between Flesh and Word and Schopenhauer's will and idea. It is necessary, however, to draw out the fact that these opposites are thought of by both Lawrence and Schopenhauer as *polar* opposites. The second book of *The World as Will and Idea*

contains an extended discussion of polarity, which Schopenhauer defines as "the sundering of a force into two qualitatively
different and opposed activities striving after reunion" (159).
Drawing on Schelling and the German *Naturphilosophen*, as well
as Goethe and Boehme, Schopenhauer describes polarity as "a
fundamental type of almost all the phenomena of nature from
the magnet and crystal to man himself" (159). Schopenhauer
finds that the will itself, the essence of all natural phenomena, is
polaric, and this polarity is manifested at each level of nature or,
as he says, at each "grade of the objectification of will." The
very constitution of space itself, the generation of opposing
directions from a point, is a result of the law of polarity, as are
gravity, crystallization, "chemical attraction," magnetism,
electricity, plant growth, sensation, instinct, and so on, in a
series of higher "powers" of polarity, up to man. In man, the
opposition of the will with itself manifests in the body as a
polarity: "man is at once impetuous and blind striving of will
(whose pole or focus lies in the genital organs), and eternal, free,
serene subject of pure knowing (whose pole is the brain)" (216).
  The same idea of a polarity between brain and genitals
appears in Lawrence's poem "Virgin Youth":

> Now and again
> All my body springs alive,
> And the life that is polarised in my eyes,
> That quivers between my eyes and mouth,
> Flies like a wild thing across my body,
> Leaving my eyes half empty, and clamorous,
> Filling my still breasts with a flush and a flame,
> Gathering the soft ripples below my breasts
> Into urgent, passionate waves,
> And my soft, slumbering belly
> Quivering awake with one impulse of desire,
> Gathers itself fiercely together;
> And my docile, fluent arms
> Knotting myself with wild strength
> To clasp – what they have never clasped.
> Then I tremble, and go trembling
> Under the wild, strange tyranny of my body,
> Till it has spent itself,

And the relentless nodality of my eyes reasserts itself,
Till the bursting flood of life ebbs back into my eyes,
Back from my beautiful, lonely body
Tired and unsatisfied.   (*Poems* 896)

As in Schopenhauer, life is a polaric force like electricity that
ebbs and flows in a circuit from the upper pole in the head to the
lower pole, the "soft, slumbering belly," which is as close as this
virginal poem gets to the phallus.

Yet it is just at this point of close contact that we can see the
two thinkers begin to diverge towards fundamentally opposite
poles. Lawrence's lament is that the consciousness focused in the
mind so easily checks the flow of life to the phallus, that the
Word thwarts the desires of the Flesh, whereas Schopenhauer's
complaint is that the head has so little control. Lawrence calls
the intellect "only a bit and a bridle," whereas Schopenhauer
is clearly on the side of the intellect, which he characterizes as
"eternal, free, serene," "perfect," "the most delightful of
things."

Given what has been said so far about the will, it may come
as a surprise to find Schopenhauer describing intellect as
"eternal" and "free." Are not consciousness and thought mere
fleeting apparitions with no substantial reality, the foam on the
surface of the wave? Is not the mind the slave of the passions, a
mere instrument of the will, incapable of deflecting it from its
ends? Is not the will the *ding an sich*, the only thing that could
rightly be called eternal and free? Apparently not, for in the
fourth and final book of *The World as Will and Idea*, Schopenhauer suddenly asserts that in man the will comes to knowledge
of itself, to "full self-consciousness, to distinct and exhaustive
knowledge of its own nature." Because of this self-consciousness,
which animals lack, man is capable of making a free choice,
between either assertion or denial of the will. Since the will
promises nothing but endless suffering, the only sensible
recourse is to deny it. How can this be possible? It is possible,
Schopenhauer maintains, through knowledge itself, which
"suddenly ... breaks free from the service of the will" (119).
"This knowledge becomes for it a *quieter*, which appeases and
suppresses all willing" (319).

The highest examples of humanity are thus the ascetic saints of Christianity and the Indian religions, those rare individuals, who through "constant mortification of will," through complete and unyielding denial of gratification of all bodily impulses, achieve the bliss of freedom from the will. Chastity is essential to this denial since "the act of generation" is "the most decided assertion of the will to live" (339). Of course if all men were ascetics, "the human race would die out," and with it, "the rest of the world would vanish into nothing; for without a subject there is no object" (380). But this is precisely the goal for Schopenhauer – the return to nothingness expressed in the Hindu "reabsorption in Brahma or the Nirvana of the Buddhists." Schopenhauer's *magnum opus* ends on this note: "to those in whom the will has turned and denied itself, this our world, which is so real, with all its suns and milky ways – is nothing" (421).

This shocking conclusion, indeed the whole turn in Schopenhauer's thinking in the fourth book, raises more questions than it answers. How can Schopenhauer, for whom God does not exist and whose attitude towards religion is positively Voltairean, suddenly appear as the espouser of what he calls "the true Christian philosophy" (*Essays* 63)? Beyond that, there is the critical question of how knowledge can overcome the will. Schopenhauer insists throughout that will and idea are utterly distinct, "*toto genere*" (119); there is no point of contact between them. It is true that in the third book, which I have had to neglect, he discusses the Platonic Idea, which comes closer to the reality of the will than do the intellect or the senses, but even the Idea remains at a remove from the *ding an sich*. As Patrick Gardner says in his *Schopenhauer*, "the Platonic Ideas do not represent the inner metaphysical essence of the world: for that is the will." Gardner describes the Idea as occupying "a curious midway position between the two poles," neither touching the will nor relating directly to the world of objects (205–7). Must there not, however, be some point of contact if knowledge and will are to interact in such a way that one negates the other?

Erich Heller says that "at this point Schopenhauer's philosophical system issues in paradox, with irony taking over from logical consistency" (*Ironic* 28). But should we not expect logical consistency from our philosophers? The more we think about it, the more inconsistent Schopenhauer's system becomes. For instance, he calls knowledge or self-consciousness "the mirror of the will" (297). But what is it that looks into the mirror and sees itself there? The will is blind. How can it see unless it too is self-conscious, unless it shares a fundamental identity with the mirror? And if the mirror is self-consciousness it must be more than a mere passive reflector. Or, to put it another way, since the mirror is self-consciousness, it follows that it too must be a subject, not the object that Schopenhauer says it is. Otherwise, we are involved in the absurdity of an object becoming a subject. This is the rock on which all materialist systems, and quasi-materialist systems such as Schopenhauer's, founder. On the assumption of an original material or bodily unconscious substrate from which all things emerge, they cannot explain how consciousness could supervene to something that is by definition the very opposite of consciousness, let alone how it could overcome or negate it.

This is an important point, for it is here that the thinkers I have described as polaric decisively depart from Schopenhauer's position. For Boehme, the creation is the result of God's need for self-reflection and for a mirror (*Spiegel*) in which to see himself. Both consciousness and nature are aspects of God, in whom they find the ground of their unity. Nature is God's projection of himself but remains unself-conscious until the appearance of man, in whom God recognizes himself. For Coleridge, too, nature is "intellect" or Reason, which is another name for God: "In the objects of nature are presented, as in a mirror, all the possible elements, steps, and processes of intellect antecedent to consciousness" ("On Poesy" 255). In man, nature becomes conscious of its true nature as "identical, and one and the same thing with our own immediate self-consciousness" (*Biographia* 1: 260). Or, as he says elsewhere, "the mind is distinguished from other things as a subject, that is its own object, an eye, as it were that is its own mirror beholding and self-beheld" (qtd. in Barfield 212).

In one of the supplements to *The World as Will and Idea* titled

"Epiphilosophy," Schopenhauer asserts that his system has succeeded in showing "the true and deepest connection" between "the external world" and "self-consciousness," thus making Schopenhauer himself the first philosopher in history to comprehend "the nature of the world in its inner connection with itself" (372). "Hitherto every philosophy has represented one or the other [materialism or idealism]. I am the first to depart from this; for I have actually established the *Third*" (379). Despite his claims, however, Schopenhauer is actually another in the long line of victims of Cartesianism. His attempt fails because his thinking is insufficiently polaric. He speaks of will and idea as polar opposites, but he has not grasped the most important implication of polarity, namely, that two contradictories must themselves be the products of an antecedent unity. His system splits apart into two disjunct halves. Or rather it stands revealed as an intoxicating brew of many incompatible elements – pessimism, atheism, Buddhism, vitalism, Kantianism, Platonism, and anti-Hegelianism – held together by style and force of character. Instead of penetrating to their common ground, he is concerned only to draw up the battle-lines between will and idea. There is no possibility of a synthesis or reconciliation; the victory of one must mean the extinction of the other.

Lawrence will eventually adopt the polaric position, but his thinking at this point in his career is similarly dualistic. Michael Black remarks that "his instinctive reaction – at this time in his life, at any rate – is to separate things into an either/or, because he could not yet think of polar opposites as combining or uniting" (*Early Philosophical* 75). Yet, even at this early point in his career, we see Lawrence's thought already transcending the Cartesian dualism – or perhaps it would be more accurate to say that he is a survival of an earlier way of thought. Black finds him to be "one of the few speakers in the twentieth century of an age-old lost language, which he has recovered ... He was born with, and miraculously managed to carry into adult life, an undissociated sensibility. He knew his kinship with the people of the Old Testament" (98–99). Black points out that Lawrence uses "blood" in the Old Testament sense, which is "naturally related to the meaning given to the physiological source and home of the blood, the heart. Cruden defines the Biblical heart as "the seat of life, or strength; hence it means mind, soul, spirit, or one's entire emotional understanding" (63). Lawrence's "flesh" is not the flesh that can be felt, his "blood" is not the blood that is shed. At the same time, to identify flesh with "mind, soul, spirit" is not to make of it something abstract or ideal. Lawrence's intuition cannot be netted in the Cartesian dichotomy. His "flesh" is neither exclusively mental nor non-mental. It is the unconscious, which, as Whyte notes, is not only "the expression of the organic in the individual," but also God: "If there is a God, he must speak there" (7).

Lawrence's different understanding of the nature of the unconscious, however, permits him to be a more consistent Schopenhauerian than Schopenhauer, in that he consistently sides with the body as opposed to the mind. He never lost this attitude to the body, just as he never lost the sense that "there is an eternal hostility" between "the intellect" and "the penis" and that "life is forever torn across by the conflict between them" (*First Lady Chatterley* 191). But, while he may have felt compelled for lack of an alternative to accept Schopenhauer's diagnosis, he could not accept the proposed cure without violating his deepest instincts. The future priest of love could never become an advocate of chastity, nor could the man for whom life is the "supreme blessing" become a life-denier. As Eleanor H. Green says in her article on "Schopenhauer and D. H. Lawrence on Sex and Love," "The difference in the basic attitude of these two men toward sex is directly related to the difference in the value they place upon life and the will to live" (338). This basic attitude will lead Lawrence eventually to a philosophy of polarity which will enable him to see that "Man need not sacrifice the intellect to the penis, nor the penis to the intellect" (*First Lady Chatterley* 191), because the two, though hostile, are nevertheless capable of reconciliation. In Green's words,

The great difference between the two thinkers is that Lawrence believes this gulf may occasionally be bridged by the Holy Ghost within man that partakes of and thus reconciles the nature of both.

Indeed, he makes "some sort of fluctuating harmony" between the two the main aim of a man's life, whereas for Schopenhauer the two poles remain forever separate. (335–36)

A passage towards the end of the "Foreword" to *Sons and Lovers* provides a glimpse of Lawrence's later position:

So there is the Father ... then the Son, who is the Utterer, and then the Word. And the Word is that of the Father which, through the Son, is tossed away. It is that part of the Flesh in the Son which is capable of spreading out thin and fine, losing its concentration and completeness, ceasing to be a begetter, and becoming only a vision, a flutter of petals, God rippling through the Son till he breaks in a laugh, called a blossom, that shines and is gone. The vision itself, the flutter of petals, the rose, the Father through the Son wasting himself in a moment of consciousness, consciousness of his own infinitude and gloriousness, a Rose, a Clapping of the Hands, a Spark of Joy thrown off from the Fire to die ruddy in mid-darkness, a Snip of Flame, the Holy Ghost, the Revelation. And so, the eternal Trinity. (470–71)

Lawrence has not really thought through the implications of the Trinity, and the entrance of the Holy Ghost throws the argument into disarray. Suddenly the Son is no longer the Word; he becomes the Utterer while the Holy Ghost becomes the Word. If the transition from Father to Son is a devolution or loss in being, the addition of the Holy Ghost to the sequence would imply for it an even greater degree of descent and hence of diminished reality. Yet the enthusiastic, ecstatic language in which Lawrence describes the Holy Ghost seems to demand a higher status for it. It is "the Revelation," the Father through the Son gaining "consciousness of his own infinitude and gloriousness."

But how is it possible for the Father, the Flesh, to become conscious of himself? This is the question we have seen Schopenhauer fail to answer. And we have seen the answers of Coleridge and Boehme: it is only possible if Father and Son are polar opposites sharing a fundamental identity. For Boehme and Coleridge the Holy Ghost or Reconciler *is* this polar relationship itself, and the Trinity, the Three-in-One, is the supreme example of polarity. As Coleridge says, "the principle of Trichotomy is necessarily involved in the Polar Logic" (qtd.

in Barfield 183). Or as Owen Barfield puts it, "another name for the principle of polarity is triunity: the two poles, with their originating unity as the relation between them" (145). This will become Lawrence's answer too, and the Holy Ghost will become his most frequently used example of polarity. For instance, in a letter of October 1915 he described the Holy Ghost as "the supreme *relation* between the Father and Son ... " (2: 408). The "Foreword," however, which was actually titled "Of the Trinity, the Three-in-One," marks only the first appearance of the Holy Ghost in Lawrence's writings – it could be called in theological terms the Annunciation of his philosophy – and he does not yet fully grasp the implications of the mystery that will become his central and abiding preoccupation from this point on.

CHAPTER 3

The passionate struggle into conscious being:
Lawrence and Nietzsche

DIONYSUS AND DARWIN

This chapter focuses on *Women in Love* and the *Study of Thomas Hardy*. The thesis of the chapter can be simply stated by saying that Nietzsche is to *Women in Love* and the Hardy study as Schopenhauer is to *The White Peacock* and the "Foreword." There is an important *relation* between Nietzsche and Lawrence, but, as in the case of Schopenhauer, the question of influence is a vexed one. The correspondences between Nietzsche and Lawrence are so striking and so extensive that several critics assume a massive, direct, and sustained influence. Harry Steinhauer concludes that Lawrence "takes over the Nietzschean 'system' in its entirety" (225), Kingsley Widmer describes Lawrence as "an English Nietzsche" (121), and Daniel J. Schneider asserts that "Lawrence's thought corresponds so closely on so many counts to Nietzsche's that it is obvious the German philosopher was one of Lawrence's greatest passions" (*Consciousness* 57). Yet, strangely, it is impossible to tell which of Nietzsche's works Lawrence actually read, or if indeed he read any. He rarely refers to Nietzsche by name and almost never mentions specific works. His references are usually to concepts, like the will to power or eternal recurrence, which appear in many places in Nietzsche and which could in fact be easily picked up without reading him at all. Sometimes Lawrence's comments on Nietzsche are so inaccurate and perverse that one wonders if he knew anything of Nietzsche at first hand. Despite the paucity of references, however, one is left with an undeniable sense of what John Burt Foster, Jr. calls a "massive unacknowledged influence" beneath the surface (185).

We know from Jessie Chambers that Lawrence discovered Nietzsche in the library at Croydon. Rose Marie Burwell reports that the library at that time possessed *Beyond Good and Evil, Thus Spake Zarathustra, Twilight of the Gods, Human, All-Too-Human, Will to Power,* and *Joyful Wisdom* ("Checklist" 69), although we obviously do not know which if any of these he read. That the local library in a London suburb should have so many volumes of Nietzsche is in itself evidence that this period was the height of what Patrick Bridgewater calls "the Nietzschean decade in English literature" (13), a time when in David Thatcher's words Nietzsche was "a tremor in the atmosphere" (3) around the leading intellectual and artistic figures, including Yeats, Shaw, Havelock Ellis, Arthur Symons, A. R. Orage, and Edward Garnett. During his years at Croydon Lawrence was immersed in the most modern thought and could not have escaped at least the indirect influence of the philosopher whose name was on everyone's lips. The influence was deepened when he visited Germany with Frieda and was exposed to the highly intellectual circle surrounding the von Richtofen sisters. Martin Green in *The von Richtofen Sisters* has shown that Nietzsche was a demigod to this circle, especially to Otto Gross, one of Frieda's former lovers, and to Frieda herself.

There is thus sufficient evidence to support Graham Hough's modest conclusion that "it is probable that his doctrine would not have been what it is if the Nietzschean influence had not been felt" (*Dark Sun* 257). But the connection remains a very odd one, perhaps because Lawrence was trying to disguise his debts, or perhaps he was trying to maintain his independence, in the belief that "We have to hate our immediate predecessors, to get free from their authority" (*Letters* 1: 509). Another explanation is Lawrence's continuing battle with Frieda. Ottoline Morrell described Frieda as having "educated herself on Nietzsche" and, to the disgust of Ottoline, proclaiming her intellectual equality with "Lorenzo" (Delany 113). And Middleton Murry records Lawrence's going into rages when Frieda tried to defend her hero Nietzsche (Nehls 1: 377). For

Lawrence, then, to preserve his independence from Nietzsche was to preserve it from his wife and to defeat Nietzsche was to defeat a rival in more senses than one.

Colin Milton's *Lawrence and Nietzsche* is the most extensive treatment of the relationship and we can accept his thoughtful conclusion that "the German philosopher did indeed profoundly affect Lawrence's whole vision and with it, the character of the fictional world he created" and that it is precisely because of the profundity of Nietzsche's influence that "it is only rarely evident in direct references or obvious borrowings. Instead it tends to appear in that more subtle and pervasive fashion which we might expect when ideas have been thoroughly assimilated and creatively used" (232). It is not necessary, however, or even particularly important to establish direct influence. Nietzsche's ideas become relevant to a study of Lawrence's ideas not because they caused them but because, as parallels, they help us to understand them.

The first point of contact between Lawrence and Nietzsche is a common early allegiance to Schopenhauer. Nietzsche was a complete Schopenhauerian from the moment that, as a young student in 1865, he discovered a copy of *The World as Will and Idea* in his landlord's shop: "I was looking into a mirror that reflected the world, life and my own mind with hideous magnificence" (qtd. in Hayman 72). His early essay *Schopenhauer as Educator* is a fervent tribute, and his first book *The Birth of Tragedy* is conscious of Schopenhauer throughout, quoting and referring to him frequently and drawing on him for its central concept. Dionysus and Apollo are direct transpositions of Schopenhauer's will and idea and are described in Schopenhauerian terminology. Nietzsche describes the Dionysian as the "eternal core of things, the thing-in-itself" (*Birth* 61); the Apollinian is the "*principium individuationis*" (36), the world of external objects. Dionysus rules over the imageless "innermost depths," while Apollo governs the world of images and "mere appearances" (34–36). Apollo is the god of boundaries, laws, conventions – all that which creates distinct entities and forms. Dionysus is the flood that overwhelms the world of distinct, separate objects and dissolves them back into their original oneness. The Dionysian is nature, the Apollinian culture (61).

While Dionysus and Apollo are Schopenhauerian opposites, they differ in one extremely important way: they are *polar* opposites capable of reconciliation while Schopenhauer's are not. The miracle of Greek tragedy for Nietzsche is precisely that there "the two antagonists were reconciled" (39). The "mystery" of "the fraternal union of the two deities" (130) Apollo and Dionysus necessarily implies an antecedent union, and art for Nietzsche is "the highest task and the truly metaphysical activity of this life" (31–2) because it gives us "the fundamental knowledge of the oneness of everything existent" and is an "augury of a restored oneness" (74). Art is the "mirror" (67) in which the will finds itself in knowledge; it is the revelation of the noumenal in the phenomenal. And Nietzsche knows that this is only possible if the opposites are "twin forces of one Power." "The Apollinian and its opposite, the Dionysian," *both* "burst forth from nature herself" (38).

In the previous chapter, we saw Lawrence in the "Foreword" to *Sons and Lovers* creating a pair of basic principles that, like Apollo and Dionysus, correspond closely to Schopenhauer, and we saw him moving away from Schopenhauer toward a clear conception of the opposites as polar opposites. Whether or not he read Nietzsche in the two years between the "Foreword" and the *Study of Thomas Hardy*, the latter work offers a fully fledged theory of polarity indistinguishable in its essentials from Nietzsche's. Dionysus and Apollo become Lawrence's Law and Love. Like Nietzsche he sees in Aeschylus' Orestean trilogy the synthesis of the opposites: "The Law, and Love, they are here the Two-in-One in all their magnificence" (89). Like Nietzsche he sees not only in Greek tragedy but "in all art ... the wonderful dual marriage, the true consummation" (*Hardy* 87) of the opposites. In fact for Lawrence all creation, every "utterance," is the product of the union of the opposites: "And everything that has ever been produced, has been produced by the combined activity of the two ... When the two are acting together, then Life is produced, then Life, or Utterance, Something, is *created*. And nothing is or can be created save by

combined effort of the two principles, Law and Love" (125).
Dionysus and Apollo, Law and Love, are principles of the
widest possible application, operative in the mineral, vegetable,
and animal kingdoms. Nietzsche like Lawrence identifies "the
Apollinian and *Dionysian* duality" with "the duality of the sexes,
involving perpetual strife with only periodically intervening
reconciliations" (*Birth* 33).

The main difference between Lawrence and Nietzsche is that
Lawrence frequently invokes the Christian Trinity as an
example of polarity, whereas Nietzsche's much fiercer animus
against Christianity prevents him from using any of its terms or
categories. The Hardy study resolves the ambiguity we noticed
in the "Foreword" about the status of the Holy Ghost as the
synthesis of the opposites. Lawrence now clearly grasps the role
of the Holy Ghost as "the Reconciler between the Father and
the Son" (79). Whenever Love and the Law, male and female,
truly conjoin, then "the two are really one again, so that any
pure utterance is a perfect unity, the two as one, united by the
Holy Spirit" (127). Lawrence finds the Trinity everywhere,
even in Aeschylus' trilogy, in which Apollo, the Erinyes, and
Athena correspond to Son, Father, and Holy Spirit (94). G.
Wilson Knight supports this identification and even suggests
that the Trinity has unconsciously influenced Nietzsche's
conception:

Dionysus is an effeminate God, Apollo a figure of masculine beauty. In
Aeschylus' *Oresteia* you get the balance: on the one side Clytemnestra
and the Erinyes, or Furies; on the other, Apollo, the rights of husband
against wife, and Orestes; Athena and the Council of the Areopagus
symbolising some higher synthesis. In the Christian scheme, God the
Father is Dionysian; God the Son, especially at the transfiguration –
for the Apollonian is visionary – Apollonian; and the Holy Spirit, the
Divine Sophia, the poetic fusion, Aeschylus' Athena. You could say
that Nietzsche was, without knowing it, reformulating Christian
dogma and simultaneously showing its relation to Attic drama. (27)

As Knight says, "These are inexhaustible categories: once
you understand them, you find them everywhere" (27). A. R.
Orage in fact pointed out (68) a passage from Coleridge's
Shakespeare lectures, in which Coleridge describes Dionysus as

"the symbol of that power which acts without our consciousness from the vital energies of nature, as Apollo was the symbol of our intellectual consciousness" (*Lectures* 1: 518). These categories, as Ronald Gray shows in his *The German Tradition in Literature*, are indeed everywhere in German literature and philosophy from Luther and Boehme through Hegel and Schelling and beyond. Nietzsche's most Germanic book, *The Birth of Tragedy*, draws deeply on this tradition, alluding to Goethe's "Zwei Seelen," Schiller's "naive" and "sentimental," Holderlin's Christ and Dionysus, and Heine's Nazarene and Hellene. Lawrence in turn, whose relationship to the German tradition is described by Gray as "both more intimate and more critical than that of any other English writer" (340), could have drawn on any number of these writers, although the repeated references in *Twilight in Italy* to Apollo and Dionysus make it clear that Nietzsche was a primary source.

Much of Schopenhauer's fascination for both Lawrence and Nietzsche lies in his unflinching view of the horror and terror of existence. Nietzsche says that Schopenhauer "has depicted for us the tremendous terror which seizes man when he is suddenly" confronted by his reality as mere appearance, when the "shuddering suspicion" overtakes him that he is a fragile apparition destined for destruction, dismemberment, and dissolution (*Birth* 36, 41). *The Birth of Tragedy* is as filled with the *frisson* of horror as is *The White Peacock*. We saw that in Lawrence, Schopenhauer's will merged with Darwin's nature to create an especially appalling picture of nature as not only enormously destructive but also as entirely lacking in any goal or meaning in accord with the specifically human aspects of man. We find the same thing in Nietzsche, who is always conscious of Darwin, having been, in Walter Kaufman's words, "aroused from his dogmatic slumber by Darwin, much as Kant was a century earlier by Hume" (*Nietzsche* xiii). Nietzsche saw Darwin as the last and climactic chapter in the history of modern nihilism and devoted his entire career to overcoming this nihilism. The Darwinian challenge is presented in terms of "the doctrines of the finality of 'becoming,' of the flux of all ideas, types, and species, of the lack of all radical difference

between man and beast (a true but fatal idea, as I think)"
("Use" 61). There is no longer any denying that man is an
animal. The critical question now becomes: does man nevertheless differ from the animals in some important way to which
we can ascribe value? Is life, including human existence, only
the struggle for dominance and survival or is there another –
specifically human yet natural – source of value, another goal
toward which men can aspire as they used to aspire toward
God?

The issue posed by Darwin and Schopenhauer can be put in
terms of the idea of waste or excess. Nietzsche more than once
characterizes the Dionysian as "nature's *excess*" itself (46),
alluding to the most salient and problematic aspect of Darwin's
nature. Nature's vast prodigality is staggeringly wasteful,
producing thousands of individuals on the off-chance that one
will survive. As Darwin says in *The Origin of Species*, "of the
many individuals of any species which are periodically born,
but a small number can survive" (78). "Every organic being
naturally increases at so high a rate, that if not destroyed, the
earth would soon be covered by the progeny of a single pair"
(80). From this central Malthusian fact flows the entire
Darwinian system. A ferocious "struggle for existence inevitably
follows" (80), in which only the fittest will survive to pass on
their traits to succeeding generations. Like Schopenhauer's will,
Darwin's nature has an utter disregard for the individual.
Individuality *per se* has no value; only the survival of the species
is important. In fact, if we have no children it follows that our
existence has been entirely futile. Evolutionarily speaking, St.
Francis, Spinoza, and Blake (or for that matter Nietzsche and
Lawrence) might as well never have existed.

This view of things was one to which Nietzsche by his very
nature was fundamentally and unalterably opposed. It eliminates meaning from the universe, and man cannot live without
meaning. In his most self-revealing book, *Schopenhauer as
Educator*, written two years after *The Birth of Tragedy*, he says
that the struggle for existence "is given meaning only by a high
and transfiguring overall goal" (26). This goal is the production
by nature of the individual in whom nature comes to con-

sciousness of herself: "This is the fundamental idea of *culture*, insofar as it sets but one task for each of us: to *further the production of the philosopher, or the artist and of the saint within us and outside us, and thereby to work at the consummation of nature*" (*Schopenhauer* 56). This is the direct antithesis of the Darwinian view. Scientific materialism purposely excludes consideration of man as a cultural being; art, religion, and philosophy are irrelevant to natural selection, reproduction, and inheritance. But it is in culture and only in culture that Nietzsche finds nature's final significance; any system of thought that excludes this dimension is necessarily vitiated and unable to find a meaning in existence compatible with man's nature and needs. Only with the appearance of man and with the creation of culture, which is "a transfigured nature [*physis*]" (322), does nature glimpse her goal. Man in fact must come to the aid of nature; he must fulfill "her compulsive need for redemption" by making "existence explicable and meaningful" (*Schopenhauer* 83–84). Culture is nature, but nature "transfigured"; man actualizes what is potential in nature, makes conscious the unconscious.

An individual human being is not just "a point in the evolution of a race" (47) destined only to be swallowed up in the stream of becoming. The goal "does not lie in the mass of specimens and their well-being, or even in the latest specimens to evolve"; it lies rather in the production of "individual great men" (59), who can hold a mirror up to existence "in which life appears no longer senseless but in its metaphysical significance" (52). Nietzsche acknowledges that, considering the rarity and relative ineffectuality of the great man, "nature's procedure seems wasteful," that "nature lacks purpose in her means." But he nevertheless affirms that the artist and philosopher are the "best proof for the wisdom of her ends" (84). By this statement Nietzsche restores the teleology that Darwinism had eliminated from nature.

Each of these conclusions reached by Nietzsche is repeated by Lawrence in the *Study of Thomas Hardy*, which becomes from its opening pages a wholesale repudiation of the Darwinian view of life. In this his second attempt to write down his philosophy, Lawrence returns immediately to the blossom of the "Foreword," as if in an effort to get it right this time. Whereas the "Foreword" emphasized the greater reality of the seed, he now declares in the opening pages that the blossom is "the be-all and the end-all" (10). He tells a little parable of an "ancient paleolithic man as he sat at the door of his cave" contemplating the red flame of the poppy blossoms:

And the flame was all the story and all triumph. The old man knew this. It was this he praised, the red outburst at the top of the poppy, in his innermost heart that had no fear of winter. Even the latent seeds were secondary, within the fire. No red; and there were just a herb, without name or sign of poppy. But he had seen the flower in all its evanescence and its being. (8)

The old man's grandson is a Darwinist who explains the vivid, beautiful red of the poppy by saying that "the red was there to bring the bees and the flies." Darwinists must explain everything materialistically in terms of reproduction. The old man merely smiles and shakes his head, knowing that if this were nature's sole aim, it could be accomplished much more efficiently: "more bees and flies and wasps could come to a sticky smear round his grandson's mouth, than to yards of poppy red." The Darwinists engage in circular reasoning: they believe that the poppies are more beautiful and more plentiful than necessary because "excess … always accompanies reproduction." But "if there is always excess accompanying reproduction, how can you call it excess?" (8–9). The biologists measure everything by their own yardstick. "They have made the measure, and the supply must be made to fit" (31). Their narrow Malthusian minds and blinkered vision entirely miss the point: "There is always excess, a brimming over. At spring-time a bird brims over with blue and yellow, a glow worm brims over with a drop of green moonshine, a lark flies up like heady wine, with song, an errand boy whistles down the road, and scents brim over the measure of the flower" (31).

Far from being excessive or secondary, such visionary phenomena are actually "the thing itself at its maximum of being" (11). The eternal thing-in-itself overflows to unite with and reveal itself in and through the temporal manifestation. It is only then that each thing – whether a poppy, a glow worm, or a man – achieves its identity, its full being.

When is a glow worm a glow worm? When she's got a light on her tail. What is she when she hasn't got a light on her tail? Then she's a mere worm, an insect.
   When is a man a man? When he is alight with life. Call it excess? If it is missing, there is no man, only a creature, a clod, undistinguished. (31)

The goal of life, its meaning and purpose, is now clearly revealed to be the attainment of maximum being, which is "true individuality" (15):

The final aim of every living thing, creature, or being is the full achievement of itself. This accomplished, it will produce what it will produce, it will bear the fruit of its nature. Not the fruit, however, but the flower is the culmination and climax, the degree to be striven for. Not the work I shall produce, but the real Me I shall achieve, that is the consideration; of the complete Me will come the complete fruit of me, the work, the children. (12–13)

"The complete Me" can only be achieved by risking the leap into being, by wasting myself in an extravagant gesture, like the "reckless, shameless scarlet" poppy that squanders itself in a brief "gaudy" moment and then is gone, "and the place thereof shall know it no more" (8). Lawrence acknowledges that "it is a wasteful ordering of things, indeed, to be sure: – but so it is, and what must be must be" (10).
   Lawrence now has his answer to Schopenhauer and Darwin. They were wrong. The aim of the will or of nature is neither sheer survival through work nor perpetuation of the species through children – it is the achievement of the individual, the "real Me." Thomas Hardy, the follower of Schopenhauer and Darwin, is also wrong, and for the same reasons. Tragedy is inevitable in Hardy's novels given his Schopenhauerian-Darwinian belief in the utter disparity between nature's will and the individual human will. For Lawrence, however, the problem lies not in nature but in Hardy, who has subdued his art to his own pessimistic metaphysics. Lawrence finds that all

of Hardy's tragic heroes and heroines have "some vital weakness, some radical ineffectuality," (45) and that their fates are a result of individual flaws rather than of a perversity built into the nature of things. Hardy has loaded the dice against his characters in order "to explain his own sense of failure" (92).

Egdon Heath in *The Return of the Native* is one of the most powerful representations in all literature of what Lawrence calls "the waste enormity of nature" (29) simply perpetuating itself with a complete indifference to the fate of the individuals that it produces. Life for Hardy is "necessarily tragic" (30) because of this background of implacable cosmic indifference (if not hostility) against which his characters play out their strange, tormented little dramas. Lawrence's beautiful description of the Heath captures this Hardy note while at the same time utterly transforming it:

What is the real stuff of tragedy in the book? It is the Heath. It is the primitive, primal earth, where the instinctive life heaves up. There, in the deep, rude stirring of the instincts, there was the reality that worked the tragedy. Close to the body of things, there can be heard the stir that makes us and destroys us. The earth heaved with raw instinct, Edgon whose dark soil was strong and crude and organic as the body of a beast. Out of the body of this crude earth are born Eustacia, Wildeve, Mistress Yeobright, Clym, and all the others. They are one year's accidental crop. What matter if some are drowned or dead, and others preaching or married: what matter, any more than the withering heath, the reddening berries, the seedy furze and the dead fern of one autumn of Egdon. The Heath persists. Its body is strong and fecund, it will bear many more crops beside this. Here is the sombre, latent power that will go on producing, no matter what happen to the product. Here is the deep, black source from whence all these little contents of lives are drawn. And the contents of the small lives are spilled and wasted. There is savage satisfaction in it: for so much more remains to come, such a black, powerful fecundity is working there that what does it matter! (25)

Instead of shuddering with horror, as he would have done earlier, Lawrence stares straight into the face of nature and finds it good beyond all human calculation.

Three people die and are taken back into the Heath, they mingle their strong earth again with its powerful soil, having been broken off at their stem. It is very good. Not Egdon is futile, sending forth life on the powerful heave of passion. It cannot be futile, for it is eternal. What is futile is the purpose of man.

Man has a purpose which he has divorced from the passionate purpose that issued him out of the earth, into being. (25)

At the very heart of things, Lawrence affirms, there is not the abyss of the will, not the blind mechanisms of natural selection, not a deity either incompetent or malevolent. "A man is a well-head built over a strong, perennial spring" (32), not a thin layer of fragile flesh rounded upon a void. At the heart of nature, in the depths of being, the *ding an sich* is a joyous fountain of ever-new life rising and flinging itself into the air, finding itself for a moment in the sunshine before disappearing into the invisible.

Just as Hardy's vision is transfigured in Lawrence, so is Schopenhauer's in Nietzsche. In *The Birth of Tragedy* Nietzsche says that "the profound Hellene, uniquely susceptible to the tenderest and deepest suffering," has looked just as deeply as Schopenhauer "into the terrible destructiveness of so-called world history as well as the cruelty of nature" (59), but what he sees there is utterly different: "If we add to this terror the blissful ecstasy that wells from the innermost depths of man, indeed of nature, at this collapse of the *principium individuationis*, we steal a glimpse into the nature of the *Dionysian*" (36). The "vast Dionysian impulse ... devours the entire world of phenomena, in order to let us sense beyond it, and through its destruction, the highest ... joy, in the bosom of the primordially One" (132). To the terror described so well by Schopenhauer we must "add ... the blissful ecstasy that wells from the innermost depths of man, indeed of nature, at this collapse of the *principium individuationis*" (36). "Life is at the bottom of things, despite all the changes of appearances, indestructibly powerful and pleasurable" (59); it is an eternal "joy" (36).

Dionysian art ... wishes to convince us of the eternal joy of existence: only we are to seek this joy not in phenomena, but behind them. We are to recognize that all that comes into being must be ready for a sorrowful end; we are forced to look into the terrors of the individual existence – yet we are not to become rigid with fear: a metaphysical comfort tears us momentarily from the bustle of the changing figures.

We are really for a brief moment primordial being itself, feeling its
raging desire for existence and joy in existence; the struggle, the pain,
the destruction of phenomena, now appear necessary to us, in view of
the excess of countless forms of existence which force and push one
another into life, in view of the exuberant fertility of the universal will.
We are pierced by the maddening sting of these pains just when we
have become, as it were, one with the infinite primordial joy in
existence, and when we anticipate, in Dionysian ecstasy, the indestructibility and eternity of this joy. In spite of fear and pity, we are
the happy living beings, not as individuals, but as the *one* living being,
with whose creative joy we are united. (104–5)

Both Nietzsche and Lawrence attain to a vision that includes
the rage for existence, the struggle, the pain, the waste
destructiveness of the will, but that utterly transfigures it: "pain
begets joy" (*Birth* 40), waste becomes exuberant excess,
destruction becomes a part of creation, the meaningless becomes
the necessary and providential.

Graham Hough says that "the ecstasy with which Nietzsche
in *The Birth of Tragedy* welcomes the merging of all separate
entities in the Dionysian flood is the only literary parallel to
Lawrence's" (*Dark Sun* 257), but in fact there are others. One
thinks of Blake's Proverb of Hell: "The roaring of lions, the
howling of wolves, the raging of the stormy sea, and the
destructive sword are portions of eternity too great for the eye of
man" (36). Or of Behemoth and Leviathan at the end of the
Book of Job, those two monstrous and fearsome embodiments of
destructiveness in whom the Lord takes such great delight and
joy. Or the vision of God granted by Krishna to Arjuna in the
Bhagavad-Gita, a vision of "Time's devouring fire" imaged as
the "blazing mouths" of Krishna into which all men rush to be
torn apart by the "jagged ghastly tusks," before which "the
worlds all shudder in affright" (84).

At these heights of vision, the relation between Nietzsche and
Lawrence is not one of literary influence but rather of each
belonging to what Nietzsche called the "republic of genius" in
which from mountain peak to mountain peak "one giant calls
to another across the desert intervals of time" and "the exalted
spirit-dialogue goes on" ("Uses" 111). Literary critics today

shy away from the word "mystic," but the vision we are describing is clearly a mystical vision. Hough rightly stresses that "the triumphant welcome Lawrence can give to the forces which are to extinguish all ordinary personal and social values is akin, or at least analogous to, the mystic's joy in the extinction of his personality" (257). This side of Nietzsche is ignored by most of his critics, but it is very prominent, especially in his early works like *Schopenhauer as Educator*:

And thus nature finally needs the saint in whom the individual ego is entirely melted away and who feels his suffering life as an identity, affinity and unity with all that is living: the saint in whom that wonder of transformation occurs, upon which the play of becoming never changes, that final and highest becoming-human after which the whole of nature strives for its redemption from itself. (57)

In the pivotal fifth chapter of the *Study of Thomas Hardy* Lawrence offers his own theory of evolution:

It seems as though one of the conditions of life is, that life shall continually and progressively differentiate itself, almost as though this differentiation were a Purpose. Life starts crude and unspecified, a great Mass. And it proceeds to evolve out of that mass ever more distinct and definite particular forms, an ever-multiplying number of separate species and orders, as if it were working always to the production of the infinite number of perfect individuals, the individual so thorough that he should have nothing in common with any other individual. (42)

"In the origin life must have been uniform, a great unmoved, utterly homogeneous infinity." The process from homogeneity to heterogeneity proceeds, after certain preliminary stages,

to naked jelly, and from naked jelly to enclosed and separated jelly, from homogeneous tissue to organic tissue, on and on, from invertebrates to mammals, from mammals to man, from man to tribesman, from tribesman to me: and on and on, till, in the future, wonderful, distinct individuals, like angels, move about, each one being himself, perfect as a complete melody or a pure colour. (43)

Michael Black finds here "Lawrence's fundamental notion of the basic progression from the unindividuated (in the Foreword, the Father) to the individuated (the Son)," a notion that Black like Ebbatson finds indebted to Spencer (*Philosophical* 174). Similarly indebted to modern biology is the reference to jelly and to cells, recalling the description in the "Foreword" of the Father as "Protoplasm" (470). There is no doubt that, as Michael Black stresses, "in his writing as a whole, Lawrence's thought is evolutionary" (*Philosophical* 183) and attempts to incorporate the results of modern science. As soon as this is said, however, it is necessary to add that, contrary to what most people think, evolutionism does not necessarily mean Darwinism and that, while he is an evolutionist, Lawrence is no Darwinist (or Spencerian).

As Henry Fairfield Osborn has shown in his *From the Greeks to Darwin*, a fully developed theory of evolution was in place long before Darwin, a theory that was largely the creation of thinkers like Herder, Goethe, Schelling, and Oken. The descent of species, the idea of a continuous transformation from lower to higher forms of life, the fact of man's anatomical kinship with the higher animals – all these ideas were well established. Romantic thought had furthermore, in its emphasis on development and becoming, created the philosophical climate without which the theory of evolution could not flourish or even exist. A. O. Lovejoy in *The Great Chain of Being* finds that "the shift from the uniformitarian to the diversitarian preconception" is "the most significant and distinctive single feature of the Romantic revolution" (297). God becomes an "insatiably creative" (296) God, realizing Himself in an eternal process of "perpetual transcendence of the already-attained," of "unceasing expansion" (306) resulting in ever-increasing individuality. Lovejoy quotes Schliermacher to the effect that "living Nature ... everywhere aims at diversity and individuality" (308), a process described by Schelling as nature's rising "from the production of more meagre and inchoate creatures to the production of more perfect and more finely formed ones" (323). Morse Peckham, drawing on Lovejoy, finds that "the idea of evolution in the nineteenth-century sense" is a direct result of these Romantic ideas (15). Darwin's contribution was a theory of the *mechanism* of evolution; his was the first explanation to be presented in entirely materialistic terms. If we look at Lawrence's theory, we see that none of the specifically Darwinian elements have survived; Lawrence's main ideas – diversitarianism, transformation, individuality – are all Romantic. Similarly Romantic – quintessentially so – is the idea of the fully evolved individual or great man at nature's apex. Behind Lawrence and Nietzsche stand Carlyle's heroes and Emerson's representative men and behind them stands the "genius" as elaborated in Schiller, Fichte, Jean Paul, Goethe, and others.

In his essay "Formation of a More Comprehensive Theory of Life," Coleridge offers an epitome of what could be called the Romantic theory of evolution, which Barfield describes as "a full-fledged theory of evolution alternative to, and largely incompatible with," the Darwinian (55). In the "Theory of Life" Coleridge seeks to reduce the "idea of Life to its simplest and most comprehensive form or mode of action; that is, to some characteristic *instinct* or *tendency*, evident in all its manifestations, and involved in the idea itself" (569). He finds this instinct or tendency, manifest through all of nature, in "*the principle of individuation*, or the power which unites a given *all* into a *whole* that is presupposed by all its parts" (573). "The tendency having been ascertained, what is its most general law? I answer – *polarity*, or the essential dualism of Nature, arising out of its productive unity, and still tending to reaffirm it, either as equilibrium, indifference, or identity" (578). The tendency to individuate progressively realizes itself through a process of "unceasing polarity," as life evolves through "an ascending series of corresponding phenomena," an ascent characterized by "progressive intensity" and "gradual enlargement of its sphere" (569). Coleridge traces this progression from the prephenomenal forces out of which matter has emerged, through the lowest "inorganic" levels where it exists in its utmost latency as "the life of metals" (572), through the vegetable and animal kingdoms where we first "perceive totality dawning into *individuation*," until the entire process reaches its apex in man, in whom "as the highest of the class, the individuality is… perfected" (577). The law of polarity operates throughout this process because "this tendency to individuate can not be conceived without the opposite tendency to connect."

If the tendency be at once to individuate and to connect, to detach, but so as either to retain or to reproduce attachment, the individuation itself must be a tendency to the ultimate production of the highest and most comprehensive individuality. This must be the one great end of Nature, her ultimate object, or by whatever other word we may designate that something which bears to a final cause the same relation that Nature herself bears to the Supreme Intelligence. (578)

In man the evolutionary process turns inward and becomes an evolution of consciousness, but remains "the same unceasing process of polarity." Consciousness is the greatest individualizer, working in the human self to produce individual men who differ as much from one another as do different species of animals – "each Soul is a Species in itself" (*Letters* 2: 1196). "The most perfect detachment with the greatest possible union" (600) is found in man, who is capable of becoming a veritable microcosm, an entire world of consciousness juxtaposed to an entire macrocosm or world of nature.

The whole force of organic power has attained an inward and centripetal direction. [Man] has the whole world in counterpoint to him, but he contains an entire world within himself. Now, for the first time at the apex of the living pyramid, it is Man and Nature, but Man himself is a syllepsis, a compendium of Nature – the Microcosm! (601)

For Lawrence and Nietzsche too the highest man is the most conscious, because consciousness is itself the individualizer in man. For Lawrence "it seems as if the great aim and purpose in human life were to bring all life into the human consciousness" (*Hardy* 41); the goal of life itself is "the production of the infinite number of perfect individuals, the individual so thorough that he should have nothing in common with any other individual" (42). Nietzsche believes that most men are not truly human. "We, together with the rest of nature, are impelled toward man as to a something which stands high over us" (*Schopenhauer* 52). That "final and highest becoming-human after which the whole of nature strives" is a man "infinite in knowing and loving" (61). Only in the infinite consciousness of such a man, the "genius," whom Nietzsche calls "the ideal expression of the species" ("Strauss" 30), does nature find her meaning, her metaphysical significance.

The difference between the truly human and the animal is not a matter of physiology – as Coleridge says, no anatomical difference, "no perceivable difference of organization is sufficient to overbridge" "the wide chasm between man and the noblest animals of the brute creation" ("Theory" 567). A qualitative leap is required. Nietzsche says that with the appearance of "those true *men, those no longer animals, the philosophers, artists and saints* ... nature, who never jumps, makes her only jump, and it is a jump for joy, for she feels for the first time to be at her goal" (*Schopenhauer* 54). This statement is in direct and conscious contravention of Darwinian dogma as expressed in *The Origin of Species*, according to which, "natural selection can act only by taking advantage of slight successive variations; she can never take a leap, but must advance by the shortest and slowest steps" (142). Lawrence is similarly heretical when he insists on the "jump beyond the bounds into nothingness" (which is somethingness), the leap into being, the sudden "brimming over" into true individuality. Any system such as Darwin's or Spencer's founded on the Cartesian dualism must necessarily be left behind at this point, where the real though immaterial polaric forces responsible for the entire process turn inward and continue their work in the invisible realms of culture and spirit.

The Cartesian dualism also prevents materialist evolutionists from seeing how the same forces could be operative in human consciousness as in nature. For Lawrence, Nietzsche, and Coleridge, however, the tendency to progressive individuation by means of polarity applies also in what Barfield calls "the *post-organic* sector," "the inner life of man" (158). The evolution of man's physical form merely provides the platform. As Coleridge says, in man "the individuality is not only perfected in its corporeal sense, but begins a new series beyond the appropriate limits of physiology" (577). Commenting on this passage, R. H. Fogle says that "the phrase 'a new series' strongly suggests a further orderly ascent from man to angels and archangels, thrones, principalities and powers as in the imagined hierarchies of *The Ancient Mariner*" (25). And Coleridge in a letter refers to the evolution of mind "through all the gradations of sentient and rational beings, till it arrives at a Bacon, a Newton, and then ... extending its illimitable sway through Seraph and Archangel, till we are lost in the GREAT INFINITE!" (*Letters* 3: 483). This may seem far from Lawrence and Nietzsche until we remind ourselves that Lawrence contemplated the evolution beyond man of "wonderful, distinct individuals, like angels" (*Hardy* 43) and that Nietzsche in Zarathustra foreshadowed the development of god-like men as high above man as man is above the animals.

Whatever one may understand by "angels," the important point is that this higher evolution takes place by means of history and culture, that history and evolution are one and the same process, governed by the same polaric forces. Nietzsche sees the phases of Greek culture as the result of "the strife of these two hostile principles" (*Birth* 47). Lawrence in the Hardy study finds the history of humanity "divided into two epochs: the epoch of the Law and the Epoch of Love" (123), to be followed by the epoch of the Holy Ghost. He also finds and traces in some detail a north-south polarity. Coleridge in his *Philosophical Lectures* develops the history of Western consciousness out of a polar opposition between the Hebrew and Greek mentalities, corresponding to the fundamental opposition between will and reason, Father and Son.

The same forces that created man's physical form and a brain capable of comprehending the idea of the infinite continue to work through history to the production of yet higher beings. What Nietzsche calls the "unconscious purposefulness of nature" becomes conscious in the higher man, who replaces "'blind instinct' by conscious will," and through continuous self-development and self-overcoming speeds nature to her end (*Schopenhauer* 63). Coleridge insists that the "enlightened naturalist" must admit "a teleological ground in physics and physiology: that is, the presumption of a something *analogous* to the causality of the human will, by which, without assigning to nature, as nature, a conscious purpose, he may yet distinguish her agency from a blind and lifeless mechanism" (*Friend* 1: 498).

THE WILL TO POWER

Despite their objections to Darwinism, Nietzsche and Lawrence are always conscious that they write within a context determined by Darwin, that Darwin has had a greater impact on man's understanding of himself and his place in the universe than anyone since Copernicus. If Copernicus displaced man from the spatial center of the universe, Darwin removed him from the temporal. Nietzsche gives brilliant expression to the new scientific vision that prevails in our culture:

> In some remote corner of the universe, poured out and glittering in innumerable solar systems, there once was a star on which clever animals invented knowledge. That was the haughtiest and most mendacious minute of "world history" – yet only a minute. After nature had drawn a few breaths the star grew cold, and the clever animals had to die.
>
> One might invent such a fable and still not have illustrated sufficiently how wretched, how shadowy and flighty, how aimless and arbitrary, the human intellect appears in nature. There have been eternities when it did not exist; and when it is done for again, nothing will have happened. (*Portable* 42)

This kind of perspective simply did not exist before the second half of the nineteenth century, and it is in their sharing of this radically altered understanding of time that Nietzsche and Lawrence are true Darwinists.

Glyn Daniel's fascinating *The Idea of Prehistory* notes that in 1802 William Paley calculated the age of the world as six thousand years, recalling Archbishop Usher's famous date for the creation as 4004 BC (31). As late as 1859, the year of *The Origin of Species*, George Rawlinson in the Bampton Lecture

> said in all seriousness that Moses's mother Jochebed had probably met Jacob who could have known Noah's son Shem. Shem, he went on, and there is no doubting his sincerity, was probably acquainted with Methuselah, who had been for 243 years a contemporary of Adam. And Adam was the first man, made on the sixth day after that great day when time began. (51)

Secular history covered three periods – ancient, medieval, and modern. There was no sense of prehistory, the term itself first being used in 1851. All of this was changed with dizzying rapidity by Darwin and the related acceptance of the fossil record. "By the late sixties prehistory was actually in existence" (49) and man's prehistory began to be calculated in the hundreds of thousands of years. The gap between ape and human was filled by primitive man, who emerged to populate the immense period before written records, and anthropology was born. It is as if man suddenly acquired an historical unconscious as well as a personal one.

Nietzsche is one of the pioneer explorers of this prehistory. *The Birth of Tragedy*, described by F. M. Cornford as "a work of profound imaginative insight, which left the scholarship of a generation toiling in the rear" (111), anticipates the researches of Jane Ellen Harrison and Frazer into the pre-Homeric matrix of primitive myth and religion out of which Greek civilization emerged. In a fragment titled "Homer's Contest," written at the same time as *The Birth of Tragedy*, Nietzsche peers into the "pre-Homeric abyss": "But what do we behold when, no longer led and protected by the hand of Homer, we stride back into the pre-Homeric world? Only night and terror and an imagination accustomed to the horrible" (*Portable* 34). Civilization is founded on "a terrifying savagery of hatred and the lust to annihilate" (*Portable* 38). Primitive man is not an animal; he is undeniably human despite his "savagery." Yet it is clearly the animal inheritance that is so visible and problematic in early man. The transition from animal to man was unimaginably bloody and slow, and any adequate idea of man must not forget or ignore the facts of his origin. Moreover, to separate the human from the natural is to cut man off from his roots and the sources of his vitality. The miracle of Greek civilization was its ability to transform "fights of annihilation" into "the activity of fights which are *contests*" (*Portable* 35). The Greeks did not seek to extirpate "jealousy, hatred, and envy," recognizing that it is these emotions that "spur men to activity" (35).

Nietzsche's philosophic instinct was always to find the

relation between the higher and the lower, the human and the natural, to see them as aspects of a single reality.

> When one speaks of *humanity*, the idea is fundamental that this is something which separates and distinguishes man from nature. In reality, however, there is no such separation: "natural" qualities and those called truly "human" are inseparably grown together. Man, in his highest and noblest capacities, is wholly nature and embodies its uncanny dual character. (*Portable* 32)

Lawrence fully shares Nietzsche's fascination with the primitive and is at one with him in his fundamental objective of grasping man in his wholeness without caricaturing him as either a noble savage or a naked ape. Lawrence like Nietzsche knows, as he says in the Hardy study, that "the greater part of every life is underground, like roots in the dark" and that "man must learn what it is to be at one, in his mind and will, with the primal impulses that rise in him" (*Hardy* 28). Any system of values or code of ethics that we construct must be naturalistic in the sense that it acknowledges "the vast, incomprehensible pattern of some primal morality greater than ever the human mind can grasp." What we call "the immorality of nature" is really "the vast, unexplored morality of life itself" (*Hardy* 29). For Lawrence and Nietzsche, the task of philosophy is to hold the terrifying and the noble in a single view, to become adequate to nature's "uncanny dual character" without lapsing into a dualism.

Both men had to struggle throughout their lives to resist a strong urge toward idealization. Nietzsche came to feel that in *The Birth of Tragedy* he had failed to adequately connect the Apollinian and the Dionysian. The Apollinian remained too much a "divine" intervention from another plane, too much an idealization. In *Ecce Homo* he says of *The Birth of Tragedy* that "it smells offensively Hegelian" (271), meaning that he had succumbed to the Hegelian dialectic, which in his view too easily overcomes oppositions in its inveterate drive to comprehend and transcend all opposition in the unity of reason. Hegel is guilty of dishonesty and "falseness"; there is in him – and in all previous German thinkers including even Schopenhauer – a "deceitfulness of instinct which *refuses* to experience these opposites as *opposites*" and to fully recognize that they "are *both* necessary" (*Ecce* 272).

Human, All-Too-Human, Nietzsche's first book after *The Birth of Tragedy*, is his attempt to reach a new level of honesty and to root out all the remaining symptoms in himself of a metaphysical need for the ideal. In *Ecce Homo* he calls the book "the monument of a crisis," in which he liberated himself from "that damned idealism" that was "the real calamity of my life" (241). He explains that the title means, "where *you* see ideal things, *I* see what is – human, alas, all-too-human!" (283). Few thinkers have been as ruthless with themselves as well as with others as Nietzsche is in this book; nothing is safe from his "merciless spirit that knows all the hideouts where the ideal is at home" (283).

The opening section sounds the new note of realism:

Chemistry of concepts and feelings. In almost all respects, philosophical problems today are again formulated as they were two thousand years ago: how can anything arise from its opposite – for example, reason from unreason, sensation from the lifeless, logic from the illogical, disinterested contemplation from covetous desire, altruism from egoism, truth from error? Until now, metaphysical philosophy has overcome this difficulty by denying the origin of one from the other, and by assuming for the more highly valued things some miraculous origin, directly from out of the heart and essence of the "thing in itself." Historical philosophy, on the other hand, the very youngest of all philosophical methods, which can no longer be even conceived of as separate from the natural sciences, has determined in isolated cases (and will probably conclude in all of them) that they are not opposites, only exaggerated to be so by the popular or metaphysical view, and that this opposition is based on an error of reason. As historical philosophy explains it, there exists, strictly considered, neither a selfless act nor a completely disinterested observation: both are merely sublimations. In them the basic element appears to be virtually dispersed and proves to be present only to the most careful observer. (13)

Science rather than art is now exalted as the closest man can come to the truth. What we need is "a *chemistry* of moral, religious, aesthetic ideas and feelings" (14). Since Darwin, we now know that "everything has evolved" (14–15). There is no eternal unchanging realm of truth; there is only the process of becoming, in which all "higher" phenomena arise out of and are indissolubly connected with their base origin. Written under the influence of Lange's *History of Materialism* (Hollingdale 55), *Human, All-Too-Human* marks the beginning of what has been called Nietzsche's positivist phase and shows him at his most materialistic. If his early work was too "idealistic," he now verges radically toward the opposite pole. "Sublimation" becomes a key concept. Drawn from chemistry, where it refers to the conversion of a substance from a solid to a vapor, the concept has unmistakeable materialist connotations.

This position soon proved as unsatisfactory as his earlier one, however, and, in a continual self-overcoming so characteristic of Nietzsche, his next books, *The Gay Science* and *The Dawn*, move in yet another direction, towards his mature doctrine of the will to power, which is announced in their successor *Thus Spoke Zarathustra*. The will to power is Nietzsche's central idea and his most important contribution to philosophic thought. It is his attempt to subsume all reality under a single principle, to account for the material and the spiritual without becoming either a materialist or an idealist. It is also extraordinarily useful in attempting to understand the philosophy expounded in the *Study of Thomas Hardy*, for the two are virtually identical.

This is true in spite of Lawrence's negative remarks about the will to power, which show little real understanding of the idea and simply subscribe to popular misconceptions. The will to power is mentioned in the *Study of Thomas Hardy*, in the course of a discussion of contrasting male attitudes towards love. In one attitude, the male feels dominant and powerful, with "the female administered to him. He feels full of blood, he walks the earth like a Lord. And it is to this state Nietzsche aspires in his *Wille zur Macht*." This attitude Lawrence contrasts with "real love," which sees the woman as "the unknown, the undiscovered, into which I plunge to discovery, losing myself." The "Nietzschean" attitude is rejected as "a spurious feeling" (103). Here we have a direct reference that establishes Lawrence's awareness of Nietzsche's central idea, but this evidence of "influence" tells us very little. Lawrence presents a caricature of Nietzsche's idea as a foil to his own, which is in fact indistinguishable from the idea that Nietzsche actually held.

The will to power can be most economically described here in terms of three concepts drawn from Coleridge that have already been discussed at some length – polarity, ideal realism, and the distinction between understanding and reason.

Polarity

The will to power is Nietzsche's attempt to solve the problem of the opposites. To be successful, his idea must first of all unmask false oppositions and "remove antitheses from things after comprehending that we have projected them there" (*Will* 76). No less importantly, it must also recognize that true opposites exist, it must in such cases experience the opposites *as* opposites that are *both* necessary to each other, and it must avoid negating one in favor of the other.

Like Schopenhauer's will, upon which it is clearly based, the will to power is "the innermost essence of being," "the world viewed *ab intra.*" The entire world, everything that exists, is "simply will to power and nothing else" (qtd. in Jaspers 294). It is the whole, not the part, and therefore "would have to be something that is not subject, not object, not energy, not matter, not spirit, and not soul" (qtd. in Jaspers 293). The will to power embraces the inorganic, the organic, the animal, and the human, dissolving the rigid divisions that are normally thought to separate these realms. The atom repulsing another atom is as much will to power as is the philosopher's quest for knowledge.

Like Schopenhauer's will, the will to power is everywhere at odds with itself, in unceasing conflict. For Schopenhauer, however, this conflict never changes and has no goal beyond sheer perpetuation of itself, whereas for Nietzsche the process is one of "*self-overcoming*" and is completely goal-oriented. Jaspers summarizes Nietzsche's argument:

What [Schopenhauer] calls "will" is merely an empty word, for in characterizing this will, he has omitted the meaning of its goal. There is no will to exist, "for what is not cannot will; and how can that which already possesses existence still will it! There is will only where there is life: not will to life but will to power." (297)

Nietzsche criticizes Schopenhauer's will for being one-sided, too exclusively focused on "craving, instinct, drive," while failing to recognize that will is just as much "that which treats cravings as their master and appoints to them their way and measure" (*Will* 52). Nietzsche's will to power is both will and that which overcomes will; it is both what Schopenhauer calls will and what he calls idea. In other words, in comparison to Schopenhauer's dualism, Nietzsche's conception is polaric, in the same way that Lawrence's is. Walter Kaufmann's excellent discussion of the will to power makes precisely this point:

Both impulse (passion) and reason (spirit) are manifestations of the will to power; and when reason overcomes the impulses, we cannot speak of a marriage of the two diverse principles but only of the self-overcoming of the will to power. This one and only basic force has first manifested itself as impulse and then overcome its own previous manifestation ... *Self*-overcoming is impossible, inasmuch as over-coming always involves two forces, one of which overcomes the other. Now, however, it appears that there are two forces, but – and this is the crucial point – they are merely two manifestations of one basic force. (235)

This is Coleridge's "two forces of one Power."

Ideal Realism

Like Coleridge's and Lawrence's, Nietzsche's thought is a thoroughgoing repudiation of the Cartesian dualism. The will to power – hence the world – is dynamic and vital through and through. Everything is alive, nothing is static or dead. Nietzsche rejects the mechanist's vision of a universe ultimately consisting of lifeless atoms moving through empty space, exerting "forces" upon each other. Like Coleridge and Lawrence, Nietzsche believes that the atom is a fiction, as is empty space. "Attraction" and "repulsion" cannot be thought of "divorced from an *intention*" (*Will* 335). The problem of *actio in distans*, which cannot be solved by the mechanist without resorting to quasi-material, quasi-spiritual "forces," is solved by Nietzsche thus: "Inorganic entities can only effect each other ... through action at a distance; hence "knowledge" is necessarily presupposed in all efficiency: What is at a distance must be perceived" (qtd. in Jaspers 312). When Nietzsche attributes "knowledge" to inorganic entities, or when he describes the inorganic as "unindividualized spirituality," or when he asserts that "memory and a sort of spirit are present in all the organic" (qtd. in Jaspers 313) – he seems to defy all of our categories and rules of logic. He is either being perversely self-contradictory, if not insane, or he is striving to express an insight that eludes the Cartesian oppositions organic-inorganic, spiritual-material.

The greatness of Nietzsche's conception is his ability to steer a course between the Scylla of materialism and the Charybdis of idealism. Unlike Freud, for instance, whose concept of sublimation is heavily indebted to Nietzsche's, Nietzsche is never reductionist. Nietzsche sees beauty, spirituality, and knowledge as indissolubly connected to the body, fueled by the body's sexual energy, yet unlike Freud he does not see all energies as reducible to libido. The difference is critical, as Walter Kaufmann explains:

Nietzsche did not decide to reduce the will to power to a sexual *libido*; for sexuality is that very aspect of the basic drive which is cancelled in sublimation, and cannot, for that reason, be considered the essence of the drive. Sexuality is merely a foreground of something else that is more basic and hence preserved in sublimation, the will to power. (222)

Nietzsche uses the term "*Vergeistigung*" or "spiritualization" as well as sublimation to designate the process of self-overcoming of the will to power, and here Plato, whose *Symposium* greatly influenced him, is a close parallel. No less than for Plato, the entire process in Nietzsche culminates in the apprehension of Beauty, "the highest sign of power" (*Will* 422), and in the philosopher's pursuit of Truth, which is "the most spiritual will to power" (*Beyond* 16). The will to power culminates in "*Geist*" – its highest manifestations are "the philosophers, artists, and saints," not the Napoleons and Borgias who are commonly thought to be Nietzsche's ideal. The will to power could just as well be characterized by its goal as by its origin. It could as well be called reason or spirit as passion or sex drive. Its higher forms are by no means simply reducible to the lower. There is a "superabundant force in *spirituality*, setting *itself* new goals, not merely commanding and leading on behalf of the lower world or the preservation of the organism" (*Will* 366). The will to power, unlike Schopenhauer's will, finds its fulfillment, not its negation, in the spiritual. Kaufmann points out that in Nietzsche, "reason is given a unique status. In the sublimation of sexual impulses, the sexual objective is cancelled. Rationality, however, is *sui generis*, and cannot be similarly cancelled in the process of sublimation" (229). Despite his closeness to Plato, however, Nietzsche never lapses into dualism.

Body never becomes merely physical, not does soul ever become disembodied. Each preserves its own identity while yet being seen in its indissoluble connection with the other. Stated negatively, the will to power is "not matter, not spirit." Matter *per se* does not exist, because "will can only act upon will and not upon matter" (qtd. in Jaspers 312). But neither does spirit *per se* exist: "If there is nothing material, there is also nothing immaterial" (*Will* 270). Stated positively, the will to power is both matter and spirit. Atoms have "knowledge," plants have "spirit" and "memory," and the philosopher's ideas are "affects" of his body. Nietzsche can be characterized as neither an idealist nor a realist. "Ideal" and "real" merely designate the extreme poles between which his thinking oscillates, in its effort to encompass the whole which is beyond this opposition and which manifests itself in terms of these opposing and mutually excluding extremes. Nietzsche's philosophy can perhaps best be described in the phrase Coleridge used in the *Biographia Literaria* to describe his own – "ideal Realism" (262).

Lawrence in the Hardy study discusses the philosophical concerns addressed by Nietzsche's will to power in terms of the relation between consciousness and life. We have already seen Lawrence assert that sometimes "it seems as if the great aim and purpose in human life were to bring all life into the human consciousness" (41), but he resists the idealist conclusion that consciousness is an aim in itself. It remains subservient to life:

> the bringing of life into human consciousness is not an aim in itself, it is only a necessary condition of the progress of life itself. Man is himself the vivid body of life, rolling glimmering against the void. In his fullest living he does not know what he does, his mind, his consciousness, unacquaint, hovers behind, full of extraneous gleams and glances, and altogether devoid of knowledge. (41)

Consciousness cannot participate in the living moment. Its glance is retrospective; it can only repeat what has already occurred; it can only reflect the already given. "The whole of human consciousness contains, as we know, not a tithe of what *is*" (44–45). Knowledge is necessary but partial and is conceived of in antithesis to the unknown, the "sentient non-knowledge" (35) that is man's "real, utter satisfaction" and which exists at the "extreme tip of life" (19), at the "fighting-line" of the soul, "where what is and will be separates itself off from what has been" (19). "Facing both ways, like Janus ... man is given up to his dual business, of being ... and of knowing" (40–41).

Yet we are not to think of consciousness or mind as simply the opposite of the body, as, for instance, something immaterial rather than material or as something abstract rather than concrete, for, we are now told, there is no ultimate distinction that can be made between them. "It must first be seen that the division ... is arbitrary, for the purpose of thought" (60). It seems as if the intellect can only think of these matters in terms of mutually exclusive opposites that contradict each other – known-unknown, backward-forward, knowing-being, *et cetera ad infinitum*. But "our view is partial" (54), and life knows nothing of these divisions that we impose on it. Though the opposites "are, in a way, contradictions each of the other," they are actually "complementary" (125).

Like Nietzsche, Lawrence wants to arrive at a single principle that will overcome all oppositions and that will account for all phenomena from the lowest to the highest. In order to express his insight into the unity beyond duality, he is forced into self-contradiction and paradox. Thus he says that "*To know* is a

force, like any other force," recalling Nietzsche's description of
knowledge as "the *most powerful* affect" or his statement in *The
Will to Power* that "every passion ... possess[es] its quantum of
reason" (208). And in a strikingly Nietzschean formulation
Lawrence describes all forces as manifestations or sublimations
of one basic force: "*To know* is a force, like any other force.
Knowledge is only one of the conditions of this force, as
combustion is one of the conditions of heat. *To will* is only a
manifestation of the same force, as expansion may be a
manifestation of heat" (41–42). Lawrence's physics of knowledge and Nietzsche's "chemistry of concepts" are parallel
attempts to express the same insight.

Understanding versus *reason*

The following passage from *Zarathustra* is one of Nietzsche's
finest attempts to express his vision:

"Body am I, and soul" – thus speaks the child. And why should one
not speak like children?

But the awakened and knowing say: body am I entirely, and
nothing else; and soul is only a word for something about the body.

The body is a great reason, a plurality with one sense, a war and a
peace, a herd and a shepherd. An instrument of your body is also your
little reason, my brother, which you call "spirit" – a little instrument
and toy of your great reason.

"I," you say, and are proud of the word. But greater is that in
which you do not wish to have faith – your body and its great reason:
that does not say "I," but does "I."

What the sense feels, what the spirit knows, never has its end in itself.
But sense and spirit would persuade you that they are the end of all
things: that is how vain they are. Instruments and toys are sense and
spirit: behind them still lies the self. The self also seeks with the eyes of
the senses; it also listens with the ears of the spirit. Always the self
listens and seeks: it compares, overpowers, conquers, destroys. It
controls, and it is in control of the ego too.

Behind your thoughts and feelings, my brother, there stands a
mighty ruler, an unknown sage – whose name is self. In your body he
dwells; he is your body. There is more reason in your body than in
your best wisdom. And who knows why your body needs precisely
your best wisdom?

Your self laughs at your ego and at its bold leaps. "What are these leaps and flights of thought to me?" it says to itself. "A detour to my end. I am the leading strings of the ego and the prompter of its concepts." (36–37)

It requires an extreme athleticism of mind to keep up with Nietzsche through such passages, as he leaps and dances, constantly shifting and moving, contradicting himself and changing his terms from one sentence to the next. The passage is built around an equivocal and contradictory use of the term "reason." Reason is "a little instrument and toy" of the body, contradistinguished from and inferior to the body, like "spirit," which is "only a word for something about the body." But, paradoxically, the body itself is also called "reason" – a "great reason." Compared to this great reason, both the "sense" of the body and the "spirit" of the soul are limited and partial. The great reason stands behind all thoughts and feelings and is called the self. It is neither body nor soul; it is rather the unified source of both that persists through their separation and rediscovers itself in the integrated man, the true individual who is no longer self-divided, whose acts are spontaneous and instinctive yet profoundly purposeful and full of reason.

Nietzsche's distinction between the great and the little reason parallels Coleridge's between reason and understanding (both in fact are drawing upon a pervasive distinction in German thought between *Vernunft* and *Verstand*). We recall that for Coleridge it is "a test and sign of a truth" of Reason "that it can come forth out of the moulds of the understanding only in the disguise of two contradictory conceptions, each of which is partially true" (*Aids* 154). The understanding is static, limited to "fixities and definites;" its logic can only deal with that which remains self-identical, the repetition of the identical being the very essence of the rational principle. In Nietzsche's words, the understanding "strives to prove that all things are fixed and unchanging." But, since reality is constantly changing, never identical with itself, the understanding is by its very nature "not designed to comprehend becoming" (qtd. in Jaspers 350). The logical principle of identity and the law of contradiction are the twin pillars of the understanding. Nietzsche attacks Aristotle's law of contradiction for the same reason that Coleridge does and baldly asserts, "Not being able to contradict is proof of an incapacity, not of 'truth'" (*Will* 279).

Nietzsche's own thought is in constant movement, every formulation being negated by a swing to the opposite pole before it has a chance to harden into a one-sided logical "position." The self-contradiction that Karl Jaspers calls "the fundamental ingredient in Nietzsche's thought" (10) is not a sign of Nietzsche's inability to think; it is rather a case of the "interplay of statements that cancel each other out while they yet strike at the heart of things" (22): "If the understanding per se is condemned, as it were, to remain on the surface of being, then being may have to become manifest through self-contradiction... A contradiction arising in this way would be necessitated by the subject-matter; it would be a sign of truthfulness rather than of incompetent thinking" (10).

In the Hardy study, Lawrence describes both matter and mind as "habits" of life. Just as "the mind itself is one of life's later-developed habits" (41), so are "gravity, or cohesion, or heat, or light." Matter itself is the result of "the movement life made in its initial passage, the movement life still makes, and will continue to make, as a habit, the movement already made so unthinkably often that rather than a movement it has become a state" (40). It is movement more than any other attribute that characterizes life, and the movement of matter and the movement of thought are equally signs of life.

If follows that thought, if it is to become adequate to this reality, must be in constant movement. It must constantly overcome itself in a dialectical movement in which every assertion has its contradictory, every Yes its No. It can be extremely difficult to follow Lawrence through the Hardy study because there are no fixed terms, no univocally defined concepts or abstractions. We can never rest in a particular idea or apprehension. For instance, no sooner do we grasp that all is motion than we are told that motion is only one half of an opposition or "dual Will," called "the Will-to-Motion and the Will-to-Inertia," that causes "the whole of life" (59). Then we are told that there is no difference between those two:

But it must first be seen that the division ... is arbitrary, for the purpose of thought. The rapid motion of the rim of a wheel is the same as the perfect rest at the center of the wheel. How can one divide them? Motion and rest are the same, when seen completely ... How can one say, there is motion and rest? If all things move together in one infinite motion, that is rest. Rest and motion are only two degrees of motion, or two degrees of rest. Infinite motion and infinite rest are the same thing. (60)

We can begin to see Lawrence's thought, like Nietzsche's, moving in what Jaspers calls "inescapable circles" (146). Is this evidence that Lawrence simply cannot think straight, as Eliot and others have said, or is it rather a case of "the interplay of statements that cancel each other out while yet they strike at the heart of things" (Jaspers 22)? Lawrence has penetrated to what Jaspers calls the "boundaries" of thought, where the understanding fails and where only the reason or imagination can carry us further. Lawrence's difficulty is the same as Nietzsche's as described by Jaspers: because his thought "penetrates to the outermost limits, he is in fact compelled either to annul his statements in consciously constructed *circles* or to leave them standing in unrecognized *contradictory* opposition to each other" (147–48).

In his treatment of consciousness, Lawrence sometimes constructs circles and sometimes simply leaves contradictory statements standing side by side. We are told that consciousness is not real, that it lacks being, containing "not a tithe of what *is*." We are told that consciousness is the opposite of being but necessary to its existence. We are told that there is no real difference between consciousness and its opposite, that they can be distinguished for the purposes of thought but not divided. Then, to complete the circle, we are told that consciousness is the "Absolute" beyond all opposition: "But except in infinity, everything in life is male or female, distinct. But the consciousness, that is of both ... the complete consciousness, which is two in one, fused. This is infinite and eternal. The consciousness, what we call the truth, is eternal, beyond change or motion, beyond time or limit" (55). And to extend the contradictions even further, the body is described in the same terms as consciousness – it also is the two in one, the "*via media*" (81).

Lawrence thus in a single extended essay occupies all of the positions that we have traced through Nietzsche's career, culminating in Zarathustra's assertion of a thoroughgoing identity between the body and the "great reason," and in such stark paradoxes as Zarathustra's "blood is spirit" and "spirit is the life that itself cuts into life" (104).

ART AND THE INDIVIDUAL

For Nietzsche it was Socrates, the "one turning point and vortex of so-called world history," who "annihilated" the synthesis attained in Greek tragic art (*Birth* 96, 106). Socrates' new and altogether unprecedented emphasis on the clarity of logic was profoundly anti-mythic and sought to destroy the old irrational gods, to drag them into the light of day and dispel their force, in the "unshakable faith that thought, using the thread of logic, can penetrate the deepest abysses of being, and that thought is capable not only of knowing being but even of *correcting* it" (95). To instinct and nature Socrates opposes reason and the "brightness" (87) of rationality, replacing myth with science.

Nietzsche believes that the consequences of Socratism and the scientific spirit have been disastrous. Without myth there is no possibility of great art and hence no possibility of true culture or creativity. "Without myth every culture loses the healthy natural power of its creativity: only a horizon defined by myths completes and unifies a whole cultural movement. Myth alone saves all the powers of the imagination" (135). Modern man's "mythless existence" has become shallow and abstract; our lives are mechanically "guided by concepts" (141), and our art has "degenerated to mere entertainment," to sensationalist realism producing "wretched copies of the phenomenon" (108). Without myth, without a rootedness in the infinite and eternal, there can be no "artistic reflection of a universal law" (108), no art in which the phenomenon both conceals and reveals, no depth or "infinitude in the background" (80), no combining of "the highest delight in clearly perceived reality" with a "longing to transcend all seeing" (140–41).

For Lawrence, too, Socrates was "the first to *perceive* the dawn" of purely mental consciousness (*Apocalypse* 75). Modern man is now trapped inside a Socratic-Cartesian consciousness that is "wide, but shallow" (*Apocalypse* 90), lacking depth or ultimate meaning. The tragic Greek culture maintained a connection with the cosmos that modern man has lost. The Dionysian constitutes what Lawrence admires in all great art, "a constant revelation," as he calls it in the Hardy study, "that there exists a great background, vital and vivid, which matters more than the people who move upon it" (29). Without myths in which the divine dimension of depth survives, the "infinitude in the background" disappears, leaving the shallow, pale, vitiated consciousness of modern man.

For Nietzsche tragic man maintains the awareness of both the light and the dark – the tragic hero is "a bright image projected on a dark wall" (67). The Socratic eye, however, "denied the pleasure of gazing into the Dionysian abysses" (89), seeks only to extend the boundaries of the small circle. "Science, spurred by its powerful illusion, speeds irresistibly toward its limits" until it reaches the "boundary points on the periphery from which one gazes into what defies illumination" (97–98). This image is echoed in Lawrence's picture of one of the protagonists of "the little human morality play" suddenly chancing "to look out of the charmed circle ... into the wilderness raging round" (*Hardy* 29).

Nietzsche and Lawrence see it as their life's task to recover the unity that the Greeks experienced, to heal the split between man and nature, man and man, mind and body, art and philosophy. It is not a matter of simply returning to the Greeks. That is an impossibility, given well over two thousand years of the history of consciousness. The synthesis must be restored at a higher level incorporating all that has gone before. Surprisingly, it is in the villain of the piece, Socrates, that the hint for a new synthesis is found. While in prison awaiting execution, Socrates – "the most questionable phenomenon of antiquity" (88) – was troubled by a daemonic voice saying, "Socrates, practice music." This voice is "the only sign of any misgivings about the limits of logic ... Perhaps there is a realm of wisdom from which the logician is exiled? Perhaps art is even a necessary correlative of, and supplement for science?" (93). The idea of a Socrates who plays music seizes Nietzsche's imagination. He realizes that there is not "necessarily only an antipodal relation between Socratism and art" and that the idea of an "artistic Socrates" is not "altogether a contradiction in terms" (92). It is clear that Nietzsche envisages himself in the role of this artistic Socrates whose task is the "regeneration of *art* – of art in the meta-physical, broadest and profoundest sense" (93). This regen-eration can only be effected through the union of science and art. The new synthesis must combine the rigor and clarity of the concept with the depth and profundity of myth. It must "cling close to the trunk of the dialectic" (91), while yet embodying a sense of infinitude in the background.

The art-philosophy opposition plays itself out through the rest of Nietzsche's career, and the struggle between the two never ceases, with now one, now the other, in the ascendant. This opposition is a prime example of the "thinking in antinomies" that Peter Putz in his essay "Nietzsche: Art and Intellectual Inquiry" identifies as Nietzsche's "methodological principle" (9). His thinking continually generates oppositions, such as Apollo and Dionysus, which in their turn generate or reveal further oppositions, such as that between Dionysus and Socrates or art and philosophy. And each opposition is related to every other because all are instances of a fundamental principial opposition designated in *The Birth of Tragedy* as "eternal contradiction, the father of things" (45). In its never-ceasing attempt to embrace the "all," the totality that is beyond all oppositions because it is the producer of them, Nietzsche's thinking employs each antinomy as a perspective. Each perspective is partial and limited yet also participates in and reveals the whole. Putz explains:

In the light of such changing perspectives, contradictions and opposites acquire a new function. Since the manifold facets of the whole can never be stated exhaustively, let alone simultaneously, the perspectivist approach first stakes out the extremes; and in this way there arises that appearance of plain contradiction. In reality, however, the opposites have the function of poles which mark off those extreme points of the whole between which a multiplicity of other perspectives are possible. And antithesis, encompassing as it does the greatest conceivable sweep, is the best suited to embrace these multifarious possibilities. Such poles do not therefore constitute absolute opposites but rather correlated extremes which stand in relation to a totality, even if it is one that cannot ultimately be encompassed. Thus contradictions not only have a solvent and relativizing function, but they also acquire a role as the necessary means of modern perspectivism, which has become an indispensable tool of knowledge and expression. Whether the sought-after totality is called "myth," as by the early Nietzsche, or "life" as in the later works, its content remains his own attempt at myth; and his method of seeking knowledge is perspectivism. The *goal* of knowledge is the *myth* of the prophet, and the *path* to knowledge is the *perspectivism* of the sceptic. (15)

Art and philosophy are thus polar opposites, not "absolute opposites but rather correlated extremes," "forever separated yet related to one another" (15). They must stand to one another "in a simultaneous relationship of hostile opposition and mutual co-operation" (16).

Nowhere is the struggle between art and philosophy more profoundly embodied than in Plato. Nietzsche makes an intriguing comment about Plato which must have galvanized Lawrence's attention: "Plato has given to all posterity the model of a new art form, the model of the *novel*" (91). Nietzsche has in mind a form that is organized dialectically, that "clings close to the trunk of the dialectic," while at the same time dramatically embodying the quest for conceptual clarity and knowledge in concrete individuals. He is also thinking about the fact that many of Plato's dialogues at their height leave dialectic behind and create new myths in their attempt to express the whole. Socrates himself, in Paul Friedlander's words, "becomes the inventor of myths," because such myths "find a necessary place wherever a ray of transcendence and, gradually, the plenitude of *Ideas* penetrate into this life" (209).

Nietzsche did not write novels or dialogues, but he achieved in *Thus Spoke Zarathustra* a unique new form, at once mythic and analytic, prophetic and sceptical. It is not, however, just in *Zarathustra* or in his poems that Nietzsche achieved a new synthesis of art and philosophy. His more conventionally philosophical works are equally artistic, containing some of the most astonishing prose in the German language, prose in which dazzling conceptual clarity and brightness is wedded to the pathos of the infinite, in which the thought is inseparable from the words and the man is fully present in the thinking. His rhythmic sentences are instinct with feeling, never abstract but saturated with metaphor, dramatically recreating the movement of thought which is carried on the feet of images as much as concepts. J. P. Stern, in his essay "Nietzsche and the Idea of Metaphor," finds that in Nietzsche's case "the alternative, poet versus philosopher, is misleading" (79). Stern finds in Nietzsche a "middle mode of discourse," "somewhere between the individuation and concern with particulars that is the language area of fiction and poetry, and conceptual generalities and abstractions which make up the language area of traditional Kantian and post-Kantian philosophy" (79). Stern considers this "literary-philosophical" mode of writing Nietzsche's greatest achievement:

> in challenging, through this mode of writing, the absurd dichotomy of "scientific" *versus* "imaginative," or again the antitheses between "concept" and "metaphor," "abstract" and "concrete," Nietzsche is at the same time intent on challenging that division in our areas of knowledge-and-experience, that fragmentation of knowledge which he … saw as one of the chief blights of modern Western civilization, as the sign of our decadence. (80–81)

The parallels and connections with Lawrence at this point are almost too numerous to elucidate – the concern to unite art and philosophy, the ambition to create a new myth, the idea of Plato's dialogues as a kind of precedent ("Plato's Dialogues are queer little novels"). Lawrence's thinking about art in the Hardy study focuses on the struggle to reconcile the artist's "metaphysic" or "theory of being and knowing" with his "living sense of being" (479). The novel for Lawrence is the supreme form because it contains the most life – it is the perspectival form *par excellence*. The novel presents the greatest challenge to the artist, who must "reveal the relation between man and the circumambient universe, at the living moment" while at the same time "viewing the universe ... in the light of a theory." "Every novel must have the background or the structural skeleton of some theory of being, some metaphysic," but this theory can never become abstract because the novel, "the highest complex of subtle interrelatedness that man has discovered," will immediately give the lie to any abstract theory imposed upon it (*Hardy* 91, 172).

For Stern "the guiding intention of [Nietzsche's] philosophical prose is to convey not the general or the average but the unique, to preserve the dynamic, unsteady, the irregular and above all the individualized nature of life" (80). Nietzsche believes that "the only 'Being' vouchsafed to us is changing, not identical with itself, it is involved in relationships" and, in Stern's words, he "sees as the task of his philosophical *and* literary undertaking ... the ever-renewed attempt to preserve these 'relationships' from petrifaction" (80). This is Lawrence's task too:

Now here we see the beauty and the great value of the novel. Philosophy, religion, science, they are all of them busy nailing things down, to get a stable equilibrium. Religion, with its nailed down One God, who says *Thou shalt, Thou shan't*, and hammers home every time; philosophy, with its fixed ideas; science, with its "laws": they all of them, all the time, want to nail us on to some tree or other.

But the novel, no. The novel is the highest complex of subtle interrelatedness that man has discovered. Everything is true in its own time, place, circumstance, and untrue outside of its own place, time, circumstance. If you try to nail anything down, in the novel, either it kills the novel, or the novel gets up and walks away with the nail. (*Hardy* 172)

Women in Love, Lawrence's greatest novel, is his most successful attempt to combine metaphysic with a "living sense of being," to combine concept and metaphor, prophecy and scepticism, myth and science. Like Nietzsche's masterpiece *Thus Spoke Zarathustra*, Lawrence's novel participates fully in what we have

seen as the central philosophical task of its creator, which is the
furthering of the evolution of man into complete individuality,
which is envisioned by Lawrence as the creation of "wonderful,
distinct individuals, like angels" and by Nietzsche as god-like
overmen as high above man as man is above the animals.

Beyond this common philosophical goal, the masterpieces of
these two writers also show striking formal similarities. Both
works attempt to articulate a new gospel through the struggles
of a protagonist who is both prophet and avatar of a new
humanity. As Jennifer Michaels-Tonks points out, Rupert
Birkin is Lawrence's overman, "the Nietzschean creator-
annihilator ... who wants to revalue all values" (100). Nietzsche
and Lawrence are able to accommodate their prophetic
intentions within a dramatic and imaginative work by creating
characters who are and are not themselves. Birkin and
Zarathustra have ideas that are identical with ideas expressed
by their authors in other writings, but they are also dramatic
creations with a life of their own. They play a role similar to that
of Socrates in a Platonic dialogue. Socrates clearly has a
privileged relationship to his creator Plato and to the truth that
Plato seeks to unveil, yet he is also a character in his own right
who interacts with other characters occupying the same plane of
the same dramatic reality. Moreover, as in a Platonic dialogue,
the driving force is a quest for truth, and the "action" is
dialectical. What Henry David Aiken says of *Zarathustra* could
be said as well of *Women in Love*:

As philosophy, *Zarathustra* somewhat resembles a Platonic dialogue:
that is to say, its ideas are developed dialectically rather than
analytically, and our primary interest lies in the dialectic itself rather
than in any specific conclusions reached in the process. In short, it is
the movement of the thought and the variable moods attending this
movement, rather than any "doctrines" formulated along the way,
that we find ultimately absorbing. (115)

By embodying ideas in "real" people, Lawrence and
Nietzsche succeed in their most important task, which is to
bring ideas into relationship with life. Ideas are put forth; they
are tested by life and by dialogue with others; and out of this

interaction of life and thought new ideas emerge to be tested in their turn in a ceaseless process that knows no terminus. This is what Jaspers calls "thinking by means of real dialectic," in which each position must be lived through with one's whole being: "Life and knowledge ... become one within the process of experimentation, are in constant movement. In this process the oppositions and contradictions are *real*. They are not subordinate from the outset to a known synthesis; rather they terminate in a synthesis that is existentially open" (390).

Central to the effort to bring forth a new man is the bringing forth of a new idea, a new revelation and redefinition of man to fit new historical circumstances. Also central is the destruction of old values and definitions that imprison and constrain new life. *Women in Love* undertakes this twofold task, as Lawrence describes it in the "Foreword":

We are now in a period of crisis. Every man who is acutely alive is acutely wrestling with his own soul. The people that can bring forth the new passion, the new idea, this people will endure. Those others, that fix themselves in the old idea, will perish with the new life strangled unborn within them. Men must speak out to one another. (486)

In the chapter "In the Train," Gerald discovers an article in his *Daily Telegraph* saying that "there must arise a man who will give new values to things, give us new truths, a new attitude to life, or else we shall be a crumbling nothingness in a few years." Birkin agrees that we need "to smash up the old idols of ourselves" and to create "a new gospel" (54). Although unnamed, Nietzsche is clearly present here, as he is throughout the novel. His presence, however, is profoundly ambiguous – he is predecessor and rival, the prophet of a preceding generation who is to be both emulated and rejected. In the canceled first chapter, "Prologue," we see Birkin "holding forth against Nietzsche" (491), much as Lawrence himself must have done many times. Yet the ideas put forth by Birkin are Nietzschean through and through.

Women in Love traces Birkin's growth into "real individuality" by focusing on two equally important and finally indistinguishable struggles, the struggle for passional fulfillment and the struggle to formulate new, living ideas. The mental aspects of the struggle are repeatedly emphasized by Lawrence, as in the following passage from the "Foreword": "Any man of real individuality tries to know and to understand what is happening, even in himself, as he goes along. This struggle for verbal consciousness should not be left out in art. It is a very great part of life. It is not superimposition of a theory. *It is the passionate struggle into conscious being*" (486).

We first become fully aware of Birkin's struggle in the third chapter, "Classroom." Up to this point we have only glimpsed him through Ursula's eyes at a wedding and have heard some of his views in conversations at the reception afterwards. He is not well, "pale and ill-looking." He is potentially a real individual, "separate" and "single," but something keeps him "subordinated ... to the common idea" (20). He espouses a doctrine of spontaneity and individuality – "to act spontaneously on one's impulses," to "act in singleness" (32–33) – but is himself hampered and self-divided. It is this man who in his Arnoldian role as school inspector enters Ursula's classroom. She is teaching a lesson in elementary biology, and the students are drawing catkins, which litter the desks. As the school day is "drawing to a close," the atmosphere is hushed and darkening. The scene is bathed in rich red-gold light from the lowering sun. Ursula is "scarcely conscious," "in a trance," "absorbed in the passion of instruction." Suddenly there is a click of the door, and she is startled to see Birkin standing in the room. He "switched on the strong electric lights," and the classroom becomes "distinct and hard." Ursula, in this new light, "looked like one who is suddenly wakened" (35–36).

After a moment of awkwardness, Birkin turns to business, observing the scholars at work and advising Ursula on teaching techniques. He says that in drawing catkins the students should emphasize the "fact," not "the subjective impression." The central fact in this case is sexual reproduction: "red little spiky stigmas of the female flower, dangling yellow male catkin, yellow pollen flying from one to the other." Hermione, who has been waiting outside in the car, enters and asks if she can observe. Birkin explains to her the way in which catkins reproduce. Hermione seems less interested in the scientific facts than in her "subjective impression." She murmurs ecstatically, "Little red flames, little red flames" (36–38).

After the class is over, the three remain in the room, and Hermione starts up a conversation about consciousness:

"Do you really think, Rupert," she asked, as if Ursula were not present, "do you really think it is worth while? Do you really think the children are better for being roused to consciousness?" A dark flash went over his face, a silent fury. He was hollow-cheeked and pale, almost unearthly. And the woman, with her serious, conscience-harrowing question tortured him on the quick.

"They are not roused to consciousness," he said. "Consciousness comes to them, willy-nilly."

"But do you think they are better for having it quickened, stimulated? Isn't is better that they should remain unconscious of the hazel, isn't it better that they should see as a whole, without all this pulling to pieces, all this knowledge?" (39–40)

This conversation between fictional characters deals with a number of issues central to Lawrence's philosophy, but the complexities made possible by this mode of philosophizing are far greater than in a treatise. Not only do we have certain ideas presented, we also see and know the people who hold the ideas. We glimpse the logical and illogical reasons people have for their beliefs. We see the same ideas expressed by different people for different reasons. We see the same person expressing contradictory ideas at different times. We see opposing ideas struggle with each other. The net effect is a real deepening of our understanding. Ideas are brought back into connection with life and measured by their ability to meet the demands of life. Most novelists do this to some extent, but Lawrence adds a further dimension by creating a character who is in many ways himself. By seeing this character, Lawrence-Birkin, in all his facets, we gain a greater ability to judge his ideas. Lawrence does not miss an opportunity to exploit the possibilities opened to him by this device, including self-criticism and self-satire. Birkin, like Zarathustra, is both inspired at times and a fool at times.

Lawrence is even able to satirize simple-minded distortions of his ideas by his so-called followers. In the conversation I have quoted, Hermione can be seen as a Lawrencean of sorts. She mouths many of the attitudes popularly conceived to be Lawrence's. It is she who goes into a mystic swoon at the sight of a flower. It is she who, like a good Romantic, believes that we murder to dissect, who condemns scientific knowledge as an abstraction, who yearns for the direct, the passionate, and the primitive. And it is her opponent Birkin, the Lawrence figure, who engages in seemingly un-Lawrencean acts. It is he who switches on the electric lights, making everything hard and distinct, and who stresses scientific fact as opposed to subjective impression.

The clash between Hermione and Birkin forces us to become more dialectical and to make subtler, more complex distinctions. Birkin points out to Hermione that, in spite of what she says, knowledge is her only reality:

"But knowing is everything to you, it is all your life – you have only this, this knowledge," he cried. "There is only one tree, there is only one fruit, in your mouth."

Again she was some time silent.

"Is there?" she said at last, with the same untouched calm. And then in a tone of whimsical inquisitiveness: "What fruit, Rupert?"

"The eternal apple," he replied in exasperation, hating his own metaphors.

"Yes," she said. There was a look of exhaustion about her. (40)

The conversation crackles with the tension of a long, difficult relationship gone bad. It also introduces a crucial distinction between two kinds of knowledge, one destructive and one beneficial, and it does this in terms of myth and metaphor. Birkin alludes to the tree of the knowledge of good and evil in the Garden of Eden, which is associated with the serpent Satan and the Fall into divided consciousness. But there is a traditional interpretation of the Eden story, alluded to later in the novel, that points to the existence of two trees, the tree of life and the tree of the knowledge of good and evil. These trees are the same tree seen under different aspects. For the fallen consciousness life is divided into opposites like good and evil, but for the paradisal consciousness there is no disjunction – good and evil are harmoniously united in the one tree of life.

Hermione is associated with the snake; she is "poisonous" and is accused by Birkin of being "the real devil who won't let life exist" (43). Her consciousness is isolated and destructive. Talking about the pupils, she gives herself away: "'But leaving me apart, Rupert; *do* you think the children are better, richer, happier, for all this knowledge, do you really think they are? Or is it better to leave them untouched, spontaneous. Hadn't they better be *animals*, simple animals, crude, violent, *anything*, rather than this self-consciousness, this incapacity to be spontaneous?'" (40). Hermione blames the mind for the nothingness that she experiences: "'Isn't the mind ... our death? Doesn't it destroy all our spontaneity, all our instincts?'" (41).

Birkin flatly rejects this idea. The self-consciousness, the nothingness, the dead incapacity to be spontaneous, that Hermione shares with her generation and culture is "not because they have too much mind, but too little." They are "imprisoned within a limited, false set of concepts" that they cannot think their way out of. But the kind of thinking that is required to escape the prison of false consciousness is a "passionate struggle into conscious being," an act of the whole, existentially engaged being. One must extend one's consciousness and knowledge; facts and ideas are essential. One must be conscious of "what *actually* is." At the same time as people are mentally imprisoned, they "haven't got any real body, any dark sensual body of life." In some as yet unexplained and unrealized way, more mind and more body go together. The effort is twofold: one must become conscious but at the same time "lapse out," "lapse into unknowingness"; "the mind and the known world" must be "drowned in darkness," in "pure sensuality" (41–44).

The rest of the novel traces Birkin's efforts to achieve the lost paradisal state of harmony between body and mind, being and knowing. At this point, early in the novel, Birkin is decidedly not there yet. The hatred and destructive passion that he turns on Hermione are also turned on the part of himself that is like Hermione. There is a shrill stridency in him; he pushes his ideas too hard, as if willing his own belief in them. There is a note of falseness and preaching: "he sounded as if he were addressing a meeting." His "thinness and his pallor" indicate a deathliness, but Ursula senses something else in him:

> There was a great physical attractiveness in him – a curious hidden richness, that came through his thinness and his pallor like another voice, conveying another knowledge of him. It was in the curves of his brows and his chin, rich, fine, exquisite curves, the powerful beauty of life itself. She could not say what it was. But there was a sense of richness and liberty. (44)

This "hidden richness," the richness of "life itself," must force its way through into being. Birkin needs to get out of his own way in order to become, as Nietzsche says, what he is. Instead of stifling his own development by imposing false ideas on himself, he needs to conceive "living ideas" (221) that will further the life already in him.

Birkin has a partial grasp of the necessary new ideas, but is also infected with the old, destructive mentality, as the unceasing intellectual discussions in the chapter "Breadalby" show. The main participants are Gerald, Hermione, Birkin, and Sir Joshua Mattheson, an acid sketch of Bertrand Russell. They are all conversational virtuosi – Sir Joshua, "whose mental fibre was so tough as to be insentient (84); Gerald, who, "on the brink of a discussion, sniffed the air with delight and prepared for action" (85); and Hermione, the high priestess of intellectual culture. Each, however, is an example of the misuse of mind. Gerald's mind is simply a well-oiled machine whose only purpose is domination. Hermione's mind is too abstract; she seeks from knowledge only spiritual uplift and release, the feeling of being "*unbounded*" (85). And Sir Joshua's "dry," "stiff," desiccated body is the sufficient comment on an intellectuality cut off from the sources of feeling. As the conversation ranges over social and educational issues, "a canal of conversation rather than a stream" (84), Birkin clearly sees the limitations of the others and senses something deeper in himself struggling for expression. Gerald and Hermione both sense this too. Hermione has a compulsion to "extract his secrets from him. She *must* know" (89). Gerald, who can find no ultimate purpose in life, says to Birkin, "I wish you'd tell me something that *did* matter" (96). Yet Birkin cannot get clear. He vacillates between moments of near "megalomania" and "bitter declamation" and moments of collapse, when "the whole tone [is] gone out of his voice" (104).

The atmosphere at Breadalby is "mental and very wearying," taking its toll on everyone except Sir Joshua, who "seemed to be thoroughly happy" (84). "There was an elation and a satisfaction in it all, but it was cruelly exhausting for the new-comers, this ruthless mental pressure, this powerful, consuming, destructive mentality that emanated from Joshua and Hermione and Birkin, and dominated the rest" (90). Hermione is the first to crack under the unceasing strain. Her tension reaches the breaking point, and, in the climax of the chapter, she crashes a lapis lazuli paperweight onto Birkin's skull. Interestingly, in "Classroom" this is precisely what Birkin said should happen to Hermione: "'You want it all in that loathsome little skull of yours, that ought to be cracked like a nut. For you'll be the same till it *is* cracked, like an insect in its skin. – If one cracked your skull perhaps one might get a spontaneous, passionate woman out of you, with real sensuality'" (42).

Birkin's prediction comes true of himself – his skull cracked, the spontaneous, sensual animal in him is released. Though he is "all fragments, smashed to bits," yet "a strong spirit in him woke him" before Hermione can deliver the fatal second blow. It is as if Birkin's fate – perhaps what Yeats called the "body of fate" – will not allow it. He is not destined to die this way. His surface mind, his self-consciousness, obliterated, there is nevertheless a larger, encompassing reality that is too strong to be killed and asserts itself. This larger reality can be described in a number of ways: it is his body that reacts reflexively to ward off the blow; it is his will that says, "No you don't, Hermione, ... I don't let you"; and it is "a strong spirit in him," "his soul," that remains "entire and unsurprised" and that directs his "perfectly coherent and clear" movements. (105–6)

After Hermione's blow, Birkin gets up, "barely conscious, and yet perfectly direct in his motion," leaves the house, and goes into the park and open countryside. With an instinctive sureness, he strips naked and saturates himself in the touch of nature, lying in the primroses and wandering through a clump of fir trees, letting them caress and sting his entire body. He "was moving in a sort of darkness," yet "all his movements were discriminate and soft" (106–7). His integral self asserts itself as the mental and social world lapse entirely out of him and he establishes a new connection with the larger world of nature. "Nothing else would do, nothing else would satisfy, except this coolness and subtlety of vegetation traveling into one's blood. How fortunate he was, that there was this lovely, subtle, responsive vegetation, waiting for him, as he waited for it; how fulfilled he was, how happy!" (107).

Although this experience is an important step in his cure, Birkin is still very sick and spends the next couple of weeks in bed. While in the woods, he feels "This was his place, his marriage place. The world was extraneous" (108). But he knows too that the woods alone are not enough: "it was necessary to go back into the world" (107). In order to become whole Birkin must establish a vital connection with at least one other person, if not yet with the larger social order. Hermione's blow having finally brought an end to their relationship, Birkin is free to turn to Ursula.

It is in the course of his encounters with Ursula that Birkin is finally delivered to himself. The process is both passional and intellectual. In fact, it is hard to think of another novel in which "the struggle for verbal consciousness" is so integral a part of love-making. The conversations usually result in confusion and anger but they are necessary. Only through engaging in this way with Ursula can Birkin elaborate and clarify a new idea of love to replace the outmoded old idea.

here was always confusion in speech. Yet it must be spoken. Whichever way one moved, if one were to move forwards, one must break a way through. And to know, to give utterance, was to break a way through the walls of the prison, as the infant in labour strives through the walls of the womb. There is no new movement now, without the breaking through of the old body, deliberately, in knowledge, in the struggle to get out. (186)

Dissatisfied with the old idea and the old experience of love, Birkin struggles to articulate and realize a new one, based on the idea of polarity. He does not want the old "*égoïsme à deux*" (352) in which each couple merges into a single unit defensively isolated in its own little house. "The merging, the clutching, the mingling of love was become madly abhorrent to him." He wants instead "to be with Ursula as free as with himself, single and clear and cool, yet balanced, polarised with her" (200). He wants them to be "clear and whole as angels ... two single beings constellated together like two stars." Lying ill in bed he meditates on the problem until he reaches a moment of clarity:

In the old age, before sex was, we were mixed, each one a mixture. The process of singling into individuality resulted in the great polarisation of sex. The womanly drew to one side, the manly to the other. But the separation was imperfect even then. And so our world-cycle passes. There is now to come the new day, where we are beings each of us, fulfilled in difference. The man is pure man, the woman pure woman, they are perfectly polarised. But there is no longer any of the horrible merging, mingling, self-abnegation of love. There is only the pure duality of polarisation, each one free from any contamination of the other. In each, the individual is primal, sex is subordinate, but perfectly polarised. Each has a single, separate being, with its own laws. The man has his pure freedom, the woman hers. Each acknowledges the perfection of the polarised sex-circuit. Each admits the different nature of the other. (201)

The emphasis has shifted from the way polarity was conceived in the earlier Hardy study. In that work, Lawrence's most optimistic and sanguine, the *unity* of the opposites was stressed; here, in a novel written *in extremis* under vastly changed personal circumstances, the *oppositeness* of the two is stressed. Polarity for Lawrence has almost become a code-word for separateness, and he has an absolute horror of mingling and merging. Yet it is always a separateness that is also a conjunction, an individu- ating that only occurs in relation to another. It is only through love that "that which is perfectly ourselves can take place in us" (147).

Birkin meanwhile remains painfully divided. There is "a violent oscillation" in him "between animalism and spiritual truth" (297). The cancelled "Prologue" describes him as "vibrat[ing] between two poles," "on the point of breaking, becoming a thing, losing his integral being":

he would not consent to sacrifice one half of himself to the other. He would not sacrifice the sensual to the spiritual half of himself, and he could not sacrifice the spiritual to the sensual half. Neither could he obtain fulfilment in both, the two halves always reacted from each other ... To save himself, he must unite the two halves of himself, spiritual and sensual. (500)

He cannot decide if his obsession with polarity is "really only an idea, or was it the interpretation of a profound yearning?" (252). At times he reacts against his theorizing. After making love, he thinks, "What did it matter, what did anything matter save this ultimate and triumphant experience of physical passion, that had blazed up anew like a new spell of life. 'I was becoming quite dead-alive, nothing but a word-bag,' he said in triumph, scorning his other self" (188). At other times he swings to the opposite extreme of total indifference to passion. Ursula fears that he will "[tear] himself in two between the opposite directions, and disappear meaninglessly out of life. It was no good – he too was without unity, without *mind*, in the ultimate stages of living" (297–98). Lawrence's emphasis on "*mind*" is highly significant. It indicates, like Nietzsche's "great reason," an encompassing reality that is neither animalistic nor spiritually abstract but is the integration of body and spirit.

Through Ursula, however, Birkin is gradually made whole. Again, the process is two-fold, their heated debates being as important as their love-making. The chapter "Excurse" rings all the changes on their relationship, starting with a car ride in which they are initially estranged, extending through moments of tenderness and intimacy when Birkin gives Ursula some rings, to a violent eruption of jealousy from Ursula when Birkin says he has to leave to see Hermione. But the fight does not take place just on the plane of personal feelings; it also passionately engages with the central philosophical themes of the novel. Animality, spirituality, the nature of love, all these are fought out in a fight to the limit. These two people can say with

Nietzsche, "All truths are bloody truths to me" (qtd. in Jaspers 386). Ursula is a worthy opponent, the only character in the novel capable of standing up to Birkin. The fight climaxes with Ursula's throwing the rings in the mud and stalking off. The fight, however, has functioned in much the same way as making love. Something in Birkin gives way. "He felt tired and weak. Yet also he was relieved. He gave up his old position. He went and sat on the bank. No doubt Ursula was right. It was true, really, what she said. He knew that his spirituality was concomitant of a process of depravity, a sort of pleasure in self-destruction" (309). Ursula has succeeded in literally changing his mind, in giving him some critical knowledge about himself and in thus altering the balance between body and mind. "There was a darkness over his mind. The terrible knot of consciousness that had persisted there like an obsession was broken, gone, his life was dissolved in darkness over his limbs and his body" (309). Earlier he had complained to Ursula that "I can't get right, at the really growing part of me ... I can't get my flower into blossom anyhow. Either it is blighted in the bud, or has got the smother-fly, or it isn't nourished. Curse it, it isn't even a bud. It is a contravened knot" (125–26). With the dissolving of this knot of false consciousness, the real life in Birkin – the real individuality – is released into expression.

Ursula returns and a mood of peace descends over them. They drift through the afternoon, Birkin driving "in a strange new wakefulness, the tension of his consciousness broken. He seemed to be conscious all over, all his body awake with a simple, glimmering awareness" (311–12). They go to an inn and in their love-making "establish a rich new circuit, a new current of passional electric energy, between the two of them, released from the darkest poles of the body" (314). This is the balanced relationship between polar opposites that Birkin has been talking about, now realized for the first time. "Mystically-physically satisfied," each comes into his "complete self" (314). Later, driving in the car again, "she was next to him, and hung in a pure rest, as a star is hung, balanced unthinkably" (319).

Lawrence attempts to further describe Birkin's state of consciousness as an integration of power and knowledge:

He sat still like an Egyptian Pharaoh, driving the car. He felt as if he were seated in immemorial potency, like the great carven statues of real Egypt, as real and as fulfilled with subtle strength, as these are, with a vague inscrutable smile on the lips ... He knew what it was to be awake and potent in that other basic mind, the deepest physical mind. And from this source he had a pure and magic control, magical, mystical, a force in darkness, like electricity.

Combined with this Egyptian power is Greek intelligence:

Nothing more was said. They ran on in silence. But with a sort of second consciousness he steered the car towards a destination. For he had the free intelligence to direct his own ends. His arms and his breast and his head were rounded and living like those of the Greek, he had not the unawakened straight arms of the Egyptian, nor the sealed, slumbering head. A lambent intelligence played secondarily above his pure Egyptian concentration in darkness. (318)

Birkin's state of unified being contains and resolves the oppositions between which he has been vacillating; from this perspective they can be seen as fortuitous and necessary. Even the most decadent sensual and the most destructive spiritual experiences have all contributed. Birkin at the zenith of his experience is a higher man in the Nietzschean sense: "the highest man ... is the one who most fully represents the antithetical nature of existence." Unlike "normal average men," who "come to grief as soon as ... the tension of the antitheses increases," the higher man is large enough to contain them, though they threaten to tear him apart. Nietzsche's description of Zarathustra in *Ecce Homo* applies to Birkin: "in him all opposites are blended into a new unity. The highest and the lowest energies of human nature, what is sweetest, most frivolous, and most terrible wells forth from one fount with immortal assurance" (305). "The wisest man [is] the richest in contradictions ... interspersed with great moments of grandiose harmony" (qtd. in Jaspers 396).

The state that the highest men reach at the zenith of their lives Nietzsche calls the Dionysian state:

The spirit then abides and is at home in the senses just as the senses abide and are at home in the spirit. ... With such perfect and well-formed men, even the most sensual acts are finally transfigured through an intoxication of highest spirituality via a simile: they experience a sort of deification of their bodies and are farthest removed from a philosophy of asceticism. (Qtd. in Jaspers 347)

Lawrence refers to the "Dionysian" but only to reject "the Dionysic ecstatic way" as a sheer letting go in an ecstasy that is ultimately destructive. It is Gerald not Birkin who is associated with Dionysus in Ursula's mind because of his yellow hair (101). And it is Gerald who displays a real capacity for the orgiastic, who is "a whole Saturnalia in himself, once he is roused" (394). In associating Gerald with Dionysus, Lawrence is apparently thinking of Nietzsche's early conception of Dionysus as the opposite of Apollo rather than Nietzsche's later conception of Dionysus as a synthesis of the Apollinian and Dionysian in opposition to Socrates and Christ.

But this is typical of Lawrence's treatment of Nietzschean terms thoughout the novel. He associates "übermenschlich" (394) and "Wille zur Macht" (105) with Gerald and rejects both ideas, one as inhuman and the other as a "lust for bullying." Bismarck, also associated with Gerald (418), is the embodiment of the will to power in Lawrence's as well as the popular mind. In every reference to Nietzsche, the German's crude, one-sided ideas are opposed to Lawrence's subtler, more comprehensive ones. Yet in each case, Lawrence's idea is indistinguishable from the real Nietzsche's as opposed to the straw man set up in the novel.

Rupert Birkin is Lawrence's answer to Hardy's Clym Yeo-bright, who is described in the Hardy study as "unable to burst the enclosure of the idea, the system which contained him" (26). To Lawrence the chief ideological bulwark of the system is Christianity, with its ethic of self-sacrifice and its denial of the desires of the body. Christianity has traditionally insisted on a divorce between the lower and the higher and has attempted to extirpate the lower. Man is not to yield to his lower desires, he is to sacrifice them to the greater good. Christianity's dualism has created divided individuals like Clym, who can never move in the direction of greater fulfillment because he represses himself out of allegiance to a higher ideal. He cannot envision a relationship between the individual and the other that would allow both to grow; either the self must be sacrificed or others must be sacrificed to the self's selfish desires. Clym ends up a pathetic figure preaching an out-worn ethic to peasants who have no idea of what he is talking about.

The only way to break out of what Lawrence in "The Crown" calls "the closed shell of the Christian conception" is to create a new conception. In a review of *Georgian Poetry* Lawrence describes Christianity as having become "pot-bound" and credits Nietzsche with "demolishing for us...the Christian religion as it stood" (*Phoenix* 304). The analysis of Christianity in *Women in Love* is indistinguishable from Nietzsche's. Lawrence presents the essential traits of the Christian in Gerald's father, the watchwords of whose life – pity, duty, and charity – are the very ideas Nietzsche singles out for his strongest attack. "He substituted pity for all his hostility" and remains "constant to charity, and to his love for his neighbor. Perhaps he had loved his neighbour even better than himself – which is going one further than the commandment" (215). Under the "armor" of his pity, however, lies a horror of death and an obscene fascination with misery:

Sometimes, it seemed to Mrs. Crich as if her husband were some subtle funeral bird, feeding on the miseries of the people. It seemed to her he was never satisfied unless there was some sordid tale being poured out to him, which he drank in with a sort of mournful, sympathetic satisfaction. He would have no *raison d'etre* if there were no lugubrious miseries in the world, as an undertaker would have no meaning if there were no funerals. (217)

As Blake says, "Pity would be no more, / If we did not make somebody Poor." In Nietzsche's analysis, pity is a mask for hatred and contempt. Pity is anti-life because it debilitates and weakens the natural impulses, and the results of this denial Nietzsche describes in *The Twilight of the Idols* as "decay, chronic degeneration, and sickness" (*Portable* 534). The Christian era has run its course and is now precipitously declining into death, as is the representative Christian Thomas Crich: "he became more and more hollow in his vitality, the vitality was bled from within him" (217).

Gerald is his father's son. He appears healthier but is really infected with the same decay; he appears more rebellious but he too is imprisoned by the old conception.

For Gerald was in reaction against Charity, yet he was dominated by it; it assumed supremacy in the inner life, and he could not confute it. So he was partly subject to that which his father stood for, but he was in reaction against it. Now he could not save himself. A certain pity and grief and tenderness for his father overcame him, in spite of the deeper, more sullen hostility. (218–19)

Gerald's feelings are a chaos because they are unacknowledged and unexpressed: underneath "a poignant pity and allegiance" lie "contempt" and "the unadmitted enmity." But his failure is as much "intellectual" as "emotional." He cannot "confute" the ideas of Christianity, cannot think his way out. He has a "cruder intelligence" and more "limited soul" (493) than Birkin. No match for Birkin's talk and "Gudrun's penetrating being," he reacts at times against his intellectual friends and wants to go back to "the dullest conservatism, to the most stupid of conventional people" (221). The Christian ethic, "the whole unifying idea of mankind, seemed to be dying with his father," but he can conceive no new "living idea" (221). Nowhere are his mental limitations more apparent than in the confrontation with Loerke, where he resorts to the most thick-headed arrogance and brutality. Gudrun finally calls him a "Dummkopf" (455).

Despite Lawrence's efforts to associate Gerald with Nietzsche, Gerald has much more in common with "the new German," whom Nietzsche constantly attacked:

The new Germany represents a large quantum of fitness, both inherited and acquired by training, so that for a time it may expend its accumulated store of strength, even squander it. It is not a *high* culture that has thus become the master, and even less a delicate taste, a noble "beauty" of the instincts; but more *virile* virtues than any other country in Europe can show. Much cheerfulness and self-respect, much assurance in social relations and in the reciprocality of duties, much industriousness, much perseverance ... (*Portable* 506)

Finally, as Nietzsche says, power, Gerald's kind of power, "*makes stupid.*"

When he takes over the mines Gerald clearly realizes that a new idea is needed: "The mines were run on an old system, an obsolete idea" (224). Unfortunately Gerald is not capable of the kind of thinking necessary to create a new, living idea: "Without bothering to *think* to a conclusion, Gerald jumped to a conclusion." He concludes that the only thing that matters is "the great social productive machine" and its efficient management.

So Gerald set himself to work, to put the great industry in order. In his travels, and in his accompanying readings, he had come to the conclusion that the essential secret of life was harmony. He did not define to himself at all clearly what harmony was. The word pleased him, he felt he had come to his own conclusions. And he proceeded to put his philosophy into practice by forcing order into the established world, translating the mystic word harmony into the practical word organisation. (227)

Gerald is not even fulfilling the first requisites of adequate thinking – defining his terms and resisting hasty conclusions. He is well educated and has a "very active" mind, but it is merely the servant of his demonic will. For him there are only two things, "two opposites, his will and the resistant Matter of the earth" (228). "Inert matter" exists only to be subjugated by the will, "for was not mankind mystically contra-distinguished against inanimate Matter, was not the history of mankind just the history of the conquest of the one by the other?"

Another way of stating Gerald's problem is that he is not capable of thinking polarically; he cannot conceive a different relation between mind and matter, the kind of relation implied by Lawrence's "mystic word harmony," which, as Stephen Miko says, "must refer, if it refers to anything, to the transcendence achieved by opposing forces" (252). A manuscript passage gives us a glimpse of Birkin engaged in a very different kind of thinking:

All is two, all is not one. That's the point. That's the secret of secrets. You've got to build a new world on that, if you build one at all. All is two, all is not one. In the beginning, all was two. The one is the result.

That which is *created* is One. That's the result, the consummation. But
the beginning is two, not one. And created is two, the whole is two, it
is not one. There you've got it. I wonder what the Priscillianists really
made of it? (Qtd. in Miko 268–69)

Birkin's effort to grasp the relation between the two and the
one is so intense and obsessive that he almost becomes
unbalanced in the struggle, but without such a struggle there
will be no new idea "to build a new world on." It is important
to notice also that Birkin does not just pull answers out of his
own guts. The casual reference to Priscillian, an obscure heretic
executed by the early Church for Manicheanism, reveals a wide
intellectual culture and informed historical context in which the
internal debate takes place.

In an essay on John Galsworthy written near the end of his
life, Lawrence makes an important distinction that is extremely
relevant to Birkin and Gerald. Lawrence finds an "abiding
antithesis" between the "social consciousness" and the "individual consciousness." The individual consciousness, the "free
human individual," preserves a state of "at-oneness" within
himself between inside and outside, "between his subjective and
objective consciousness": "there is no *me or you*, no *me or it* in his
consciousness, but the *me and you*, the *me and it* is a living
continuum, as if all were connected by a living membrane"
(249). Neither self-conscious nor isolated, the free individual has
a "mysterious naive assurance" and a "natural innocent
pride." In the social consciousness, on the other hand, "the
psyche splits in two," producing "creatures which are ... always
aware of the 'you' set over against the 'me,' always conscious of
the 'it' which the 'I' is up against" (*Hardy* 250).

Gerald is the social individual, always aware of the cleavage
between himself and the world.

From time to time, in a manner characteristic of him, Gerald lifted his
head and looked round. Even though he was reading the newspaper
closely, he must keep a watchful eye on his external surroundings.
There seemed to be a dual consciousness running in him. He was
thinking vigorously of something he read in the newspaper, and at the
same time his eye ran over the surface of the life round him, and he
missed nothing. Birkin, who was watching him, was irritated by this

duality. He noticed, too, that Gerald seemed always to be at bay against everybody, in spite of his queer, genial, social manner when roused. (53)

At bay and tense, he completely lacks Birkin's ability to occasionally "get free from the weight of the people present," as he does at Breadalby, allowing him to recapture a state of "naive assurance" and to break into spontaneous dancing with a "real irresponsible gaiety" (92).

The individual consciousness, like Coleridge's reason, reconciles subject and object in a living organic unity. It preserves the continuum in which subject and object are "different, but not separate: different as the eye is different from the nose" (*Hardy* 250). The social consciousness, by contrast, is like Coleridge's understanding, essentially fixed and dead: it "can only be analytical, critical, constructive but not creative, sensational but not passionate, emotional but without true feeling. It can know, but it cannot be. It is always made up of a duality, to which there is no clue." Lacking the clue (Lawrence's favorite word for the Holy Ghost), "one half of the duality neutralises, in the long run, the other half. So that, whether it is Nebuchadnezzar or Francis of Assisi, you arrive at the same thing, nothingness" (251). This is Gerald's state long before his death. At the end of "The Industrial Magnate" chapter he is described as suffering from "a strange pressure ... as if the very middle of him were a vacuum, and outside were an awful tension" (233). "The queer nuclear spark in the protoplasm, which is life itself, in its individual manifestation" is dead: "And, of course, the moment you cause a break-down in living tissue, you get inert Matter. So, the moment you break the continuum, the naïveté, the innocence, the at-oneness, you get materialism and nothing but materialism" (*Hardy* 251). This "queer nuclear spark" is referred to in the novel as Gerald's "divine reason" or "mystic reason" – that which gives his life meaning and without which "his centres of feeling were drying up" (232). The terrible strain and lack of equilibrium are contrasted with Birkin's "odd mobility and changeableness which seemed to contain the quintessence of faith" (232).

The distinction made in the Galsworthy essay and in *Women*

in Love is, like so much else in Lawrence, Nietzschean, as he himself suggests in the essay: "The free moral and the slave moral: the human moral and the social moral: these are the abiding antitheses" (210). This alludes to Nietzsche's "noble-morality" and "slave-morality," as well as to his distinction between the "single one" and the "herd animal." But a halt must be called to the drawing of parallels, which, in the case of Lawrence and Nietzsche, could be continued indefinitely. I will only point out in closing this chapter that "noble" and "slave," individual and social, are conceived of as opposites that are, like the other opposites we have examined, polar in nature.

CHAPTER 4

"A dry soul is best": Lawrence and Heraclitus

COSMIC FIRE

Nietzsche existed for Lawrence as a kind of atmospheric presence diffused over many years and absorbed from many directions, a presence to which Lawrence's response was highly ambivalent. Heraclitus provides a complete contrast. We can identify with precision the moment and the place where Lawrence first encountered him, and there is no mistaking the nature of his reaction. The encounter occurred in July of 1915 in the pages of John Burnet's *Early Greek Philosophy*, which had been loaned to Lawrence by Bertrand Russell. The effect on Lawrence was electric – a classic instance of what Edmund Wilson called "the shock of recognition." We have already seen his response: "I shall write out Herakleitos on tablets of bronze," he exclaimed to Russell in a letter (2: 364). He wrote to Lady Ottoline Morrell, "I shall write all my philosophy again. Last time I came out of the Christian camp. This time I must come out of these early Greek philosophers" (2: 367).

Pre-Socratic thought in general struck Lawrence as a new revelation, but, as George A. Panichas observes in his essay on "Lawrence and the Ancient Greeks," it is clearly Heraclitus of all the Greeks who is "closest in spirit to Lawrence" (341) and who made by far the greatest impression. It is Heraclitus whose influence is discernible in "The Crown", on which Lawrence was working at the time, and it is Heraclitus whom Lawrence quotes in *Women in Love*, on which he was also working. After repeating Heraclitus' strange statement that "a dry soul is best," Rupert says to Ursula, "I know so well what that means.

Do you?" (173). It is a brief moment but a highly significant one. In Birkin's words we can feel Lawrence's own deep sense of kinship with the thinker whose prophetic words reached across two and a half millennia to strike a resonant chord in his own being. Lawrence knows "so well" what Heraclitus means because he recognizes himself in the features of the ancient Greek. Unfortunately the printed record has preserved only a few brief references by Lawrence to Heraclitus, so that we do not know the details of Lawrence's reaction. We have to rely instead on indirect evidence, and consequently much of this chapter will be devoted to tracing Heraclitus' palpable but mostly unnamed presence in "The Crown" and *Women in Love*.

There is, however, another approach, by way of Nietzsche, who shares the same sense of kinship with Heraclitus and who, as we have seen, is so close to Lawrence. Nietzsche's reaction to Heraclitus should tell us something about Lawrence's because they are both looking at him with the same or very similar eyes. Nietzsche's relation to Heraclitus was one of virtually complete self-identification. Heraclitus is *the* thinker for Nietzsche, "in whose proximity I feel altogether warmer and better than anywhere else" (*Ecce* 273). Heraclitus is present from beginning to end of Nietzsche's career, and the only thinker whom he never criticizes or attacks. Nietzsche in his early unfinished *Philosophy in the Tragic Age of the Greeks* presents the major pre-Socratic philosophers as "the archetypes of philosophic thought" (31), and he makes it clear that he sees himself as belonging to the same type as Heraclitus. As a way into Heraclitus, I will therefore draw upon Nietzsche's account to supplement what we know of Lawrence's reaction. Nietzsche's discussion has the additional advantage of presenting in brief compass the essential features of the philosophy with which we are concerned throughout this study. These features have already been discussed under three major headings – Polarity, Ideal Realism, and Imagination/Reason *versus* Understanding – to which we will add a fourth, called Participation.

Polarity

Nietzsche says that Heraclitus conceived the world "under the form of polarity, as being the diverging of a force into two qualitatively different opposed activities that seek to re-unite. Everlastingly, a given quality contends against itself and separates into opposites; everlastingly these opposites seek to re-unite" (*Philosophy* 54). This everlasting contention between opposites results in a world of strife and flux, the two qualities for which Heraclitus' world is best known. He celebrates strife because "all things come to pass through the compulsion of strife" (29) between opposites, and all things constantly change because this strife is never-ending. In one of Lawrence's favorite quotations, Heraclitus asserts that "Homer was wrong in saying, 'Would that strife might perish from amongst gods and men.' For if that were to occur, then all things would cease to exist" (Heraclitus 29). Nothing is permanent, there is no realm of Being, there is only coming-to-be and passing away. In Nietzsche's words,

Ordinary people fancy they see something rigid, complete and permanent; in truth, however, light and dark, bitter and sweet are attached to each other and interlocked at any given moment like wrestlers of whom sometimes the one, sometimes the other is on top ... the definite qualities which look permanent to us express but the momentary ascendency of one partner. (55)

Another of Heraclitus' most famous statements asserts that "You cannot step twice into the same river, for other waters are continually flowing on" (29). Nothing is exempt from being swept up in the river of change, not even the gods, for "Immortals become mortals, mortals become immortals" (68). Everything is ceaselessly turning into its opposite. This is true not only of gods and men but also of the natural world, where we observe, according to Heraclitus, that "Cool things become warm, the warm becomes cool; the moist dries, the parched becomes moist" (29). These contrary qualities – hot, cold, wet, dry – are central to early Greek thinking and are associated with the four elements, fire, air, water, and earth, which are the

basic constituents of all things. They too are warring opposites
whose relations are characterized by intense dynamism and
violence. The life of one is literally the death of the other: "Fire
lives in the death of earth, air in the death of fire, water in the
death of air, and earth in the death of water" (37).

Lawrence's "The Crown", his next extended attempt after
the *Study of Thomas Hardy* to write out his philosophy, differs
from the Hardy essay by placing a much greater emphasis on
these twin Heraclitean themes of flux and strife. "All is flux"
(413), Lawrence now declares. This is true "in Time and in
Eternity" (413). This is true of matter, which is "a very slow
flux" (412), and of consciousness, which is "no more than an
accidental cohesion in the flux of time" (384). Flux is the result
of the constant war being waged by the opposites that constitute
life. These opposites Lawrence now symbolizes in the lion and
the unicorn which are battling for the crown on the British
national crest. Each seeks with all its being to destroy the other
and to gain the crown for itself – the very *"raison d'être* of each of
them is to obliterate the other." Neither antagonist realizes,
however, that to finally destroy its opponent would be to
destroy itself, for each achieves its identity only in the continuing
struggle with its opposite.

But think, if the lion really destroyed, killed the unicorn: not merely
drove him out of town, but annihilated him! Would not the lion at
once expire, as if he had created a vacuum around himself? Is not the
unicorn necessary to the very existence of the lion, is not each opposite
kept in stable equilibrium by the opposition of the other? (366)

Neither victory nor peace is the answer. The lion can neither
devour the unicorn nor lie down with him – it is only "the fight
of opposites which is holy" (374). To attempt to reconcile the
opposites is to "blaspheme against the *raison d'être* of life ... to try
to destroy the essential, intrinsic nature of God" (374). God is
strife, or, as Heraclitus says, "Zeus and war are the same
thing," and Homer was indeed wrong to wish for an end to strife
because that would mean the end of the world: "Remove the
opposition and there is collapse, a sudden crumbling into
universal nothingness" (368).

If "the whole history is the fight," if "the whole field is occupied by the lion and the unicorn," what then of the crown for which they are contending? "The crown that binds them both" is the "perfect union in opposition," the "two-in-one." "The direct opposites... by their very directness, imply their own supreme relation. And this supreme relation is made absolute in ... the Crown, the Absolute" (371). The crown is the "consummation" that "comes from perfect relatedness." It is "a glimpse of the Holy Ghost" (396). "The crown is upon the perfect balance of the fight, it is not the fruit of either victory. The crown is not prize of either combatant. It is the *raison d'être* of both. It is the absolute within the fight" (373).

"The Crown" is largely a restatement of the philosophy with which we are already familiar. It does, however, in its ceaseless attempts to formulate and express the idea of polarity, provide new opportunities and new terms with which to catch a glimpse of the Holy Ghost. At times Lawrence's prose catches fire and carries us with him past our normal mental categories into a vision of life that reveals the opposites in their sheer interaction and underlying unity:

Unless the sun were enveloped in the body of darkness, would a cast shadow run with me as I walk? Unless the light lay within the embrace of night, would the fish gleam phosphorescent in the sea, would the light break out of the black coals of the hearth, would the electricity gleam out of itself, suddenly declaring an opposite being? ... when the opposition is complete on either side, then there is perfection. It is the perfect opposition of dark and light that brindles the tiger with gold flame and dark flame. It is the surcharge of darkness that opens the ravening mouth of the tiger, and drives his eyes to points of phosphorescence. It is the perfect balance of light and darkness that flickers in the stepping of a deer. But it is the conquered darkness that flares and palpitates in her eyes. (370–71)

It is the fiery dynamism of this vision that we also find in Heraclitus. Fire, in fact, is Heraclitus' central reality: "This universe, which is the same for all, has not been made for any man or god, but it always has been, is, and will be – an ever-living fire, kindling itself by regular measures and going out by regular measures" (37). The most volatile and active of the elements, fire best represents the cardinal principle of ceaseless change. But fire is more than just a symbol of a philosophical idea. It is itself the fundamental reality underlying all things: "There is exchange of all things for fire and of fire for all things, as there is of wares for gold and of gold for wares" (37). The other elements – earth, water, air – are "transformations of fire" (37). Fire is the one and the many – at one and the same time both one of the elements and the only element. We are once again in the midst of statements that seem to cancel each other out in mutually irreconcilable opposition. Virtually every statement Heraclitus makes embodies a paradox and is contradicted either by itself or by another statement. Variety, contrariety, strife, flux – these characterize the nature of things, yet "all things are one" (102). "Into the same rivers we step and we do not step" (90). "It is in changing that things find repose" (29). "Strife is justice" (29). "Opposition brings concord. Out of discord comes the fairest harmony" (90).

As Philip Wheelwright in his brilliant presentation of *Heraclitus* expresses it, "it is misleading ... to stress his doctrine of change, chance, and strife without adding that these characteristics, real and basic though they are, exist somehow counterbalanced by a tendency toward order, pattern, and harmony, which is equally inherent in what we must call (knowing that words fail us here) reality." We cannot "call Heraclitus a pluralist without adding that he is somehow a monist as well"; his position "cannot be indicated by any of the usual philosophical labels" (103). Heraclitus cannot be enmeshed in such oppositions as one-many, unity-diversity, monism-pluralism. The truths of polarity, as we have seen in preceding chapters, can only be communicated in ways that elude the logical oppositions of the understanding. Paradox and symbol are necessary, not signs of Heraclitus' wilful obscurity. The next sections will take up these topics. It is sufficient for now to note simply that Heraclitus' is a philosophy of polarity. As Charles H. Kahn says in his *The Art and Thought of Heraclitus*, "the characteristic achievement of Heraclitus lies in articulating a view within which the opposites can be seen together as a unity" (14). He is, as Coleridge called him, the "first promulgator of the law of polarity." It was a fact of the highest significance to Coleridge, as well as to Nietzsche and Lawrence, that the first great philosopher in the Western tradition, the most ancient philosophic voice that still speaks to us with challenge and profundity, should have been speaking of polarity.

Ideal Realism

In *Philosophy in the Tragic Age of the Greeks* Nietzsche asserts that the early Greeks present the complete range of possible philosophical positions; they are "pure types" in contrast to the "mixed" type of Plato, with whom "something entirely new has its beginning" (34). Thales is the scientist, Anaximander the mystic, Parmenides the idealist, and so on. Heraclitus, who rouses Nietzsche to his highest flights of enthusiasm, is the philosopher-artist and the greatest thinker of them all. "The world forever needs the truth, hence the world forever needs Heraclitus" (68). Nietzsche creates a kind of portrait gallery in which Heraclitus stands between Anaximander and Parmenides, superior to each. Nietzsche's Anaximander is a combination of Kant and Schopenhauer, a "true pessimist" who views "all coming-to-be as though it were an illegitimate emancipation from eternal being, a wrong for which destruction is the only penance" (46). Anaximander flees from the ephemerality and pain of existence "into a metaphysical fortress" (48), into the "mystic night" of that which truly is, which can only be designated negatively as "the indefinite" and which Nietzsche compares to Kant's *ding an sich*. Anaximander is thus the first in a long line of religious dualists who deny this world for a higher one. In Heraclitus, on the other hand, Nietzsche finds "not the punishment of what has come-to-be... but the justification of that which is coming-into-being" (51). "By a divine stroke of lightning" Heraclitus illuminates the problem of becoming. "He denied the duality of totally diverse worlds... He no longer distinguished a physical world from a metaphysical one, a realm of definite qualities from an undefinable 'indefinite.'" There is no realm of being, there is only becoming, only one world, which "flows upward and downward in brazen rhythmic beat" and "nowhere shows a tarrying, an indestructibility, a bulwark in the stream" (51). This world is one of ceaseless motion and strife, but, like Nietzsche's Zarathustra, Heraclitus is able to take this "terrible, paralyzing thought" and transform it into its opposite, "into sublimity and the feeling of blessed astonishment" (54).

Just as Heraclitus on the one side is opposed to Anaximander, so on the other he is opposed to Parmenides. Parmenides was the first human being to experience "a moment of purest absolutely bloodless abstraction, unclouded by any reality" (69). In this moment, "un-Greek as no other in the two centuries of the Tragic Age," Parmenides experienced the perceived world of various qualities as entirely false and illusory. Before this moment, his earlier philosophy had attempted to explain coming-to-be as the interaction of opposing qualities. But even here he differed crucially from Heraclitus because he divided the opposites into positive and negative, whereas for Heraclitus both opposites of any pair are positive existents. "Comparing, for example, light and dark, he found the latter obviously but the *negation* of the former" (71). Those qualities corresponding to light were positive, those to dark were negative. Thus in the case of light and heavy, light is positive and heavy negative. "The very method," says Nietzsche, "exhibits a defiant talent for abstract-logical procedure, closed against all influences of sensation. For heaviness surely seems to urge itself upon the senses as a positive quality; yet this did not prevent Parmenides from labelling it as a negation" (72). But if a given quality is negative, how can it exist? Logically, it cannot. And here Parmenides, driven by logical necessity, took the fatal step from which Western thought has not recovered. "Thus before his gaze our empirical world divided into two separate spheres," and, "instead of the words 'positive' and 'negative,'" he began to "use the absolute terms 'existent' and 'non-existent'" (72). The world given us by our senses is thus unreal, illusory, condemned at the bar of logic.

If Anaximander is like Kant and Schopenhauer, Parmenides is like Hegel, who in Nietzsche's view attempts to seize the

absolute by means of abstract concepts, in the mistaken belief
that the logical and the real coincide, that "man has an organ
of knowledge which reaches into the essence of things and is
independent of experience" (82). "Henceforward truth shall
live only in the palest, most abstracted generalities, in the empty
husks of the most indefinite terms, as though in a house of
cobwebs" (80). Behind all such attitudes Nietzsche discerns "a
hatred for phenomena including oneself, a hatred for being
unable to get rid of the everlasting deceitfulness of sensation"
(80). All pure "conceptions lead to contradictions" as soon as
they are brought to bear on the empirical world, but thinkers
like Parmenides, unable to accept the fact that "knowing and
being are the most opposite of all spheres" (83), "hold fast to
the truth and universal validity of the concepts and discard the
perceivable world as the antithesis to all true and universally
valid concepts, as the objectification of illogic and contradiction" (86–87).

Heraclitus' preeminent value for Nietzsche (and, we can
infer, for Lawrence) is his artist's love of phenomena, his refusal
to yield up the perceivable world given by our senses, his refusal
to "distinguish a physical world from a metaphysical one."
Unlike the mystics who condemn the world on moral grounds or
the idealists who condemn it on logical grounds, Heraclitus
embraces the world, which for him is largely what it appears to
be. The thinker's goal is to be as wide awake and with his eyes
as wide open as possible. Heraclitus' anti-mysticism and anti-
idealism, however, do not make him a materialist. He has as
little in common with the later atomists like Leucippus and
Democritus as he has with Parmenides. In fact, he differs from
the materialists in the same way he differs from the idealists, and
this is because there is no essential difference between the two
philosophies in their relation to the world in which we all live.
John Burnet, whose *Early Greek Philosophy* was Lawrence's chief
source, makes clear the historical link between the atomists and
Parmenides, whom he paradoxically calls "the father of
Materialism." The "main thesis" of Burnet's book is that "the
'matter' of the Materialist is not a possible object of sense at all;
it is as much, or more, an *ens rationis* as Spirit, and the 'being' of

Parmenides is the first clear attempt to apprehend this non-sensuous reality" (v-vi). Once Parmenides made the decisive break with the senses, the way was clear to postulate, on the basis of logical "necessity," either a world of abstract Ideas or a world of atoms, both of which are more real than the familiar world in spite of being imperceivable. "Ideal" and "material" are both the result of the same act of abstraction, in which the world of perceivable qualities is sacrificed to conceptual reasoning. Burnet makes it clear that after Parmenides the

primary substance of which the early cosmologies were in search has now become a sort of "thing in itself." It never quite lost this character again. What appears later as the elements of Empedokles, the so-called "homoeomeries" of Anaxagoras and the atoms of Leukippos and Demokritos, is just the Parmenidean "being." Parmenides is not, as some have said, the "father of idealism"; on the contrary, all materialism depends on his view of reality. (182).

Whether or not dependent on Burnet, with whom he was quite familiar, Lawrence makes the same argument in *Psychoanalysis and the Unconscious*. He asserts that "pure idealism is identical with pure materialism" (12) and that, moreover, materialism is a result of idealism. Both are the products of minds cut off in some essential and ultimately disastrous way from the living world around them. Life has been subjugated to the abstracting intellect and its logical imperatives; "idealism has no escape from logic" (12). But, Lawrence insists again and again, life "is never an abstraction, *never to be abstracted*. It is never an ideal entity. It is always concrete" (42). Life is always "a specific individual, not a mathematical unit" (13). Lawrence's "answer to materialism and idealism alike" is that life itself is beyond such logical alternatives; it brings "forth organs and consciousness alike" (36). We can distinguish but we cannot divide "psychic and physical [which] run parallel, though they are for ever distinct" (29). In life itself, as opposed to the conscious mind,

we have none of that tiresome business of establishing the relation between the mind and its own ideal object, or the discriminating between the ideal thing-in-itself and the mind of which it is the content. We are spared that hateful thing-in-itself, the idea, which is at once so all-important and so *nothing*. We are on straightforward solid ground; there is no abstraction. (29)

Coleridge's paradoxical "ideal realism" involves overcoming a distinction that is built into our thinking, that has become second nature to us, but for Heraclitus the distinction between the physical and the spiritual simply does not exist. He cannot conceive of the "material" as such. For him anything that has motion has life and soul. As Nietzsche explains Heraclitus' position, "the many perceivable qualities" (Coleridge's "real and very object") are "neither eternal substances nor fantasms of our senses" (58). There is a "third possibility ... which cannot be guessed by dialectic guesswork nor figured out with the help of calculations" (58). It can only be grasped by "the creative imagination" (40), which brings us to our next topic.

Imagination/reason versus *understanding*

We have seen Coleridge, Nietzsche, and Lawrence each explicitly dissociate his kind of thinking from that represented by Aristotle. Each contends that his thinking violates Aristotle's law of contradiction without thereby falsifying reality. Heraclitus has the distinction of actually being condemned by Aristotle – and precisely for violating the law of contradiction. In his *Metaphysics* Aristotle calls the law of contradiction "the most certain of all principles" and then mentions Heraclitus: "for it is impossible for any one to believe the same thing to be and not to be, as some think Heraclitus says" (737). In Aristotle's view, Heraclitus is simply irrational at best and perhaps a madman at worst for believing what no one who is rational would believe. Nietzsche takes the exact opposite view of Heraclitus:

Heraclitus' regal possession is his extraordinary power to think intuitively. Toward the other type of thinking, the type that is accomplished in concepts and logical combinations, in other words toward reason, he shows himself cool, insensitive, in fact hostile, and seems to feel pleasure whenever he can contradict it with an intuitively arrived-at truth. He does this in dicta like "Everything forever has its opposite along with it," and in such unabashed fashion that Aristotle accused him of the highest crime before the tribunal of reason: to have sinned against the law of contradiction. (52)

Heraclitus' kind of thinking is "lightning-quick" and leaps boldly from insight to insight, while "calculating reason lumbers heavily behind, looking for better footholds" (40).

It is not necessary to labor the point that Nietzsche is distinguishing between reason and understanding and that he believes that the truths of the higher faculty (intuition, reason) can only appear to the Aristotelean understanding as contradictions. Also like Coleridge, he sees a necessary alliance between this higher faculty and the imagination. The power of Heraclitus' thought is "the power of creative imagination" (40), which for Nietzsche as for Coleridge shares reason's power of direct insight into truth. Heraclitus' supreme greatness is the result of an intuitive power combined with a symbolic imagination that creates symbols with a unique ability to seize upon and express the most hidden and elusive aspects of reality. The world is "mastered by him with a sublime metaphor" (62). It is as necessary that he be a poet as a philosopher, because, as Coleridge says, the truths of reason "cannot be conveyed but by a *symbol.*"

Fire, the chief metaphor by which Heraclitus masters the world, is an excellent example of what Coleridge calls a symbol. In Wheelwright's words, when Heraclitus mentions "fire" he means both "actual physical fire, which burns and flares," and a "symbol to denote incessant change" (14). "As is quite generally the case with ancient thinkers he did not distinguish between vehicle and tenor sharply, and it is evident that he thinks of fire not only as meaning something other than itself, but also as a physical thing (albeit a fast moving and elusive thing) playing a definite role in the natural world" (38). Wheelwright cites Coleridge's "union and interpenetration of the universal and the particular" as a description of Heraclitus' "central image-idea of fire." Wheelwright points out that distinctions that are second nature to us – like those between things and qualities, subject and object, concrete and abstract

– do not exist for Heraclitus. They "coalesce" in his "concretely philosophical imagination" (30). Concrete and abstract coalesce in Heraclitus' fire in a way that is literally inconceivable to us, a fact that is illustrated by Wheelwright's having to resort to a makeshift hybrid term like "image-idea" to convey his meaning. This recalls Coleridge's definition of symbols as incorporating "the reason in images of the sense," as "consubstantial with the truths of which they are the conductors." Fire is a concrete entity that is nevertheless consubstantial – coalescent – with its own meaning, a meaning revealed within the phenomenon itself to the contemplative gaze of the artist-philosopher.

Wheelwright refers again to Heraclitus' fire in his *Metaphor and Reality*, which explores the implications of what he calls "*metapoetics*," which is "an ontology not so much of concepts as of poetic sensitivity" (20). Wheelwright finds that the "tensive language" of poetry can more adequately capture the dynamism and depth dimension of reality than can the "steno language" of science and logical philosophy. Fluidity, plurisignation, ambiguity, intensity – "connotative fullness and tensive aliveness" (17) – are all necessary. Even more necessary are symbol and metaphor, if we are to combine "physical perception" and "spiritual insight" (67). Only in the symbol does "the particular, without losing any of its bright actuality, tend also to be, or at least to suggest overtones of, something more" (167). To "the poetical mode of awareness," to the symbolic imagination, "particular things bulge with significance, to whatever extent they participate in, coalesce with, a something more that is consubstantial with themselves" (168). And in *The Burning Fountain* Wheelwright extends this understanding of symbol, calling it a "concrete universal":

The concrete universal should not be confused either with the abstract universal or with allegory. An abstract universal, which is a universal in the logical sense, is a class-concept, every member of which is an instance of the class and necessarily possesses, by virtue of its subsumption under the universal, such characteristics as are shared by all the other members of that class. In a concrete universal, on the contrary, the universal subsists in the individual not *qua* abstract but *qua* concrete. The individual as concretely sensed or imaged or described is the important thing, the bulwark of poetic consideration; the universal is not announced explicitly, but stays implicit in, and yet is strongly affirmed by, the very individuality of the individual. (83)

Wheelwright's fascinating work provides another angle of approach to the constellation of ideas with which we have been concerned. We can see again why it is that, as Coleridge says, "an IDEA, in the highest sense of that term, cannot be conveyed but by a *symbol*" or concrete universal. An Idea in Coleridge's sense of the term is not something separate from the particular but rather something that exists only in and through the particular. In Wheelwright's words, it is "at once genuinely universal and undivorcably concrete" (53). And it is only the imagination that can communicate this reality, the imagination that "incorporates the reason in images of the sense" and creates symbols that are "consubstantial with the truths of which they are the conductors." The union of image and idea is of course an impossibility to the understanding. That is why Coleridge says that "all symbols of necessity involve a contradiction." That is also why the artist-philosophers with whom we are concerned are all ineluctably paradoxical.

Wheelwright observes that concrete universals are "the natural and usual terms of thought in a pre-sophisticated civilization" (*Metaphor* 168). Language in its beginnings is inherently symbolic, and only slowly does it evolve the capacity for abstraction, the clear distinction of particular from universal. As Nietzsche points out, the Greeks "found it unbelievably difficult to comprehend concepts as such" (41). The thinkers who preceded Heraclitus, particularly Thales and Anaximander, took the first halting steps, but it was only after Heraclitus that the process of abstraction began in earnest, with Parmenides, Plato, and Aristotle. Heraclitus' thought thus represents a unique moment, poised between two opposing worlds, the world of myth and the world of the logos. Again, it is by way of fire that we can see this. For fire on the one hand is conceived mythically, as Zeus's thunderbolt, and on the other hand it is the *logos*, the principle or reason by which the universe is ordered and which is reflected in Heraclitus' own rational thought. Fire in one of its most sensorily arresting forms is the "thunderbolt," which "pilots all things" (37). In another fragment this function of piloting all things is served by "the intelligence by which all things are steered through all things" (102). And in yet another fragment he says that "all things come to pass in accordance with the Logos" (19). An identity is thus established between Zeus (the thunderbolt), intelligence, and the Logos. As F. M. Cornford says in his influential *From Religion to Philosophy*, for Heraclitus "the living Fire ... actually *was* Reason" and "its chief embodiment was the Sun" (189). Yet, as always with Heraclitus, this is true and not true, for the "wisdom" that understands – is one with – the Logos is "unwilling and yet willing to be called by the name of Zeus" (102).

Lawrence's *Apocalypse*, which contains his most extensive discussion of the pre-Socratics, makes it clear that he had a profound understanding of the necessarily symbolic nature of primitive or mythic thought and that he appreciated Heraclitus' place in the transition from myth to logos. For "the old human conscious-process," he says, "everything is concrete, there are no abstractions" (95).

> The pre-Greek ancient world had not the faintest inkling of the lengths to which mental activity could be carried. Even Pythagoras, whoever he was, had no inkling: nor Herakleitos nor even Empedokles or Anaxagoras. Socrates and Aristotle were the first to *perceive* the dawn.
>
> But on the other hand, we have not the faintest conception of the vast range that was covered by the ancient sense-consciousness. We have lost almost entirely the great and intricately developed sensual awareness, or sense-awareness, and sense-knowledge, of the ancients. It was a great depth of knowledge, arrived at direct, by instinct and intuition, as we say, not by reason. It was a knowledge based not on words but on images. The abstraction was not into generalisations or into qualities, but into symbols. And the connection was not logical but emotional. The word "therefore" did not exist. Images or symbols succeeded one another in a procession of instinctive and arbitrary physical connections ... and they "get nowhere" because there was nowhere to get to ... (91)

The last sentences could serve as an excellent description of Heraclitus' style, which does not build an argument but rather proceeds paratactically from image to image, each of which is meant to sink into the mind, not propel it onwards.

Of the pre-Socratics, it is Heraclitus in particular in whom Lawrence finds "a revelation of the old symbolic mind" (131), and it is in Heraclitus' cosmic fire that Lawrence finds a particularly compelling example of an ancient symbol. Lawrence is fascinated throughout *Apocalypse* with "the effulgence of the cosmic fire" (98), as we might expect in a thinker for whom life is a flame. Drawing on Heraclitus, he associates lightning and its accompanying thunder with both "the Almighty" (Zeus) and "the fiery Logos." And he makes it quite clear that the lightning bolt is not merely a sign or emblem or allegory of the divine power. "It was a being in itself: another aspect of the Almighty or the Demiurge." It is consubstantial with what it symbolizes. When Lawrence first read Heraclitus, he found there an affirmaton of his own desire to create a poetic philosophy and an example of the union of image and idea in the symbol. As he wrote to Lady Cynthia Asquith while working on "The Crown," "And the Lion and the Unicorn are at any rate better than 'the universe consists in a duality, but there is an initial element called polarity etc etc'" (2:411). And Heraclitus and the pre-Socratics remained with him to the end of his life. In preparing to write *Apocalypse*, in many ways his last testament, he arranged to have Burnet's *Early Greek Philosophy* sent to him in Italy and quoted freely from it. Burnet was a reminder that, as Lawrence says, the "pagan thinkers were necessarily poets" (86) and that living thought must be concrete thought.

Participation

In a passage I have already quoted, Wheelwright describes the concrete universal as a "participation" of the particular "in the universal reality that gives it its main significance": "Particular things bulge with significance, to whatever extent they participate in, coalesce with, a something more that is consubstantial with themselves" (168). He observes further that concrete universals are "the natural and usual terms of thought in a pre-sophisticated civilization." Closely related to the lack of

separation between particular and universal is another aspect of
the primitive mind, which Wheelwright describes as the lack of
"an intellectual cleavage between subjective mind and objective matter" (166). Mind "participates" in external reality
in the same way that the particular participates in the universal.
Such a participatory way of knowing is extraordinarily difficult
for our minds to grasp, conditioned as they are by a long history
of abstraction which has made a rigid distinction between mind
and matter the *sine qua non* of rationality. Yet we find in each of
the thinkers with whom we are concerned an assertion of the
union of mind and nature, and I would like to approach this
difficult topic by way of the concept of participation. Not only
will it help us to understand Heraclitus, in whom primitive
thought still lives in delicate balance with a more developed
rationality, it will help us understand Lawrence and Nietzsche.
For, as Wheelwright says, the participatory mode of the
primitive mind persists in "the poetic mode of thinking of times
thereafter."

Wheelwright's choice of the term "participation" has been
influenced by Levy-Bruhl's formulation of the "Law of Participation" as "a governing condition of all primitive thought"
(*Burning* 162), and it is to this French thinker's classic work on
How Natives Think that I will turn for a further understanding of
participation. My discussion at this point closely parallels
Michael Bell's in his *D. H. Lawrence: Language and Being*. Bell
draws on Cassirer and Heidegger rather than on Wheelwright
and Levy-Bruhl, but his main points are the same: that
Lawrence shares the primitive mode of thought which experienced the "external world as in fluid continuity with the life
of man" (3) and that Lawrence, like Heidegger, "had a
powerful vision of a pre-metaphysical mode of being that he
struggled to express in modern terms," a vision that was in
"radical opposition to Cartesian dualism" (10).

The law of participation as Levy-Bruhl describes it exhibits a
number of striking similarities with the polaric thinking that is
the subject of this study. First of all, primitive thinking "does
not bind itself down, as our thought does, to avoiding
contradiction" (78). For the primitive, "phenomena can be,

though in a way incomprehensible to us, both themselves and something other than themselves" (76). The Bororo tribe of Northern Brazil, for instance, believe that they are at one and the same time human beings and red parakeets, that the relation between them and their totem animal is one of actual identity. And this is true of all totemism, the one identity extending to the many members of a totemic group. The primitive experiences

a community of essence in which the actual individual, the ancestral being living again in him, and the animal or plant species that forms his totem, are all mingled. To our minds, there are necessarily three distinct realities here, however close the relationship may be. To the primitive minds, the three make but one, yet at the same time are three. (92)

Levy-Bruhl is acutely aware of the survival of participation in the thinking of later periods, and the obvious relationship to the Christian Trinity is brought out elsewhere in his book. As another example of participation, Levy-Bruhl points to the primitive's reaction to a picture or portrait – "every picture, every reproduction 'participates' in the nature, properties, life of that of which it is the image" (79). The picture is a "symbol" coalescent with that which it represents, just as a word can be an actual being with the effective force of that which it names. For the totemic or participatory mind there is no problem of the one and the many, there is no difficulty with more than one object occupying the same space at the same time, and there are no abstract concepts to contradict one another. There is instead a "community of essence" in which all things participate, with which they merge and coalesce.

The very world that we live in, the world of distinct and separate objects, each occupying its own portion of space, is the result of a long evolution of consciousness. As the anthropologist Lawrence O'Keefe puts it in his *Stolen Lightning*, for the primitive "it is possible to be two persons or in two places at once," but we moderns live in "isotropic, three-dimensional space," whose very essence is that no two objects can occupy the same space at the same time. Just as two mutually irreconcilable ideas cannot both be true, so no two objects can occupy the same space.

O'Keefe suggests that "the principle of contradiction became a Western institution which progressively hardened our concepts of all the physical entities so as to build contradiction right into them. The sharp edges that objects have for us are all conceptual ... [They] obey the principle of contradiction because such exclusion is built right into our concepts of them" (86–88).

Levy-Bruhl also discusses as examples of participation the related ideas of the *mana* of the Melanesians, the *orenda* of the Hurons, and the *wakonda* of the North American Indians. He quotes Alice Fletcher's description:

"The Indians regarded all animate and inanimate forms, all phenomena as pervaded by a common life, which was continuous and similar to the will power they were conscious of in themselves. This mysterious power in all things they called *Wakonda*, and through it all things were related to man, and to each other. In the idea of the continuity of life, a relation was maintained between the seen and the unseen, the dead and the living, and also between the fragment of anything and its entirety." (103)

We cannot help but think of Nietzsche's will to power, which conceives all things as partaking of the same life that is experienced by man as will. Nietzsche's "mystical sense of oneness," Lawrence's "oneness with all life," Heraclitus' "ever-living fire" "common to all," and Coleridge's "one Life within and abroad" clearly have a familial relationship with the primitive's sense of participation.

Lawrence was well aware of his own relationship to primitive thought, in which he showed an intense interest throughout his life. In the years 1915–16, this interest reached a peak as he immersed himself in the classical anthropologists Frazer and Tyler, read the Cambridge anthropologists, including Gilbert Murray, who interested him "enormously" (*Letters* 2:559), and any number of others including the eccentric Bachofen. What he learned confirmed his deepest intuitions, as he states in a remarkable letter to Bertrand Russell. The letter needs to be quoted at length:

I have been reading Frazer's *Golden Bough* and *Totemism and Exogamy*. Now I am convinced of what I believed when I was about twenty –

that there is another seat of consciousness than the brain and the nerve system: there is a blood-consciousness which exists in us independently of the ordinary mental consciousness, which depends on the eye as its source or connector. There is the blood-consciousness, with the sexual connection, holding the same relation as the eye, in seeing, holds to the mental consciousness. One lives, knows, and has one's being in the blood, without any reference to nerves and brain. This is one half of life, belonging to the darkness... when I *see*, there is a connection between my mental-consciousness and an outside body, forming a percept; but at the same time, there is a transmission through the darkness which is never absent from the light, into my blood-consciousness...

... All living things, even plants, have a blood-being. If a lizard falls on the breast of a pregnant woman, then the blood-being of the lizard passes with a shock into the blood-being of the woman, and is transferred to the foetus, probably without intervention either of nerve or brain consciousness. And this is the origin of totem: and for this reason some tribes no doubt really *were* kangaroos: they contained the blood-knowledge of the kangaroo...

This is very important to our living, that we should realise that we have a blood-being, a blood-consciousness, a blood-soul, complete and apart from the mental and nerve consciousness.

Do you know what science says about these things? It is *very* important: the whole of our future life depends on it. (2: 470–71)

The word "very" in the last sentence was underlined three times, reinforcing the sense that we are at the heart of what Lawrence has to say. In an age completely given over to mental consciousness, he somehow preserved an earlier way of "seeing" that exists alongside the mental, that is in fact inseparable from it ("the darkness which is never absent from the light"). Lawrence's remarkable descriptions of American Indian dances in *Mornings in Mexico* are proof that he shared in what he calls there "the mystery of participation" (60), which he describes as perceiving with the blood. In addition to the knowledge of external objects that comes to us through the eye and other senses, there is an "extra-sensory" knowing that is more like a direct transmission or "communion of essence." Levy-Bruhl likens *wakan* to "a fluid which courses through all existing things, and is the mystic principle of the life and virtue of all things" (133). Lawrence's blood is just such a fluid, through

which transmissions pass, directly connecting "knower" and
"known." The same "blood-being" is shared by "all living
things."

As we have already noted, Heraclitus is not far removed from
this "primitive" mode of perception – a point made by F. M.
Cornford, who also draws upon Levy-Bruhl's thought and
specifically links Heraclitus' fire with the primitive *mana* (188).
Even Plato is not yet completely cut off from participatory
knowing. His theory of Ideas is a theory of participation, as
Wheelwright explains:

> Plato, who in the Dialogues of his middle period manages to combine
> the poetic and the logical mode of thinking in so distinctive a manner,
> recognizes the fact of coalescence between particulars and universals.
> For a particular exists, according to his teaching, by participation
> (*methexis*) in the universal reality that gives it its main significance, and
> conversely the universal reality permeates all particular things to
> different degrees, much as the pure light of the sun illuminates the
> different objects of a landscape to different degrees, each according to
> its capacity for receiving. (*Metaphor* 168)

Coleridge's own theory of Ideas is directly related to Plato's,
and he describes the Reason as the power that enables human
nature to stand "in some participation of the eternal and the
universal" (qtd. in Barth 35). Heraclitus and Plato share the
ancient Greek maxim that like can only be known by like, that
"if the Soul is to know the world, the world must ultimately
consist of the same substance as Soul. *Physis* and Soul must be
homogeneous" (Cornford 133). The mind participates the
phenomena. It perceives the sun because it is itself of the same
nature. As Lawrence said, "I am part of the sun as my eye is
part of me" (*Apocalypse* 149). Or as Coleridge said, "Never
could the eye have beheld the sun, had not its own essence been
soliform" (*Biographia* 1: 115).

THE WAY UP AND THE WAY DOWN

The "Water-Party" chapter of *Women in Love* mentions Heraclitus at the end of a conversation between Birkin and Ursula,
who are

sitting together by the boats, talking and laughing. Birkin had been teasing Ursula.

"Do you smell this little marsh?" he said, sniffing the air. He was very sensitive to scents, and quick in understanding them.

"It's rather nice," she said.

"No," he replied, "alarming."

"Why alarming?" she laughed.

"It seethes and seethes, a river of darkness," he said, "putting forth lilies and snakes, and the ignis fatuus, and rolling all the time onward. That's what we never take into count – that it rolls onwards."

"What does?"

"The other river, the black river. We always consider the silver river of life, rolling on and quickening all the world to a brightness, on and on to heaven, flowing into a bright eternal sea, a heaven of angels thronging. – But the other is our reality –"

"But what other? I don't see any other," said Ursula.

"It is your reality, nevertheless," he said; "the dark river of dissolution. – You see it rolls in us just as the other rolls – the black river of corruption. And our flowers are of this – our sea-born Aphrodite, all white phosphorescent flowers of sensuous perfection, all our reality, nowadays."

"You mean that Aphrodite is really deathly?" asked Ursula.

"I mean she is the flowering mystery of the death-process, yes," he replied. "When the stream of synthetic creation lapses, we find ourselves part of the inverse process, the flood of destructive creation. Aphrodite is born in the first spasm of universal dissolution – then the snakes and swans and lotus – marsh-flowers – and Gudrun and Gerald – born in the process of destructive creation."

"And you and me – ?" she asked.

"Probably," he replied. "In part, certainly. Whether we are that, in toto, I don't yet know."

"You mean we are flowers of dissolution – fleurs du mal? – I don't feel as if I were," she protested.

He was silent for a time.

"I don't feel as if we were, *altogether*," he replied. "Some people are pure flowers of dark corruption – lilies. But there ought to be some roses, warm and flamy. – You know Herakleitos says 'a dry soul is best.' I know so well what that means. Do you?" (172–73)

The question troubling Birkin here is the central question asked by the novel: what is the relation between the two couples? Is there a fundamental difference between them, and if so what is the nature and extent of that difference? Gerald and

Gudrun, according to Birkin, belong to the "dark river of dissolution." Rupert and Ursula also belong to that river, at least "in part," but whether "in toto" Birkin does not yet know. The passage is deeply meditative, in imitation of the circling and deepening movement of Birkin's own thinking. Ursula does not understand, and we feel Birkin's frustration in communicating what he himself does not yet clearly grasp. He quotes Heraclitus, whom he understands "so well," although it is doubtful whether the strange statement that a dry soul is best will help Ursula get what he is driving at. We on the other hand are in a much better position to understand Heraclitus and, by extension, Birkin.

Heraclitus' entire remarkably organic doctrine is implicit in the judgment that a dry soul is best. A dry soul is best because it is closest to fire, the ultimate "substance," as well as the "intelligence" or "Logos" that guides the world and is embodied in Zeus. On the principle that like can only know like, man can most truly know the nature of things when his intelligence is the most fiery – active, dry, light, and clear. Heraclitus believes that a man should be awake and sober; the highest awareness is simply observing the normal waking world illuminated by the sun of the Logos. His contempt is reserved for those souls who flourish at night, in whom the light is extinguished, like "night-walkers, magicians, bacchantes, revellers, and participants in the mysteries" (58). And for drunks: "A drunken man has to be led by a young boy, whom he follows stumbling and not knowing whither he goes, for his soul is moist." Even though "it is death to souls to become water," "souls take pleasure in becoming moist." Men therefore must "fight against impulsive desire; whatever it wants it will buy at the cost of soul" (58).

We have already explored the ways in which for Heraclitus the soul participates in nature. When Heraclitus speaks of moist or dry souls he is not being fanciful or allegorical. He is pointing to a literal identity between the soul and the elements of nature – the same processes prevail in both. Nature is in a process of continual transformation which Heraclitus understands as "the way up" and "the way down." The way up is towards the warmth, lightness, and dryness of fire; the way down, toward the coldness, heaviness, and moisture of water. Soul participates in the same dual process, as Wheelwright summarizes the doctrine:

soul has its natural place somewhere in the area between water and fire, and contains within itself the possibilities of self-transformation in either direction ... Since soul is a dynamical something, always tending by a sort of inner urgency to become other than what it was and is, it may (if it be wise and excellent) struggle upwards to become drier, brighter, and more fiery, or (if it yield to degeneration) it may slip downwards to become more sodden and moist. (62)

"The Crown" presents Lawrence's own version of the way up and the way down as a "stream flowing in opposite directions," either toward "the glad warm confluence of creation" or toward "the cold flowing apart of corruption." In a cosmological-philosophical perspective, the two directions can be characterized as matter and spirit: "Matter is a slow, big wave flowing back to the Origin. And Spirit is a slow, infinite wave flowing back to the Goal, the ultimate Future" (412). The two directions are also psychological, and, as Birkin says, human beings, like all other things, either find themselves part of "the black river of corruption" or of "the silver river of life." Most fundamental to Lawrence's as to Heraclitus' imagination, however, is the opposition between water and fire, between the cold, watery lily of the river of dissolution and the "warm and flamy rose" of creation. The passage from *Women in Love* that we have been looking at is like a nodal point or an eddy in the stream of the novel where undercurrents of meaning gather and rise to the surface. Moving outward from this passage we can see an incredibly detailed and rich pattern of fire and water imagery throughout the novel. With a Shakespearean density, the images cluster about Gerald and Gudrun, who are associated with water, and their fiery counterparts Rupert and Ursula. If we see this pattern of images, and if, guided by our knowledge of Heraclitus, we can understand the nature of the opposition between fire and water, then we will have less difficulty seeing the relation between the two couples that is a central crux of the novel.

Gerald's and Gudrun's natural element is water. One of our
first glimpses of Gerald, in the chapter "Diver," has a vivid
picture of him at home in his natural element: "He was alone
now, alone and immune in the middle of the waters, which he
had all to himself. He exulted in his isolation in the new element,
unquestioned and unconditioned. He was happy, thrusting
with his legs and all his body, without bond or connection
anywhere, just himself in the watery world" (47). Gudrun,
watching, envies him his possession of "the grey, uncreated
water." "Even this momentary possession of pure isolation and
fluidity seemed to her so terribly desirable" (47). In "Water
Party" Gerald is diving again, this time for his dead sister. He
discovers "a whole universe under there; and as cold as hell"
(184). This is the universe of icy death in which he is fated to end
his life.

Gudrun too has a premonition of her own final state as she
watches Gerald diving:

Gudrun sat, sick at heart, frightened of the great, level surface of the
water, so heavy and deadly. She was so alone, with the level, unliving
field of the water stretching beneath her. It was not a good isolation,
it was a terrible, cold separation of suspense. She was suspended upon
the surface of the insidious reality until such time as she also should
disappear beneath it. (182)

Just before this episode, in the lantern which Birkin lights for her
and which she insists on exchanging with Ursula, she has
another terrifying glimpse of her essence:

Birkin went and kindled it. It was of a lovely deep blue colour, with a
red floor, and a great white cuttle-fish flowing in white soft streams all
over it. The cuttle-fish had a face that stared straight from the heart of
the light, very fixed and coldly intent. (175)

These aspects of the water principle – isolation, fixity, coldness – are crystalized in the terrible last chapters in the Alps. By
the end of the novel, Gerald, who has been described as being
"like a plant whose tissue is burst from inwards by a frost"
(345), has literally become a chunk of ice, "frozen like an ice
pebble" (477). He has become a piece of "cold, mute Matter"
(480) that can only be described in the abstractions of physics:

The first days passed in an ecstasy of physical motion, sleighing, skiing, moving in an intensity of speed and white light that surpassed life itself, and carried the souls of the human beings beyond into an inhuman abstraction of velocity and weight and eternal, frozen snow.

Gerald's eyes became hard and strange, and as he went by on his skis he was more like some powerful, fateful sigh than a man, his muscles elastic in a perfect, soaring trajectory, his body projected in pure flight, mindless, soulless, whirling along one perfect line of force. (421)

If Gerald is obviously frozen, Gudrun is no less so, although by a different means: "the cold devil of irony ... froze her soul" (476). She too experiences ecstatic communion with the essence of her being in the snow and ice: "she seemed to pass altogether into the whiteness of the snow, she became a pure, thoughtless crystal" (420).

In studied contrast, Birkin and Ursula have throughout the novel the warmth, changeableness, and vitality of fire, even though the wick at times burns very low. Ursula has the "brightness of an essential flame" (7), and this is how she is revealed to Birkin more than once:

He looked up at her. He saw her face strangely enkindled, as if suffused from within by a powerful sweet fire. His soul was arrested in wonder. She was enkindled in her own living fire. (130)

She was so quick, and so lambent, like discernible fire, and so vindictive, and so rich in her dangerous flamy sensitiveness. (151)

Ursula has a golden yellow light in her that is repeatedly compared to the sun. "A yellow light flashes up" (158) in her eyes. She has "a light of her own ... within which she looked radiant as if in sunshine" (259). She is "all golden. She was as happy as the sun that has just opened above clouds" (407). Birkin realizes this quality in Ursula, "the beauty of her eyes, which were sometimes filled with light, like spring suffused with wonderful promise" (249). He is able to perceive the light in her because he shares the same light, as Ursula knows when she sees his face "gleaming like fire." Like can only be known by like. Birkin belongs to the sign of fire, like the chameleon to which he is compared by the Contessa: "He is not a man, he is a chameleon, a creature of change" (92). The important word "lambent," repeatedly applied to Ursula, is also applied to Birkin: "There was something in his presence, Ursula thought, lambent and alive" (375). The flame flickering in Ursula and Birkin keeps them spontaneous, lambent, changeable – saves them from the mechanical, deathly fixity of will that afflicts Gerald and Gudrun.

Wherever we turn in the novel we see the same pattern, as in this richly evocative scene:

One morning the sisters were sketching by the side of Willey Water, at the remote end of the lake. Gudrun had waded out to a gravelly shoal, and was seated like a Buddhist, staring fixedly at the water-plants that rose succulent from the mud of the low shores. What she could see was mud, soft, oozy, watery mud, and from its festering chill, water-plants rose up, thick and cool and fleshy, very straight and turgid, thrusting out their leaves at right angles, and having dark lurid colours, dark green and blotches of black-purple and bronze. But she could feel their turgid fleshy structure as in a sensuous vision, she *knew* how they thrust out from themselves, how they stood stiff and succulent against the air.

Ursula was watching the butterflies, of which there were dozens near the water, little blue ones suddenly snapping out of nothingness into a jewel-life, a large black-and-red one standing upon a flower and breathing with his soft wings, intoxicatingly, breathing pure, ethereal sunshine; two white ones wrestling in the low air; there was a halo around them; ah, when they came tumbling nearer they were orange-tips, and it was the orange that had made the halo. Ursula rose and drifted away, unconscious like the butterflies. (119)

Gudrun "*knows*" the water plants "as in a sensuous vision"; Ursula becomes "like the butterflies." These are not just analogical or metaphorical associative links; they are rather the signs of a communion of identical substances.

Such passages communicate a wealth of doctrine effortlessly and naturally. When Lawrence's art is operating at this level of density and ease, we find an abundance of images that seem to organize themselves spontaneously into patterns of controlling significance. We feel that the patterns are not planned and calculated, but rather the natural expression of an organic imagination. Which does not mean that Lawrence is not quite conscious of what he is doing. In *The Symbolic Meaning*, for instance, he spells out the distinction we have noticed between the two couples: "It is obvious, however, that some races, men and women alike, derive from the sun and have the fiery principle predominant in their constitution, whilst some, blonde, blue-eyed, northern, are evidently water-born, born along with the ice crystals and blue, cold deeps, and yellow, ice-refracted sunshine" (185).

The Symbolic Meaning makes another relevant connection, between the water principle and phosphorus. Lawrence calls phosphorus "a sheer apparition of water" and describes the phenomenon of phosphorescence as the final expression of the water principle just before it passes off in "watery smoke" (182–83). The connection between water and phosphorus is important to *Women in Love*, as in a passage following the sketching scene just quoted. Gerald and Hermione row up to the two sisters, and they, like Gudrun, are identified with the marsh and the water plants. Gerald "started out of the mud."

And as if in a spell, Gudrun was aware of his body, stretching and surging like marsh-fire, stretching towards her, his hand coming straight forward like a stem. Her voluptuous, acute apprehension of him made the blood faint in her veins, her mind went dim and unconscious. And he rocked on the water perfectly, like the rocking of phosphorescence. (120)

The "marsh-fire," the phosphorescent *ignis fatuus* given off by decomposing matter, is a motif repeated at several points, as in Hermione: "Her face was soft and pale and thin, almost phosphorescent" (140). And in the Chinese drawing of geese that Birkin is copying:

"I know what centres they live from – what they perceive and feel – the hot, stinging centrality of a goose in the flux of cold water and mud – the curious stinging heat of a goose's blood, entering their own blood like an inoculation of corruptive fire – fire of the cold-burning mud – the lotus mystery." (89)

Evidently, there are two kinds of "fire" in question, one corruptive, one creative. The corruptive watery fire is white and cold, phosphorescent; the creative fire is yellow and warm. It is important to realize that in Lawrence's imagination phosphorescence is the same as the cold white light reflected from ice, that both are expressions of the water principle and the way down. Gerald in particular is repeatedly associated with phosphorescence and cold light:

In his clear northern flesh and his fair hair was a glisten like sunshine refracted through crystals of ice. (15)

she seemed like a soft recipient of his magical, hideous white fire. (242)

There seemed a faint, white light emitted from him, a white aura ... He was such an unutterable enemy, yet glistening with uncanny white fire. (331–32)

He looked at her, and the whitish, electric gleam in his face intensified. (241)

Gerald is even compared to "a piece of radium" (396). His body is "radioactive" (332). Like the phosphorescent *ignis fatuus*, radioactivity is also a by-product of decay. The appearance of this white fire is deceptive – it looks alive but is actually an embodiment of the death principle.

Michael Black's two books on Lawrence have traced the image patterns we have been describing back to Lawrence's earliest fiction and up through his early philosophical writings. Black shows conclusively that

the candle-flame, golden and warm, associated with the sweetness of honey and the warmth of the sun, is a cardinal point to which Lawrence's compass naturally sets. It is opposed in Lawrence's associative world to the fierce white light of the pressure lamp, to the coldness of moonlight, and the corrosive power of salt glittering in that light like the pillar which once was Lot's wife. The cold white light is identified with mind, the warm gold one with being. (*Fiction* 35)

Failure to distinguish between these two kinds of fire has resulted in confused explications of the novel. Stephen Miko, in his *Toward Women in Love*, finds two patterns of imagery in the novel, which he calls the light and the dark. He finds both the light and the dark in Gerald, "the only figure who fully embodies both these patterns" (222). Gerald has, in the words of the novel, "a glisten like sunshine refracted through crystals of ice," as well as, in Miko's words "a sinister, wolflike ... darker power." According to Miko, "the two sides of Gerald … become the two sides of the book," and, by the end, "the themes of darkness become increasingly revealed and identified with the themes of light" (222). Miko further asserts:

Although the Lawrentian ideal seems to remain in a principle of balance, at the end of the book we are unable to find the elements of that balance in the extremes implied by the apparent opposition between sensuality and intellectuality. Both are mainly destructive in this book and are finally identified with one another, just as in "The Crown" Lawrence tended to collapse his forces of light into reduction processes dominated by dark and sensual images. (239)

Not only is this reading of the novel confused, it seriously misperceives Lawrence's achievement. Miko is right that the light and dark as we find them in Gerald do collapse into one another. That is because, as we have seen, the light in Gerald is the light of "reduction processes," but it is most decidedly not the light of creation, of the way up. Miko is moreover oblivious of the presence of the opposite fire principle in the golden light shared by Birkin and Ursula. It is incorrect to say that there is no balance at the end of the book; the two principles are clearly established and carefully balanced throughout.

Another passage from *The Symbolic Meaning*, one that alludes to Heraclitus, establishes again the fact that for Lawrence the distinction we are insisting upon was fundamental: "Life – and salt – and phosphorus – and the sea – and the moon. Life – and sulphur – and carbon – and volcanoes – and the sun. The way up, and the way down" (213). Whether or not this distinction is realized in the actual text of the novel is of course a different matter. I find it throughout, as in the chapter "Moony," where Lawrence brings the two kinds of light into direct juxtaposition and contrast. At the begining of the chapter Ursula is in one of her lowest states; the death stream in her has gained the ascendancy. She feels "just like a rock in a wash of floodwater. The rest was all nothingness. She was hard and indifferent, isolated in herself." She feels only "contemptuous mockery." At this point she is virtually indistinguishable from Gudrun, who is also hard, isolated, and mocking. "The strange bright-

ness of her presence ... was a luminousness of supreme repudiation." She arrives at Willey Water in this state.

> She started, noticing something on her right hand, between the tree-
> trunks. It was like a great presence, watching her, dodging her. She
> started violently. It was only the moon, risen through the thin trees.
> But it seemed so mysterious, with its white and deathly smile. And
> there was no avoiding it. Night or day, one could not escape the
> sinister face, triumphant and radiant like this moon, with a high smile.
> (245)

Ursula in her state of repudiation is symbolically linked with
the moon; their community of essence is reflected in shared
characteristics – hardness ("she wanted another night, not this
moon-brilliant hardness"), mockery (the moon has a "high
smile"), and luminous or white light (the moon is "incandescent," "a white body of fire") (245–47).

The spell is broken by Birkin violently and angrily throwing
stones at the moon's reflection in the water, cursing the moon as
Cybele, "the accursed Syria Dea!"

> He stood staring at the water. Then he stooped and picked up a stone,
> which he threw sharply at the pond. Ursula was aware of the bright
> moon leaping and swaying, all distorted, in her eyes. It seemed to
> shoot out arms of fire like a cuttle-fish, like a luminous polyp,
> palpitating strongly before her. (246)

We have seen the cuttle-fish before, in the lantern that horrifies
Gudrun with a glimpse of herself. The polyp is mentioned again
in the next chapter, when Birkin is describing a "Jap" he used
to wrestle with: "'He was very quick and slippery and full of
electric fire. It is a remarkable thing what a curious sort of fluid
force they seem to have in them, those people – not like a
human grip – like a polyp — '" (268–69). To the cluster of
images associated with the water principle – phosphorescence,
radium, cold white light – we can add moonlight and luminous
polyps. These images are not arbitrarily linked; each bears a
clear, articulable relationship to the others and to their common
principle.

The moon is also linked with Ursula's detached observing
mind and hard, self-conscious ego. The moon's light is reflected

light; it and the conscious ego both merely reflect a light that is not theirs, that comes from some other, more vital source. Birkin's stoning the moon's image is in part his attempt to destroy the moon-aspect of Ursula. His fury reaches a climax as he throws stone after stone in such rapid succession that he succeeds momentarily; "there was...no moon any more." At this moment, we are told, "Ursula was dazed, her mind was all gone" (247–48). Ursula's repelling, frozen ego has to be reduced down before Birkin can enter her consciousness at its deeper levels. The two would-be lovers have been completely separated, but now they are able to interact again, and Ursula speaks to Birkin. As they talk, Birkin "remembered the beauty of her eyes, which were sometimes filled with light, like spring, suffused with wonderful promise. So he said to her, slowly, with difficulty: 'There is a golden light in you, which I wish you would give me'" (249). This golden light comes from her elemental self and can only shine through when the reflecting white light of her ego-consciousness is dispersed. The following pages mention the golden light several times and link it with the "Paradise" that Birkin and Ursula are seeking:

In Ursula the sense of the unrealized world ahead triumphed over everything. In the midst of this profound darkness, there seemed to glow on her heart the effulgence of a paradise unknown and unrealised. Her heart was full of the most wonderful light, golden like honey of darkness, sweet like the warmth of day, a light which was not shed on the world, only on the unknown paradise towards which she was going, a sweetness of habitation, a delight of living quite unknown, but hers infallibly. (388)

Lawrence explicitly, consciously, and repeatedly distinguishes between the warm yellow light of fire and the cold white light of water. This needs repetition because a number of recent influential critics blur the distinction. Like Miko, Colin Clarke in his *River of Dissolution* argues that the forces of darkness prevail in *Women in Love* and that finally there is only the river of dissolution. Clarke finds Birkin deeply and inextricably immersed in the stream of dissolution. Here is his discussion of Birkin stoning the moon's image:

It may be granted that Birkin's violence has no immediate and obvious relevance to the activity of *decay* or *corruption*; and yet, intricately and variously, the language refers us back to numerous occasions where we have registered human or non-human activity as lethal and corruptive. "Burst," "exploded," "white and dangerous fire," "incandescent," "not yet violated," "violent pangs," "white-burning," "tormented," "convulsive": one thinks how closely this vocabulary has been associated with Gerald and Gudrun; it is partly in these terms that Birkin defined for Ursula that "inverse process" of "destructive creation" in which (at this moment in history – "at the end of a great era or epoch") we all of us in some degree find ourselves involved. This is that rhetoric of disruption that Lawrence uses for his most equivocal purposes – a marvellously sensitive medium for suggesting, among other things, a quality of dangerous, non-organic vitality. (109)

Clarke attempts to create an impression of a Lawrencean rhetoric that conflates essential distinctions. Only some of the phrases he quotes apply to Birkin, and those that do refer only to one aspect of Birkin, admittedly a very important aspect but not finally the most important one. Far from being identified with the moon – the object to which most of the phrases refer – Birkin is in active opposition to it and succeeds – momentarily at least – in destroying it. Birkin is engaging in violence of a sort but there is all the difference in the world between struggle in the service of greater life and mere destruction.

Clarke emphasizes what he calls the "satanic Lawrence" (xiv). He finds the novel a "haunting celebration" of the beauty of degeneration; "*Women in Love* discovers a virtue in degradation" (xi-xii). Clarke's extremely subtle, sometimes forced readings consistently make the case that the distinctions Lawrence intended – between creation and dissolution, the demonic and the paradisal – do not stand up, that, as Miko says, the "forces of light" "tend to collapse" into "reductive processes." Clarke focuses on the passage with which we began:

it is the inverse process that the *fleurs du mal* are a product of, and the notion that this is at the same time a necessary life-process seems muted. But in fact the notion is by no means as muted as the initial disjunction between the rivers of life and corruption would seem to suggest... The substance of Birkin's complaint is not so much that we belong to the death-process as that we belong to it entirely; there are two realities – the demonic and the paradisal – and today we know only one of them. This, at all events, is what he is saying on one level. Yet he also hints at the possibility that there *is* only one river after all – the river of corruption – and that the other is merely a myth. (80)

Birkin does find a virtue and necessity in knowledge of the death process – it is an undeniable part of life – and he does wonder if there is only the river of dissolution. At this point early in the novel, Birkin, who is after all a character and not the author, is confused about the two realities he posits. But if Birkin is not entirely clear, the novel itself, in its patterns of imagery, makes it abundantly clear that Birkin belongs in the final analysis to the bright river of life, and that it is not "merely a myth."

Despite a keen eye for ambiguity and a penchant for paradox, Clarke's thinking is not sufficiently polaric. Fire and water are polar opposites. One cannot exist without the other, and both are eternally necessary to life itself. We can and must distinguish them but we must also realize that they cannot be divided. They exist in each other as well as at the expense of each other. An undeniably real part of Ursula does belong to the death stream; she cannot deny her past or the existence of its fixed product, her ego. But her ego never achieves the final victory; the opposite creative force in her keeps struggling until she is at last able to break down her old self and allow something deeper and more vital to emerge. The same is true of Birkin. He is deeply implicated in the stream of corruption. That, however, is the prerequisite for becoming creative. As Lawrence says in "The Crown," "there must always be some balance between the passion for destruction and the passion for creation, which means that we must know both" (405). It is only the preponderance of one element over the other that reveals to which stream an individual belongs. Only in consummation is one's true elemental nature revealed. The sheep are separated from the goats only at the end. At the end of the novel, the two streams decisively diverge, one taking Ursula and Birkin to Italy and the sun, the other holding Gerald and Gudrun fixed and frozen in the north.

It is also true that, from another perspective, the two are one;

the two forces are the two forces of one power. Or, as Heraclitus says, "the way up and the way down are one and the same." Heraclitus' paradox is something very different from Clarke's conflation of creation and dissolution, because it is at the same time equally true that a dry soul is best. As Philip Wheelwright says, it is a question of two different perspectives –

the one ethical and personal, the other cosmological and universal. In the perspective of here and now, with a choice of paths before me, it is pertinent to judge one path better than the other; in fact, a failure to do so is even self-delusory, because a self that tries to avoid choosing makes a choice in that very avoidance, in letting its action be determined by dark impulses instead of by lighted reason ... On the other hand, each moral struggle and moral choice, and the unique truth it expresses, is embedded in time as an event amidst innumerable other events. From the cosmic point of view the individual event, whatever its quality and temporal importance, is insignificant ... Of all the paradoxes in Heraclitus' philosophy there is none more fundamental than this one of the simultaneous validity of the two attitudes, valuational and trans-valuational. (65–66)

We find the same paradox in *Women in Love*. From a human and ethical point of view, Gerald and Gudrun stand sharply condemned for slipping downward. Far from discovering a virtue in degradation, the novel insists that "a dry soul is best." There is a norm of positive value shining through the novel in the fiery yellow light. Yet at the same time I think Lawrence has succeeded in creating a novel remarkably free of conventional moral judgments. He achieves the quality he most admired in the great writers like Hardy, Shakespeare, Sophocles, and Tolstoi,

the setting behind the small action of his protagonists the terrific action of unfathomed nature; setting a smaller system of morality, the one grasped and formulated by the human consciousness within the vast, uncomprehended and incomprehensible morality of nature or of life itself, surpassing human consciousness. (*Hardy* 29)

In terms of the morality of life itself, it is not a matter of praise or blame, only of compassion and understanding. Gerald and Gudrun are what they are, and so are Birkin and Ursula – passional phenomena on the face of the earth neither good nor bad but complementary halves of the eternal and necessary opposition between life and death, fire and water. To give Heraclitus the last word: "To God all things are beautiful, good, and right; men, on the other hand, deem some things right and others wrong" (90).

CHAPTER 5

The science of the soul: Lawrence and Boehme

THE SUBTLE BODY

If one were forced to describe the thought of the later Lawrence in one word, that word would have to be "theosophical." During the period from *Women in Love* to his death, the important new influences on him were theosophical, and his most important writings were based on ideas drawn from theosophical sources. His basic ideas did not change appreciably – in fact they were confirmed – but there is a distinct new emphasis and vocabulary as a result of a distinct new influence, which is theosophy. P. T. Whelan in his *Myth and Metaphysic in "The Rainbow" and "Women in Love"* says that "Lawrence lived at a time when occultism was a pervasive interest, almost a preoccupation among intellectuals" (103). Whelan thinks that Lawrence first became aware of theosophical and occult thought as early as 1908, but it was not until as late as 1917 that there are references to specific works that we know Lawrence read. The redoubtable Madame Blavatsky, founder of the Theosophical Society, was his chief source, although, as Tindall has documented in *D. H. Lawrence and Susan His Cow*, he was familiar also with other contemporary theosophists such as Annie Besant, Ouspensky, Gurdjieff, and Rudolf Steiner. His major philosophical works after "The Crown" are all consciously and explicitly theosophical. The psychology constructed by Lawrence in *Psychoanalysis and the Unconscious* and *Fantasia of the Unconscious* is based on the esoteric doctrine of *chakras* that he found in Blavatsky and in her friend James Pryse's *The Apocalypse Unsealed*. *The Symbolic Meaning* (the title given by their editor to early versions of the essays that later became *Studies in Classic American Literature*) draws centrally on Blavatsky's presentation of an occult symbolic knowledge once known to initiates throughout the world. And *Apocalypse* began as an introduction to *The Dragon of Revelation* by Frederick Carter, a theosophist who had become a friend of Lawrence's. Towards Blavatsky herself Lawrence always maintained a critical distance, but not towards the ideas he found in her encyclopedic writings. As we have seen, he found her writings "not *very* much good" (*Letters* 3: 299), "in many ways a bore, and not quite real. Yet one can glean a marvelous lot from [them], enlarge the understanding immensely" (3: 150). Her ideas, he exclaimed, were "marvelously illuminating" (3: 143). The last time we saw this kind of enthusiasm in Lawrence, it was for Heraclitus.

The term theosophy tends to be associated with Blavatsky but has a much wider reach. In this chapter I would like to keep the term but dissociate it from Blavatsky and from the occult and spiritualist emphasis that she gave it. The OED defines theosophy simply as "wisdom concerning God or the divine." Theosophy needs to be distinguished from philosophy and from theology, two other ways of thinking about God or the divine. It differs from philosophy in that theosophers derive their wisdom from sources higher than the intellect and are often mystics and visionaries. Theosophy differs from theology in that it is not an attempt to reconcile revelation with the categories of reason but is rather a revelation or vision in its own right, often in competition with orthodoxy, and expressed mythically and symbolically rather than rationally. Theosophy, however, differs crucially from primitive myth by virtue of its immensely greater philosophical sophistication. The most important theosophical systems, such as Gnosticism, Hermetism, the Kabbalah, and alchemy, were all formulated in the Hellenistic centuries before and after the birth of Christ and show the influence of such elaborate systems of thought as Aristotel-eanism, Stoicism, and Neoplatonism. In addition to being mythic and symbolic, these systems have a highly complex, systematic quality and clearly bear the stamp of minds nurtured

on philosophy. Theosophy in fact represents a unique reconciliation of poetry and philosophy, managing to satisfy the
demands of both the poetic and the rational mind. We have seen
this as Lawrence's own goal, and much of theosophy's powerful
appeal to him lies in its solution of the problem. In theosophy
Lawrence saw a way of preserving the virtues of ancient myth
without sacrificing reason.

We have Coleridge's support for our use of the term
"theosophical." In the margins of the William Law edition of
the writings of Jacob Boehme, Coleridge wrote: "Theosophy,
from Heraclitus (500 AC) to S. T. C. (1817 PC)" (*Marginalia* 1:
588), thus placing himself and Heraclitus and Boehme in the
same theosophical tradition. It is Boehme who provides the link
between Heraclitus and the nineteenth century, and we have
already noted Boehme's immense influence on Coleridge's
philosophy of polarity. But Boehme was important to Coleridge
as more than just another thinker. He credited him with helping
"to keep alive the *heart* in the *head*," of saving him from the
"mere *reflective* faculty [which] partook of DEATH" (*Biographia* 1:
152). In other words, Coleridge found in Boehme the same
philosophic imagination that he found in Plato the poet-
philosopher. The humble, unlearned shoemaker who was yet
"a stupendous human being" possessed perhaps a "greater
genius even [than] Plato himself." For "fulness of heart and
intellect" (*Philosophical* 329) he is unmatched; and his writings
have a rare power to directly convey authentic spiritual
intuitions. His words are the "immediate echoes of his feelings"
(329), emerging with an astonishing directness, seemingly free
of all influence of other thinkers or systems.

This characteristic of Boehme's style – its spontaneity and
immediacy – is one of the most striking similarities between him
and Lawrence. They share what we could call the style of left-
wing Protestantism. In both writers one feels a direct, head-on
attempt to seize the ground of being without intermediaries.
Both depend on the Holy Spirit to animate their words. Boehme
says, "if the Spirit were withdrawn from me I could neither
know nor understand my own Writings." The Spirit moves
where and when it will. Great unevenness characterizes their
literary output – there are arid stretches when the writer is

struggling darkly, waiting for the Spirit, followed by beautiful
passages when the Spirit is present. The impression is one of
dark rolling thunderclouds lit up by intermittent flashes of
lightning. A concern for system or terminological consistency is
secondary to the attempt to capture the immediate and
momentary intuition. They attempt to bring down ideas on the
wing, and there are hits and misses. They are both expansive,
repetitious, energetic. Each new book is a fresh start, a new
attempt to restate the entire philosophy from the present
vantage point. There is a strong feeling of emotional turmoil
and struggle reflected in the style that is mimetic of the great
turbulent forces they feel within themselves and in the world of
nature.

In these and other ways Lawrence is even closer to Boehme
than to the other figures in this study, in spite of the fact that he
probably read none of Boehme's writings. There is one reference
to Boehme in a letter (4: 460), but no evidence of any direct
acquaintance. By contrast, one can point to any number of
direct borrowings from Madame Blavatsky, as Richard J.
Kuczkowski does in his dissertation *Lawrence's "Esoteric" Psychology*. Yet it is to "the Teutonic Theosopher" that we must
turn for a deeper understanding of theosophy – and of Lawrence – than Blavatsky provides. Boehme and Lawrence share a
philosophical position and a Weltanschauung, whereas Blavatsky cannot be said to have an identifiable position. Her
Theosophy is a chaotic mix of undigested elements representing
prodigious learning but little philosophic depth or order. The
choice of Boehme is further supported by Rene Guenon's
informed opinion that Blavatsky's ideas are largely drawn from
Boehme (*Théosophisme* 8). Blavatsky indiscriminately mixes the
profound and the absurd, as in the following passage from *Isis
Unveiled*, which lists different versions of the idea of an "all-
pervading subtile principle" or "UNIVERSAL ETHER," also called
FOHAT, from which the physical world is formed:

The chaos of the ancients; the Zoroastrian sacred fire, or the *Antusbyrum*
of the Parsees; the Hermes-fire; the Elmes-fire of the ancient Germans;
the lightning of Cybele; the burning torch of Apollo; the flame on the
altar of Pan; the inextinguishable fire in the temple on the Acropolis,
and in that of Vesta; the fire-flame of Pluto's helm; the brilliant sparks

on the hats of the Dioscuri, on the Gorgon head, the helm of Pallas and the staff of Mercury ... the Egyptian Phtha or Ra; the Grecian *Zeus Cataibates* (the descending); the pentecostal fire-tongues; the burning bush of Moses; the pillar of fire of the *Exodus*, and the "burning lamp" of Abram; the eternal fire of the "bottomless pit"; the Delphic oracular vapors; the Sidereal light of the Rosicrucians; the AKASA of the Hindu adepts; the Astral light of Eliphas Levi; the nerve-aura and the fluid of the magnetists; the *od* of Reichenbach; the fire-globe, or meteor-*cat* of Babinet; the *Psychod* and ectenic force of Thury; the psychic force of Sergeant Cox and Mr. Crookes; the atmospheric magnetism of some naturalists; galvanism; and finally, electricity, are but various names for many different manifestations, or effects of the same mysterious, all-pervading cause – the Greek *Archeus* ... (125)

Blavatsky's fantasias can be quite exciting, even exhilarating, although there is finally more smoke than fire. She is pointing to profound connections, such as those between the fire of the ancients and the ether and electricity of more recent systems, but these connections are buried under a load of often questionable learning rather than elucidated.

In Boehme, by contrast, we have a direct apprehension or vision of the reality of cosmic fire. He is a primary rather than secondary source – the fire that Blavatsky merely talks about is actually experienced by Boehme, and his many books are attempts to articulate and explain that experience. As Boehme's best modern commentator Alexandre Koyre observes, fire is the "symbole central de sa doctrine" (362). Hundreds of times in his many books the observation is repeated that "life is a fire." The two most salient features of his doctrine – the idea that life is a struggle between polar opposites and the omnipresence of the Trinity – are expressed in the fire symbol. Fire first of all has two opposing aspects: it is heat and light, a painful burning and a joyful illumination; it is wrath and love, hell and heaven. Fire is a "*contrarium*," a synthesis of polar opposites that can be distinguished but not separated.

The power in the light is God's love-fire and the power in the darkness is God's anger fire; yet it is but one and one only fire, but divided into two principles, that the one might be manifest in the other. For the flame of anger is the manifestation of the great love; and in the darkness is the light made known else it were not manifest of itself. (Qtd. in Brinton 161)

We must know wrath in order to experience love; the light can only manifest by contrast to its opposite the dark.

The *Lebens-Feuer* is a perfect expression for the dynamism and vitality that characterize life for Boehme. Just as life is a product of inextricably linked opposites, so is fire in its dual aspect. There is no writer more aware of life's duality than Boehme. "In Yes and No stand all things," he declares over and over. Everywhere he looks he sees double; he discovers "in all things, Evil and Good, Love and Anger." "There are two *qualities in Nature*... The one is pleasant, heavenly, and holy; the other is fierce, wrathful, hellish, and thirsty" (*Aurora* 32). These two qualities or principles are embodied in the Father and Son of the Trinity, the Father being a dark, burning, centripetal source, and the Son a bright, centrifugal light. The opposition that is found everywhere in life is extended daringly into God's very essence, the Father being the source of the wrathful, hellish, burning fire. The Father is comparable to the dark at the center of the candle flame; he is the wick, his the substance that is consumed. The Son is the yellow flame itself, the offspring and opposite of the dark source, yet coeternal and one with it. The Holy Ghost on this analogy becomes the light itself that moves out from the flame, the product of the struggle between the first two principles in God's interior. Or, in another formulation, Boehme calls it the air which is necessary to the existence of both the light (which needs a medium) and the fire (for which it provides fuel). This is not the place to explore all of the complexities of Boehme's thought or to create the impression that he is more clear than he is. There is in fact no important writer who can be less clear or more confusing that Boehme, unless it is Paracelsus, who unfortunately served as one of his models. Boehme's writing itself is like a fire, at times smoldering darkly, at times emitting smoke, at times bursting into clarity. What does emerge again and again is a powerful apprehension of life in its essence as a fire.

In this regard, as Nicolas Berdyaev, Boehme's foremost modern disciple, says, "the only thinker to whom he is close is Heraclitus" (xxxvii). It is as if Boehme somehow, inexplicably, were able to circumvent centuries of Aristoteleanism and to return directly to pre-Socratic thought. His thinking is always in images, always concrete, never abstract. His thought is living and vital, as is the natural world in which he lives, which is alive in every aspect. And nowhere is he closer to Heraclitus than in his fire-doctrine. For both men, fire is the one (Boehme's *quinta essentia*) that transforms itself into the many, into the four elements from which all things are created and into which they are reabsorbed. As Boehme describes it in *Mysterium Magnum*:

The fire is the workmaster thereunto, which putteth forth from a small power a little sprout out of the earth, and displayeth it into a great tree with many boughs, branches and fruits; and doth again consume it, and reduceth it again to one thing, viz. to ashes and earth, whence it first proceeded: and so also all things of this world do enter again into the one whence they came. (1 : 53)

Fire is the driving force behind all change and motion, that which in Heraclitus' words "pilots" all things. As we have seen, for Heraclitus the thunderbolt is the most striking manifestation of fire, the emblem and instrument of Zeus who is himself the "ever-living fire." Heidegger explains Heraclitus' lightning as "what brings everything to appearance" (122), and this is the role played by lightning in Boehme. Just as on a dark night the lightning momentarily flashes and reveals things in their articulated outline, so the world itself is a manifestation of the hidden god, an out-flashing from his inner life. Without going into the technicalities of his seven nature-spirits or "qualities," we can justly describe Boehme's account of the generation of external nature, which is the third principle or Holy Spirit, as the result of a tremendous tension between the first two principles. As in a thundercloud, the tension builds until it is finally released in the bolt of lightning, the central event of cosmogony:

Now both these [principles, wills] dash together in one another. The sharp will eagerly and mightily desireth the free lubet, and the lubet desireth the austere will; and as they enter into and feel each other, a great flagrat is made, like a flash of lightning, in manner as the fire or lightning is enkindled in the firmament.
And in this flagrat the fire is enkindled. (*Mysterium* 1 : 11)

Boehme's English translators have made him even more difficult than he is in German by introducing their own terms – "lubet" for "*Lust*" and "flagrat" for "*Schrack*" – diminishing the force of the original, which conveys a grand cosmic drama whose crisis is, in Howard Brinton's words, "a sudden release of a mighty pent-up force accompanied by a terrifying sound (*Schrack*) and a great flash of light (*Blitz*)" (142).

Bergson describes how all true philosophies arise from a vision or intuition that is both simple and rich but which the philosopher cannot at first translate into the terms of rational discourse. This intuition, however, transforms itself in his spirit into a symbolic image, an image which underlies his deductions and forms the center of his thought (qtd. in Koyre 283). This is the role played by fire in each of the thinkers in this study, all of whom are born under the sign of fire, are in Blavatsky's term "fire-philosophers." This is Nietzsche's description of himself:

> Yes, I know from whence I came!
> Discontented as a flame,
> Upon myself I live and glow.
> All I grasp like lightning flashes,
> All I leave behind is ashes:
> Flame I am – that much I know!
>
> (Qtd. in Jaspers 414)

Life is preeminently a flame for Lawrence, for whom all phenomena are bright sparks thrown off from the central dark fire at the source, and for whom the central cosmogonic event – the act of coition – is "a great flash of interchange ... like lightning out of the densely surcharged clouds" (*Fantasia* 141). This is true from the beginning to the end of his life – a fundamental intuition that he was born and buried with. Joyce Carol Oates notes a "strange unity" in Lawrence's *Collected Poems*, from the first phrase, "quick sparks," to the last, "immortal bird" (45). The unity is that of fire, embracing everything from gorse bushes to Lawrence's emblem the phoenix, the creature that is born, lives, and dies in flame. He especially loves flowers and birds because in them life's flaminess is more apparent than in other things (although the other things are simply slower flames). The "quick sparks" (33) of the gorse bushes of "The Wild Common" are, like the rose, "only a running flame" (182), or like the almond trees "aflame with blossom" (244). Lawrence's remarkable "Turkey-Cock" emerges into vision straight from its "firing in the furnace of creation," its wattles "bits of slag still adhering" (370). It is the same fire that burns in nature and in our spirits:

> And the same fire that boils within this ball
> Of earth, and quickens all herself with flowers,
> Is womb-fire in the stiffened clay of us:
>
> And every flash of thought that we and ours
> Send suddenly out, and every gesture, does
> Fly like a spark into the womb of passion,
> To start a birth, from joy of the begetting.   (89)

The poet and his wife create each other in the fire of passion. She is the wick, he the flame. "Where I touch you, I flame into being." Together, they are "a bonfire of oneness, me flame flung leaping round you, / You the core of the fire, crept into me" (245).

Bergson speaks of the transformation of the thinker's original intuition into a symbol, but we need to remind ourselves that this is a symbol in Coleridge's sense of symbol as consubstantial with the symbolized, as participating in the same reality. As Koyre states, Boehme is not a Cartesian: "For him there is a union between spirit and matter and, even if there is opposition, it is an opposition of contrary and not contradictory terms" (my translation, 109). The relation between fire and God is not one of analogy but of identity. Boehme's symbol is not an example of a certain similarity brought in to aid the understanding; fire is the expression and incarnation of God in nature. God the source of life acts and is in the sun that acts in nature: "As in the earth also there is a subtle good virtue, which is like the sun and is one and the same with the sun; which also in the beginning of time did spring and proceed out of the divine power and virtue, from whence all the good virtue of the body is likewise derived" (*Way* 151). This "subtle virtue" or "divine power" fills all space. Boehme reasons simply and even primitively: Where God acts, there he must be, and if he acts in the world then he must be in the world as a real, creative force, the source of life. Moreover, if God is a living God – and Boehme's is above all a living God – then he must have a body, and this body must pervade all nature. Boehme nowhere reasons like a philosopher. His God is not a lifeless abstraction arrived at as a *terminus ad quem* of syllogistic logic, like Aristotle's Unmoved Mover.

But if God is not pure disembodied spirit, neither is He matter as we ordinarily conceive it. Koyre's masterful exposition cannot be improved upon:

> God possesses a body (*Leib*). This body is invisible, intangible, and possesses none of the properties that constitute matter properly speaking. However, this divine "matter," this divine body possesses the character of spatiality, although God does not become for all that a spatial being, any more, moreover, than the fact of possessing a material body reduces the human being to an exclusively material existence or makes of man a simple body ...
>
> It is extremely difficult to render the exact sense of this idea ... to represent this immaterial matter, this subtle matter that is not a body in our sense of the term – that is to say an impenetrable and delimited part of space – but is something intermediate between gross matter and spirit. For too long there has been for us an uncrossable abyss between body and spirit, between extension and thought. We are all cartesians, whether we wish it or not. However, it is not impossible to reconstruct this notion, the last residue of a primitive mentality. (My translation, 113–14)

Koyre then refers to Levy-Bruhl's work, reminding us that what we find in Boehme's subtle matter is a survival in the seventeenth century of the primitive's participatory way of thinking. As we saw in the previous chapter, the primitive's *Wakan* or *mana* is a "community of essence" that is like a "fluid" that courses through all things. And we saw the fundamental identity between this fluid that is neither spiritual nor material and Lawrence's "blood," Nietzsche's "will," and Heraclitus' "fire."

How are we to think of this literally (to us) inconceivable immaterial matter? It helps to recall the traditional threefold distinction spirit-soul-body. Pure Spirit can only be described in terms of the negation or absence of all categories or images drawn from the world; it is beyond all specification of human thought, beyond imagination and conception, beyond space and time. Matter on the other hand exists in time and space, can be perceived by the senses and described by the mind; it is visible and tangible and undergoes constant change. Soul, between the other two, corresponds to the subtle. As David V. Tansley puts it in his *Subtle Body*, "When these two polar opposites [spirit and matter] come into union, their interaction gives birth to the soul" (6). Existing as it were between spirit and matter, the soul shares some of the characteristics of each. The soul or subtle could be described as existing in time but not in space, although it possesses a "spatiality" of sorts since souls or subtle bodies have "form" and are distinct from one another. Most theosophical sources discriminate a series of subtle bodies or subtle worlds, usually seven in number, bridging the gap between spirit and matter, to which they give names such as "astral" or "etheric" or "mental" bodies. For our purposes it is enough to simply refer to a single subtle body or realm of "immaterial matter" between spirit and matter. We are to think of the individual subtle body as inhabiting a subtle world that encompasses the *anima mundi* as well as the individual soul.

The subtle is the source of both the form and the energy of the phenomena that we witness in the realm of the material. It is the realm of Plato's Ideas, the archetypes of the visible. It is *natura naturans*. Like spirit it is invisible and penetrable; like matter it has articulate form. From the spiritual standpoint, it is the means by which the spirit manifests in the material. From the standpoint of the material, it is an extremely fine attenuation and subtilization, an etherealization. In the transition from solid to liquid to gas, it is the next step. It is the quintessence (*quinta essentia*) or ether that is the source of the four visible elements. It has survived in the history of modern science in a number of guises, including the caloric fluid, the electric fluid, and the ether.

Lawrence draws centrally upon this idea of the subtle body in all of his later philosophical writings, most elaborately and systematically in his two works on the unconscious. He explicitly identifies the "unconscious" with what has traditionally been called the "soul" – "by the unconscious we do mean the soul" (*Psychoanalysis* 15). However, he uses the term soul sparingly because it has been vitiated by our modern idealism which can only conceive of the soul as something abstract when in fact the soul or "pristine unconscious" is the source of all life and must be at least as real as its product. The soul, the unconscious, is "only another word for life" (42), which is "never an abstraction, *never to be abstracted* ... It is always concrete" (42). We can in fact, Lawrence insists, "quite tangibly deal with the human unconscious. We trace its source and centres in the great ganglia and nodes of the nervous system" (43) – the solar plexus, the lumbar ganglion, the cardiac plexus, and the thoracic ganglion. Although these centers have a real existence, they are not to be thought of as identical with the physical organs that the anatomist dissects. Lawrence calls them "chakras" (35), a term taken from yoga. *Chakras* can most easily be understood as the point of intersection or transition from the material to the subtle. In the words of Alain Danielou in his *Yoga: The Method of Reintegration*, they are the points at which "the subtle body is connected with the gross body" (123). Pryse's *The Apocalypse Unsealed*, Lawrence's chief source, explains that there are seven principal *chakras* arranged in ascending order along the spine. The yogi or spiritual initiate progresses by awakening these centers in his body. This is the awakening of the *kundalini*, "which in the *Upanishads* is poetically said to lie coiled up like a slumbering serpent" (16). The *kundalini* is subtle energy, "which in energizing becomes what may be described as living, conscious electricity, of incredible voltage and hardly comparable to the form of electricity known to the physicist" (11–12). As the *kundalini* "passes from one ganglion to another its voltage is raised, the ganglia being like so many electric cells coupled for intensity" (16). The goal of this process is the transmutation of man's physical being "ultimately into a divine being bodied in a deathless ethereal form of ineffable beauty ... a self-luminous immortal body" (9). This subtle body is "formed of etheric fire, and is in direct relation with, and is sustained by, the cosmic and divine forces" (215).

Lawrence modifies Pryse's seven centers into his own ingenious scheme of four primary centers, but his understanding of the nature of these centers differs in no significant way from that found in any number of theosophical and occult sources. At one point he describes the *chakras* as "the points of vital contact between my rider and my machine: between my invisible and my visible self" (96) – in other words, the points of contact between the soul or subtle body and the physical body. He characterizes the force that passes through and between these centers as "vital magnetism" (21) and as "a lovely, suave, fluid, *creative* electricity" (22). But he also realizes quite clearly that this "dynamic polarized flow of vitalistic force" (140) is not identical to what the physicist knows as electricity or magnetism: "we know no word, so say 'electricity,' by analogy" (141). Electricity and magnetism are for Lawrence, as for Coleridge, *natura naturata* masquerading as *natura naturans*. They do, however, point us to the essential nature of the formative creative force as dynamic and polaric. Yet, we must repeat, the fact that this subtle power is invisible does not make it unreal. That which connects the centers within man, which connects one individual with another, which connects the perceiver with the perceived, is all one "definite vital flow, as definite and concrete as the electric current whose polarized circuit sets our tramcars running and our lamps shining, or our Marconi wires vibrating" (163). It is compared elsewhere to "plasm," to "blood," and to "fire," but perhaps the best term – a term used several times by Lawrence – is "subtle" (70–72).

For Boehme man is embedded in a field of invisible, subtle forces that directly influence him through his own subtle body. The forces charted by astrology are real. Man's gross body composed of the physical elements is separate from other objects in space, but his "sidereal" body is "from the stars" and participates in the divine life of the universe.

This twofold outward body is now to be considered if we would understand nature ... The sidereal body is the highest excepting the divine in man; the elemental body is its dwelling house ... the sidereal spirit is the true rational life in all creatures ... This substance is the spirit of the stars which the elements receive into themselves and coagulate it in themselves and hatch it as a hen her eggs ... (Qtd. in Brinton 123)

As Boehme says in *Aurora*, "the whole nature," including the earth and heavens, "is together the *body* or corporeity of God;

and the powers of the stars are the fountain veins in the natural body of God in this world " (56). Just as the blood flows through the arteries, so the sidereal forces flow through God's body. The homology between heart and sun is neither accidental nor a mere analogy.

Lawrence criticism has not sufficiently appreciated the extent to which Lawrence shares these ideas expressed by Boehme. In *The Symbolic Meaning* he speaks respectfully of astrology and dwells repeatedly and at length on man's "subtle faculty for perceiving the greater inhuman forces that control us" (19). It is not the conscious surface mind that perceives these forces – it can only perceive sense objects located externally in space – but rather the "physical soul" (24), which is Lawrence's oxymoron for the subtle body localized in the ganglia and plexuses. "Fine waves of vital effluence" (23) are transmitted across space. These "rarest impressions ... from the invisible ether" act upon the "unthinkably sensitive substance," the "finest tissue," of man's physical soul, which, again, is the subtle body (23–24). Lawrence attacks "the modern, scientific attitude," which "has brought about the materialization and emptiness of life" by its belief only in lifeless particles and empty space as its ultimates. "God made heaven and earth" and "did not disappear" at that point. He continues to exist and must continue to exist as long as the universe does, because He is its life. And "If we try to conceive of God," Lawrence insists, "we must conceive some homogeneous rare *living* plasm, a *living* self-conscious ether, which fill[s] the universe" (163).

In the last chapter we described this worldview under the rubric "participation." Owen Barfield also uses this term, which he also – like Wheelwright, Cornford, and Koyre – borrows from Levy-Bruhl. In his *Saving the Appearances* Barfield defines participation as "the extra-sensory relation between man and the phenomena" (40): "in the act of perception, [primitives] are not detached, as we are, from the [phenomena]. For us the only connection *of which we are conscious* is the external one through the senses. Not so for them" (31). Empty space does not exist for the primitive, for whom it is a matter of immediate experience that he and the phenomena he perceives are linked in a continuum, albeit an "extra-sensory" one. We, on the other hand, perceive the object as "out there," separated from us in a uniform, three-dimensional, empty space. We experience ourselves as a center of consciousness "in here," "situated at some point in space," cut off by our skin from the world outside us (78). For Barfield, man's awareness of his participatory relation to phenomena survived through the Middle Ages and came to an end with the scientific revolution. Boehme, although living in the seventeenth century, is really a late representative of the medieval worldview. Here is Barfield's attempt to get inside the medieval mind looking at the sky:

> We do not see it as empty space, for we know very well that a vacuum is something that nature does not allow, any more than she allows bodies to fall upwards. If it is daytime, we see the air filled with light proceeding from a living sun, rather as our own flesh is filled with blood proceeding from a living heart. If it is night-time, we do not merely see a plain, homogeneous vault pricked with separate points of light, but a regional, qualitative sky, from which first of all the different sections of the great zodiacal belt, and secondly the planets and the moon (each of which is embedded in its own revolving crystal sphere) are raying down their complex influences upon the earth, its metals, its plants, its animals and its men and women, including ourselves ... our own health and temperament are joined by invisible threads to these heavenly bodies we are looking at. We probably do not spend any time thinking about these extra-sensory links between ourselves and the phenomena. We merely take them for granted. (76–77)

Lawrence has the same understanding of participation. In *Apocalypse* he says that primitive man lived in "an ancient tribal unison in which the individual was hardly separated out, then the tribe lived breast to breast, as it were, with the cosmos, in naked contact with the cosmos, the whole cosmos was alive and in contact with the flesh of man" (130). Modern man has lost this connection with the cosmos; isolated and cut off, he no longer lives in "responsive connection" (76). But the ancient Chaldeans in their star lore and even the medieval Christian in his astrology still had

> the experience of the living heavens, with a living yet not human sun, and brilliant living stars in *live* space ... It may seem an absurdity to

talk of *live* space. But is it? While we are warm and well and "unconscious" of our bodies, are we not all the time ultimately conscious of our bodies in the same way, as live or living space? And is not this the reason why void space so terrifies us? (51)

(Pascal's "these infinite spaces terrify me".) For the participative consciousness, the sun is not a dead ball of gas, but rather "the sun of the Old Testament, coming forth like a strong man to run a race" (52). Rays of influence link us to the sun: "There is an eternal vital correspondence between our blood and the sun ... The cosmos is a vast living body, of which we are still parts. The sun is a great heart whose tremors run through our smallest veins" (77).

Koyre says that "we are all cartesians" and that the "uncrossable abyss between body and spirit" makes it extremely difficult for us to understand what is meant by the subtle body. The name of Descartes has appeared frequently in these pages as both the prime architect and the most convenient symbol of a dualistic worldview that is the direct antipode of the polaric. The Cartesian revolution of which we are all the heirs was brought about by, in Barfield's words, the "partition of all being into the two mutually exclusive categories of extended substance and thinking substance – which is another way of saying: between matter and spirit" ("Matter," 149). All that exists on the far side of the partition (or gulf) is matter; everything on this side is self-consciousness. On one side is the objective, on the other the subjective. Descartes also formulated the distinction between primary and secondary qualities, or between what can be considered to be objectively "out there," as opposed to what our subjectivity projects onto it. The scientific materialism that developed out of these Cartesian distinctions believes that what is "really" out there in every object we perceive is an aggregate of atoms that can only be talked about in quantifiable terms like "mass" and "motion." Everything else that we perceive, all qualities – the blue of the sky, the smell of the earth, the sound of the robin – are artifacts of our subjectivity and hence unreal.

As Rene Guenon describes it in his brilliant *The Reign of Quantity*, Cartesian rationalism is the result of a twofold reduction – "the reduction of the whole nature of the spirit to 'thought' and that of the body to 'extension'" (112). This reduction has led to what Coleridge called "the epoch of the understanding and the sense," in which the Understanding has usurped the place of Reason, and the "real and very object" given us by our senses has been replaced by "a *mote dance* of abstractions" ("Theory of Life" 579), of fictitious entities called atoms. There is clearly no place in such a scheme for what we have been calling the subtle, and the scientific revolution initiated by Descartes has proceeded by rigorously excluding what became known as "occult qualities." Again in Barfield's words, "all that is not either objectively observable 'matter' on the one hand, or simply the observer himself perceiving and thinking on the other, comes under the heading of 'occult qualities'" ("Imagination," 116–17). Aquinas' hierarchies of angels must be eliminated as well as all the unseen forces considered by alchemy and astrology. Once the split between spirit and matter had been decisively effected, spirit tended to drop out of existence because science concerns itself only with material objects, and spirit is by definition immaterial. The Understanding, moreover, cannot bring these two mutually contradictory realms into any kind of relationship. Descartes for instance thinks of the pineal gland as the point of contact between body and soul, but cannot explain the nature of the interaction. In yoga, the pineal gland coincides with one of the *chakras* and is understood in terms of the subtle body. In Descartes's mechanistic terms, however, the soul would have to be stapled or glued to the body. In any case, his ideas about the pineal gland had no influence on later thinkers, and what we find in Descartes is the last survival of the subtle body in official Western thought.

As M. H. Abrams says, Coleridge found the Cartesian view of the ultimate structure of reality "both incredible to human experience of the world and intolerable to human needs" ("Coleridge's" 170). As Coleridge says of "the Mechanic or Corpuscular Scheme":

In order to submit the various phenomena of moving bodies to geometrical construction, we are under the necessity of abstracting from corporeal substance all its *positive* properties, and obliged to consider bodies as differing from equal portions of space only by figure and mobility. And as a *fiction of science*, it would be difficult to overvalue this invention ... Descartes [however] propounded it as *truth of fact*: and instead of a World *created* and filled with productive forces by the Almighty *Fiat*, left a lifeless Machine whirled about by the dust of its own Grinding: as if Death could come from the living Fountain of Life. (*Aids* 268–69)

A true science, or "metascience," would account for the "positive properties" or qualities that we actually experience, and it would account for life as the product of "productive forces" that are themselves living.

It was to Descartes's slightly older (by twenty-one years) contemporary Jacob Boehme that Coleridge turned for a completely different understanding of nature. In what could be called Boehme's "science of qualities" he found what he could not find in Descartes's science of quantities – a satisfactory explanation of the *powers* by which life comes into existence. Boehme shares fully the scientific impulse of his time and desires to account for the world of nature in terms of real forces that are logically related to each other. His forces, however, are qualities (*Qualitaten*) that are thought of as characteristic forms of activity or kinds of energy that operate through all things. A quality to Boehme is not something that adheres to an underlying thing or material substrate. A quality is not a static property or accidental attribute; it is rather the power that makes a concrete object what it is. In Coleridge's words, "By Quality Behmen intends that act of each elementary Power, by which it energizes in its peculiar kind" (*Marginalia* 1: 567–68). Brinton lists some of the many names given to these forces by Boehme: "Essences," "Spirits of the Eternal Nature," "Fountain Spirits" (*Quellgeister*), "Properties," "Forms" (*Gestalten*), "Species," and "Mothers" (135). The objects that we perceive are incarnations of qualities, "coagulations," materializations, so to speak, of qualities, the means by which qualities communicate to our senses. These qualities are the fundamental elements of nature, beyond which it cannot be reduced. They differ crucially from the elements of modern chemistry in that they are not further reducible into atoms.

Boehme's "qualities" or "Nature spirits" are intricately

connected to the traditional four elements, which themselves can only be understood as active forces that are essentially qualitative, as opposed to the elements of modern chemistry which are distinguished from one another only quantitatively, in terms of their different arrangements of atoms that are themselves lifeless and quality-less. To Heraclitus, for example, fire and water are at one and the same time physical entities and qualities. In fact, as Wheelwright observes, there is no real distinction in Heraclitus between things and qualities, between, for instance, "cool and warm things and the resident qualities of coolness and warmth" (*Heraclitus* 14). A thing is largely what it appears to be, that is, the synthesis of the qualities that make themselves visible in the object.

A poem by Lawrence expresses the difference between the traditional and the modern elements:

The Four
To our senses, the elements are four
and have ever been, and will ever be
for they are the elements of life, of poetry, and of perception,
the four Great Ones, the Four Roots, the First Four
of Fire and the Wet, Earth and the wide Air of the world.

To find the other many elements, you must go to the laboratory
and hunt them down.
But the Four we have always with us, they are our world.
Or rather, they have us with them.   (*Poems* 706)

The elements created in the laboratory are products of analysis, the end result of a process of decomposition, not the origin of life. In "Introduction to These Paintings" Lawrence says:

The very statement that water is H_2O is a mental *tour de force*. With our bodies we know that water is *not* H_2O, our intuitions and instincts both know it is not so. But they are bullied by the impudent mind. Whereas if we said that water, under certain circumstances, produces two volumes of hydrogen and one of oxygen, then the intuitions and instincts would agree entirely. (574)

In the ancient and alchemical sense water is a living power creative of what we perceive as water, which is indistinguishable from the quality of wetness. "The Third Thing" that makes

water water is missing in chemical analysis, as he says in a poem
by that title:

> Water is H_2O, hydrogen two parts, oxygen one,
> but there is also a third thing, that makes it water
> and nobody knows what that is.
>
> The atom locks up two energies
> but it is a third thing present which makes it an atom.
>
> (*Poems* 515)

Coleridge makes precisely the same point in more philosophical
language:

> Thus Water is neither Oxygen nor Hydrogen, nor yet is it a
> commixture of both; but the Synthesis or Indifference of the two: and
> as long as the copula endures, by which it becomes Water, or rather
> which alone *is* Water, it is not less a *simple* Body than either of the
> imaginary Elements, improperly called its Ingredients or Com-
> ponents. It is the object of the mechanical atomistic Philosophy to
> confound Synthesis with *synartesis*, or rather with mere juxta-position
> of Corpuscles separated by invisible Interspaces. I find it difficult to
> determine, whether this theory contradicts the Reason or the Senses
> most: for it is alike inconceivable and unimaginable. (*Friend* 1 : 94)

The elements of modern chemistry are "imaginary," just as
the atom is an "*ens fictitium*," "a fiction formed by abstraction"
("Theory" 575, 579). A law of nature must be *causal*, must be
able to account for the "actual *generation* of the phenomena of
which it is the law" (*Theory* 562). Modern science, which seeks
the cause in "unproductive particles" defined only by quantity,
cannot do this. Life itself – and "what is *not* Life that really *is*?"
– can only be defined qualitatively. In fact, quality " (the word
is here used in the active sense) " "belongs to Life." More than
that, "the ideas of Quality and Life" are "identified" with each
other (and with the ideas of power and productivity) (571). As
we saw in the chapter on Nietzsche, the all-important word Life
can only be understood as partaking of the same formative level
of reality as Plato's Ideas, which is the level of Boehme's
"qualities," which is the level of *natura naturans*, which is also the
level of the subtle body.

We cannot talk about this "level" (to use an inappropriate
visual metaphor) of reality without talking about polarity, the

"most general law" of productive nature. In explicit contrast to
Descartes, who, "speaking as a naturalist...said, give me
matter and motion and I will construct you the universe,"
Coleridge says, "grant me a nature having two contrary forces
...and I will cause the world...to rise up before you"
(*Biographia* 1 : 296–97). For all of the thinkers with whom we are
concerned here, this initial opposition at the origin of life can be
expressed as the opposition between the two primary quality-
elements, fire and water. Thus Boehme: "this outward world is
as a smoke, or vaporous steam or exhalation of the fire-spirit and
water-spirit, breathed forth both out of the holy world and then
also out of the dark world; and therefore it is evil and good, and
consists in love and anger" (*Mysterium* 1 : 25). And Lawrence,
commenting on *Genesis*:

> The living cosmos divided itself, and there was Heaven and Earth: by
> which we mean...an inexplicable first duality...Then the Spirit of
> God moved upon the face of the waters. As no "waters" are yet
> created, we may perhaps take the mystic "Earth" to be the same as
> the Waters. The mystic Earth is the cosmic Waters, and the mystic
> Heaven the dark cosmic Fire. The Spirit of God, moving between the
> two great cosmic principles, the mysterious universal dark Waters and
> the invisible, unnameable cosmic Fire, brought forth the first created
> apparition... (*Symbolic* 176–77)

These two initial qualities or "spirits" give rise to two more, air
and earth, and thence in a sequence of steps to the entire
manifested universe. Each step is to be understood in terms of
polarity: the two are a polarization of the original unity, the
four are a polarization of the initial two. Boehme and Lawrence
understand the four as a cross. "When the blaze or flagrat
ariseth out of the first two principles, then it...maketh in the
twinkle a cross" (*Mysterium* 13).

> If we conceive of the first division in Chaos, so-called, as being
> perpendicular, the inexplicable division into the first duality, then this
> next division, when the line of the firmament is drawn, we can
> consider as horizontal: thus we have the ... elements of the Rosy Cross,
> and the first enclosed appearance of that tremendous symbol, which
> has dominated our era, the Cross itself. (*Symbolic* 177)

"The cross of all existence and being" (*Psychoanalysis* 44) is
necessarily to be found in all created things, including the

human body. Lawrence modifies the Indian idea of *chakras*, which exist only in a vertical relation to each other, by adding a horizontal dimension, thus creating a cross.

Barfield explains this process in which "polarities are themselves polarized" as follows:

> Every polarity, while being a duality from the point of view, so to speak, of either pole alone, is nevertheless a unity... Diagrammatically, if a commencing polarity is represented by a line, then the two extremities of the line represent its duality, its poles. But the whole line nevertheless remains a unity and can itself be polarised. Its whole length then becomes the *axis* of a new polarity... and this genesis is symbolised on the diagram by taking it into a second dimension. (*What* 53–54)

We are touching here upon the Pythagorean and Platonic tradition of the generation of life out of number. The sequence dictated by pure geometric reasoning – from the point to the line to the surface to the depth, from the dimensionless point to one to two to three dimensions (and beyond – to Lawrence's "fourth dimension") – is also the sequence found in nature, for example in the egg as Lawrence describes it:

> From the perfect oneing of the two parent nuclei in the egg-cell results a recoil or new assertion. That which was perfect *one* now divides again, and in the recoil becomes again two... Then, this [vertical] division having taken place... there is a horizontal division across the whole egg-cell, and the nuclei are now four, two above, and two below. (*Symbolic* 75–77)

Lawrence is seeking what he calls the union of "the science of mathematics... with life itself." By mathematics, however, he means not that based on abstract Cartesian quantity, which is "only the skeleton fabric of the living universe," but rather number as understood by "the Pythagoreans" when they assert that "all is number" (*Symbolic* 184). Coleridge similarly praises Boehme for "the union of the natural with the transcendental Philosophy" (633), and by transcendental Coleridge means "the system of Pythagoras and of Plato revived" (*Biographia* 1: 263). The Pythagorean number, no less than the Platonic Idea, is a *power* that is invisible and immaterial. Phenomena cannot be explained by other phenomena – that which produces the phenomenon must be of a higher, non-phenomenal order. But it is precisely this point that the Cartesians cannot grasp. Their science is a result of what Coleridge calls "that despotism of the eye (the emancipation from which Pythagoras by his *numeral*, and Plato by his *musical* symbols, and both by geometric discipline, aimed at, as the first *propaideutikon* of the mind)" (qtd. in Barfield 19). The atom exercises such a strong hold on modern thinking because it can at least hypothetically be seen: "we are restless because invisible things are not the objects of vision; and metaphysical systems, for the most part, become popular, not for their truth, but in proportion as they attribute to causes a susceptibility of being *seen*, if only our visual organs were sufficiently powerful" (qtd. in Barfield 19–20).

The true scientist must be a seer, but his seeing is not with the physical eye alone. "Sensation itself is but vision nascent" (*Biographia* 1 : 286). As we contemplate them and penetrate to their true causes, the "phaenomena themselves become more spiritual" (*Biographia* 1 : 256). Lawrence offers us an example of such vision in one of his Tortoise poems:

> *Tortoise shell*
> The Cross, the Cross
> Goes deeper in than we know,
> Deeper into life;
> Right into the marrow
> And through the bone.
>
> Along the back of the baby tortoise
> The scales are locked in an arch like a bridge,
> Scale-lapping, like a lobster's sections
> Or a bee's ...
> Four, and a keystone;
> Four, and a keystone;
> Four, and a keystone;
> Then twenty-four, and a tiny little keystone.
> It needed Pythagoras to see life playing with counters on
> the living back
> Of the baby tortoise;
> Life establishing the first eternal mathematical tablet,
> Not in stone, like the Judean Lord, or bronze, but in
> life-clouded, life-rosy tortoise shell.   (*Poems*, 354–55)

This union of the *a priori* and the empirical is true natural philosophy, the perfection of which, in Coleridge's words, "would consist in the perfect spiritualization of all the laws of nature into laws of intuition and intellect" (*Biographia* 1 : 256).

ALCHEMICAL TRANSMUTATION

Lawrence believed that the ancients possessed a wisdom that we have lost. Because there was as yet no split between inner and outer, between man and nature, because nature was a *participated* nature, "the religious systems of the pagan world" did what modern science has been unable to do: "they gave the true correspondence between the material cosmos and the human soul" (*Symbolic* 176). In a remarkable passage, Boehme says the same thing: "The mysteries of nature were not so deeply hidden to those (prehistorical) peoples as they are to us, because they were not so deeply hidden (immersed) in materiality and sin. Therefore they knew the relationship between the paradisiacal (ethereal) forms of nature and their corporeal visible embodiment" (qtd. in Hartmann 220). Boehme's science of the soul is devoted to explicating the relationship between these ethereal or subtle forms and their corporeal embodments. This is Lawrence's concern as well:

We need to find some terms to express such elemental connections... We need to put off our personality, even our individuality, and enter the region of the elements.
    There certainly does exist a subtle and complex sympathy, correspondence between the plasm of the human body, which is identical with the primary human psyche, and the material elements outside. (175–76)

Alchemy is perhaps the most important of the ancient sciences of the soul devoted to exploring the correspondences between microcosm and macrocosm, between the psyche and the material elements. Both Boehme and Lawrence were strongly drawn to alchemy and use its language and concepts extensively, although it is not so much a case of alchemy determining the character of their thought as it is of their finding in alchemy a symbolic language in which they could express their preexisting intuitions. It is true, as Czeslaw Milosz says, that "Boehme springs directly from Renaissance alchemy" (109), but it is also true that, as Coleridge notes, Boehme seized on the language of the alchemists and struggled to express "the inward Seeing in *their* phrases" (*Marginalia* 1 : 631). The same is true of Lawrence, who found in alchemy and the other traditional sciences of the soul a confirmation of what he already believed and knew.

James C. Cowan's essay "Alchemy and *The Plumed Serpent*" discusses Lawrence in terms of Jung's influential studies of alchemy, but I have chosen instead to draw on Titus Burckhardt's *Alchemy* because Burckhardt's lucid exposition is clearer than Jung's and because his metaphysics is closer to Lawrence's (and to alchemy's). Burckhardt says that alchemy pursues the "analogy between the mineral realm and that of the soul," and it does this by looking on "material things qualitatively" and by grasping "the things of the soul 'materially'" (27). Alchemy

looks on the play of the powers of the soul from a purely cosmological point of view, and treats the soul as a "substance" which has to be purified, dissolved, and crystallized anew... With its "impersonal" way of looking at the world of the soul, alchemy ... regards the "I"-bound soul "objectively," instead of merely experiencing it subjectively. (27)

As early as 1914, in a well-known letter, Lawrence viewed the soul in this essentially alchemical way – materially, cosmologically, objectively:

There is another ego, according to whose action the individual is unrecognisable, and passes through, as it were, allotropic states which it needs a deeper sense than any we've been used to exercise, to discover are states of the same single radically-unchanged element. (Like as diamond and coal are the same pure single element of carbon. The ordinary novel would trace the history of the diamond – but I say "diamond, what! This is carbon." And my diamond might be coal or soot, and my theme is carbon.) (2: 183)

According to Lama Govinda in his *Foundations of Tibetan Mysticism*, "certain schools of alchemy" have used precisely the same example:

The relationship between the highest and the ordinary state of consciousness was compared by certain schools of alchemy to that between the diamond and an ordinary piece of coal. One cannot imagine a greater contrast, and yet both consist of the same chemical substance, namely, carbon. This teaches symbolically the fundamental unity of all substances and their inherent faculty of transformation. (Qtd. in Klossowski de Rola, 21)

Alchemists of course most commonly speak of gold rather than of diamond, but the goal is the same, and the means to the goal is transmutation of the lower into the higher, of lead or coal into gold or diamond. Since the material and the psychic essentially correspond, one can also speak of the transmutation of the soul. According to Burckhardt, in the symbolic language of alchemy "the base metals are regarded as being analogous to one-sided and imperfectly 'coagulated' states of the soul" (97), and these imperfectly coagulated states are referred to as the limited "ego" (185). The individual ego is a transitory form, a passing and momentary appearance, a manifestation or "accident" of an underlying substance. As Burckhardt explains it, in alchemy, this underlying substance – Lawrence's "single radically-unchanged element" – is "the soul in its original state, as yet unconditioned by impressions and passions, and 'uncongealed' into any definite form" (97). Alchemy is "the art of the transmutations of the soul," whose goal is "the rebirth of the soul" (23). "Spiritually understood, the transmutation of lead into gold is nothing other than the regaining of the original nobility of human nature" (26) – the soul in its original unfallen state.

To call alchemy a science of the soul is to call it a science of the subtle body, since as we have seen soul and subtle body are the same thing. The alchemical transmutation of the soul, therefore, is also, in the words of G. R. S. Mead, "the process of regeneration, or the bringing to birth of man's perfected subtle body" (31). Mead's useful *The Doctrine of the Subtle Body in Western Tradition* identifies the subtle body as the "very soul" (9) of alchemy, an identification repeated in Burckhardt's work, which also approaches alchemy from the perspective of the subtle body. For Boehme too the goal of alchemy is regeneration, which is a resumption by man of the paradisiacal or subtle body that he lost with the Fall. Before the Fall, which was a fall into materiality, man was a part of God's substance or "body." Adam like the angels had a subtle body. What Boehme calls "the precious gold of heavenly corporeity" (*Signature* 44) is the paradisiacal or subtle body that man lost with the Fall and seeks to regain.

The alchemical process of regeneration or transmutation that occupies so many of Boehme's pages is also the subject of *The Plumed Serpent*, the major novel of Lawrence's theosophical period. The heroine Kate Leslie undergoes a process of change that is identical to the alchemical process, which can be summarized in the adage *solve et coagula*. In alchemy the base metals must be first dissolved, reduced to their common underlying substance, before they can be recoagulated in the nobler form of gold. This underlying (psychic or subtle) substance is also known as *materia prima* or the *quinta essentia*, which is "the common basis of the four elements" (67), that which precedes their separation and manifestation in the physical world. As Boehme says, "There is in the four elements no perfection, till the body is changed again into the pure element; therefore it must enter again into that from whence the four elements arise" (*Signature* 169). On the psychic level, *solve et coagula* means a dissolving of the lower self, the death of the ego, followed by a reconfiguration, which is an assimilation to a higher self. This is the process undergone by Kate.

At the beginning of the novel, her ego is in the ascendancy, an ego so hard and enclosed that it threatens to cut off access to further life. The hard, *ironic* style of the opening chapters reflects Kate's one-sided state of mind, repelled and repellant, struggling against being overwhelmed by disgust and anger. She suffers likewise from the iron will of the *Gringos* that is "like their machines of iron" (257). The homology between inner and outer is beautifully expressed by Lawrence in his description of Mexico City. The culmination of all that is wrong with modern civilization, this Mexico City is composed entirely of repellent, hard, material surfaces, like the concrete amphitheater where the sordid and debased ritual of the bullfight takes place. Iron is evoked repeatedly, in the "horrible machine of the world" (104), in the railway and motor cars racing mindlessly about, and even in the iron cacti (100). It is this base metal, this hardened ego, that must be dissolved. For Boehme too it is the ego, the separate selfhood (*Selbheit*), which is associated with the "self-will" (*Eigenwille*), that must be broken down and dissolved; it is the self-will that separates man from God and that was responsible for man's loss of Paradise and of his paradisiacal body, and responsible also for the eventual fall into the iron age.

In alchemy the base elements are placed in an *athanor* or oven, in which, under the influence of fire – what Boehme calls "a very subtle drying fire" (*Way* 64) – they are slowly melted down. Mexico itself, a land where things are "in chemical conflict" (214), is the fiery furnace in which Kate is smelted down, beaten upon by the unrelenting sun, exposed to the electricity in the air, subject to the influence of subterranean volcanoes. The very spirit of place – "the serpent tangle of sun and electricity and volcanic emission" (135) – works relentlessly upon her spirit to pull it down into the matrix from which it originally emerged. This transmutation of the soul is bodily and spiritual at once: "For it was not her spirit alone which was changing, it was her body, and the constitution of her very blood. She could feel it, the terrible katabolism and metabolism in her blood, changing her even as a creature, changing her to another creature" (421).

The process is long, slow, dangerous, and painful. "It has to be a slow, organic process. Anything sudden or violent would destroy her" (417). Ramon is at a further stage in the alchemical process: "inside him was a slow, blind imperative, urging him to cast his emotional and spiritual and mental self into the slow furnace, and smelt them into a new, whole being" (206). We get a glimpse of the goal of the process in the mysterious god-like man – we do not know if it is Ramon or Quetzalcoatl or a peasant – who emerges from the lake glistening with new life and with a body that "shone like gold" (56).

If Mexico for Kate is the *athanor*, then Cipriano is the fire. It is in the fiery bath of sex with him that Kate is finally reduced down. At his touch, "her soul melted like fused metal" (311).

She trembled, and her limbs seemed to fuse like metal melting down. She fused into a molten unconsciousness, her will, her very self gone, leaving her lying in molten life, like a lake of still fire, unconscious of everything save the eternality of the fire in which she was gone. Gone as the burning bush was gone. Gone in the fadeless fire, which has no death. Only the fire can leave *us*, and we can die. (320)

The "lake of still fire" expresses in an image the union of the primal opposites fire and water. Kate has become one with what Boehme calls "the inward and spiritual element, from whence the four elements proceed and are produced." He calls this one element (*materia prima*) "paradise," because "no one property was predominant over another, neither was there any strife or contrariety" (*Way* 95).

Fire and water initially "manifest their opposition in a certain outward tension" (Burckhardt 129), dramatically represented by Lawrence in the shifting tensions between Kate and Cipriano. The tension is necessary, however, for only in overcoming is there joy. The struggle becomes an embrace which restores the paradisal state. This takes place when the properties of Sulphur and Quicksilver [masculine and feminine, fire and water] mutually penetrate each other" (Burckhardt 127). "The two powers, when they have so grown that one can embrace the other, reunite on a higher plane, so that their opposition, which previously had bound the soul, now becomes a fruitful complementarism" (129). This reunion on a higher plane Lawrence represents in the marriage of Kate and Cipriano, who are described throughout the novel in terms of archetypal opposites: spirit-blood, light-dark, water-fire, green-red, Venus-Mars, mercy-wrath.

Burckhardt says that "the marriage of Sulphur and Quick-silver, Sun and Moon, King and Queen, is the central symbol of alchemy" (149), and he reproduces common alchemical illustrations showing this marriage, including one (152) which shows the King and Queen married under the presence of a hovering dove representing the Holy Ghost, and another (65) showing the marriage of Sun and Moon with the star of the Spirit hovering between, reconciling the opposition. *The Plumed Serpent* recreates this central icon in the marriage of Kate and Cipriano by and in the presence of Don Ramon, who is repeatedly associated both with the Holy Ghost and the Morning Star.

"There!" said Ramon. "That is the symbol of Quetzalcoatl, the Morning Star. Remember the marriage is the meeting-ground, and the meeting-ground is the star. If there be no star, no meeting-ground, no true coming together of man with the woman, into a wholeness, there is no marriage...But if the meeting comes to pass, then whosoever betrays the abiding place, which is the meeting-ground, which is that which lives like a star between day and night, between the dark of woman and the dawn of man, between man's night and woman's morning, shall never be forgiven, neither here nor in the hereafter." (331)

Don Ramon is the Morning Star, "the hoverer between" (441), "the clue" (one of Lawrence's favorite words for the Holy Ghost), "the quick of the whole" (399). The opposites meet in his "tent of the cloven flame" (441). He is "the star that shall not be betrayed," the one unforgiveable sin being the sin against the Holy Ghost.

The "action," then, of *The Plumed Serpent* is the transmutation of the soul or subtle body. This action necessarily can only be presented symbolically, but this "deepest soul process" is always Lawrence's subject, one he attempts to convey in a number of ways. One of the most important of these ways in the novel is in terms of race, and our understanding of the soul or subtle body will help us understand what Lawrence means by race. Like the subtle body, race exists at the causal, formative, archetypal level. Existing at a deeper level than the personality or ego, a person's race manifests both psychically and physically, yet is neither exclusively one nor the other. To understand the role played by race in the novel, we need to turn to *The Symbolic Meaning*, Lawrence's study of American literature, which is virtually a blueprint for *The Plumed Serpent*, Lawrence's American novel.

The first chapter of *The Symbolic Meaning*, "The Spirit of Place," explains the characteristics unique to American literature as a product of the American "Spirit of Place." "All art partakes of the Spirit of Place in which it is produced" (16), and America, like "every great locality has its own daimon," which

works at the deepest levels to produce an indigenous consciousness or race-soul. This is how Lawrence explains the effect
of place on the newcomers to America:

> They walked a new earth, were seized by a new electricity, and laid in
> line differently. Their bones, their nerves, their sinews took on a new
> molecular disposition in the new vibration.
>   They breathed a savage air, and their blood was suffused and burnt
> … Their subtlest plasm was changed under the radiation of new skies,
> new influence of light, their first and rarest life-stuff transmuted.
>   Thus, through hundreds of years, new races are made, people slowly
> smelted down and re-cast. There is the slow and terrible process of
> transubstantiation. (29–30)

This transmutation of the Americans' "subtlest plasm" is
clearly linked to Kate's transmutation.

Lawrence insists that the European-Christian "ideal" consciousness that has held sway for the last two thousand years is
being superseded in America by a "new way of feeling" (17).
There is "an unthinkable gulf," "an inconceivable difference
in *being*," between Europe and America. America is the
beginning of a new epoch. Historical epochs are determined by
what he calls "psycho-magnetic polarities," "circuits of vital
magnetism," that connect distinct regions. For instance, the
German-Italian circuit was "the main polarity of Europe, from
the time of Diocletian to the Renaissance," when "the old circle
of vital flow was broken. It was then that Europe and America
became the great poles of negative and positive vitalism" (21).
In America, this vital polarity which pulled the first Europeans
across the ocean, is creating a new race or consciousness. This
new consciousness, however, is only mythically foreshadowed in
American literature. It is not yet fully born into actuality, and
Lawrence is trying to assist it: "Look at me trying to be mid-
wife to the unborn homunculus" (*Studies* viii).

The new consciousness is to arise from the encounter between
the white Europeans and the dark natives. The next three
chapters of *The Symbolic Meaning* present a series of encounters
between white men and Indians. With Benjamin Franklin, the
encounter altogether fails. To him Indians are only drunken
savages. Franklin's moral complacency and absolute inability
to get outside his own consciousness render him incapable of

confronting the Indian on any real level. He is merely a transplanted eighteenth-century rationalist on whom the spirit of place has had no effect, a mechanical man, a "monster" (54).

Unlike Franklin, Hector St. John de Crèvecoeur, who wrote *Letters from an American Farmer*, is strongly attracted to the Indian. He has something of the artist in him and is able to glimpse, if only in a limited way, the other pole of being that the Indian represents:

> Crèvecoeur the artist, however, glimpsed some of the passional dark mystery which Crèvecoeur the idealist completely ignores. The artist is no longer European. Some little salt of the aboriginal America has entered into his blood. And this aboriginal Crèvecoeur sees as the savage see, knows as they know, in the dark mystery of division, difference, culmination, and contest. (61)

Crèvecoeur, however, never really got beyond his idealistic notions of the Noble Savage, and it is only in James Fenimore Cooper that we first get the "true marriage with the aboriginal psyche" (96). At the center of Cooper's vision Lawrence sees "the two impressive figures of the middle-aged men, Natty and Chingachgook." "Two mature, silent, expressionless men, they stand on opposite shores of being, and their love, the inexpressible conjunction between them, is the bridge over the chasm."

> Each of them is alone, and, since the death of Uncas, conclusive, concluded in himself. They are isolated, final instances of their race: two strangers, from opposite ends of the earth, meeting now, beholding each other, and balanced in unspeakable conjunction – a love so profound, or so abstract, that it is unexpressed; it has no word or gesture of intercommunion. It is communicated by pure presence alone, without contact of word or touch. This perfect relationship, this last abstract love, exists between the two isolated instances of opposite race.
>
> And this is the inception of a new race. Beyond all expression, save the pure communion of presence, the abstract love of these two beings consummates itself in an unimaginable coalescence, the inception of a new psyche, a new race-soul that rises out of the last and first unknowable intercommunion of two untranslatable souls. That which Chingachgook was, Natty was not; nor could he ever know. In the same way, Natty himself was the untranslatable unknown to Chingachgook. Yet across this unsuperable gulf in being there passed some

strange communion between the two instances, invisible, intangible, unknowable – a quality of pure unknowable embrace. And out of this embrace arises the strange wing-covered seraph of new race-being. From this communion is procreated a new race-soul, which henceforth gestates within the living humanity of the West. (103)

This moment of gestation of a new "race-soul" that clearly means so much to Lawrence is central to the conception of *The Plumed Serpent*. Kate and Cipriano are Lawrence's Natty and Chingachgook, but the use of race is even more specific than the mere conjunction of Indian and European. In *The Symbolic Meaning* Lawrence says that two European races remained outside the German-Italian circuit – the Celtic and the Iberian. These two races are located on the Atlantic coast closest to the pull of America:

Therefore they placed themselves in a polarity with the great invisible force of America, they looked to their positive pole into the west, the land of the setting sun, over the great sea to the unknown America. Their heaven was the land under the western wave, the Celtic Tir na Og. (22)

It is no accident that the two race-individuals who establish vital contact with the Indian Cipriano are Don Ramon, who has Iberian blood in his veins, and Kate, a Celt.

There is much talk about race in the novel. During an after-dinner conversation in Ramon's house, Toussaint raises the topic by saying that most Mexicans are half-breeds: "'Now, the half-breed is a calamity. For why? He is neither one thing nor another, he is divided against himself. His blood of one race tells him one thing, his blood of another race tells him another'" (64). Mexico is hopeless, according to Toussaint, because of the destructive and despairing spirit in which these half-breeds have been begotten. Everything depends on the spirit "at the moment of coition": "At the moment of coition, either the spirit of the father fuses with the spirit of the mother, to create a new being with a soul, or else nothing fuses but the germs of procreation" (64). Toussaint concludes that it would take a "miracle" to create this new soul.

Kate then turns to Ramon: "'Do you think one can make this miracle come?' She asked of him. 'The miracle is always there,' he said, 'for the man who can pass his hand through to it, to take it'" (68). In fact, the miracle has already been realized in Ramon. He is "almost pure Spaniard," while "Don Cipriano is pure Indian," yet Kate notices a relationship between them like the one Lawrence described between Natty and Chingachgook: "she had noticed that usually, when an Indian looked to a white man, both men stood back from actual contact, from actual meeting of each other's eyes. They left a wide space of neutral territory between them. But Cipriano looked at Ramon with a curious intimacy, glittering, steady" (67).

Ramon is the *via media* for a similar conjunction between Kate and Cipriano. "The Lord of Two Ways," he seems European to Kate and Mexican to Cipriano. Kate says to Cipriano:

"I *don't* think he is Mexican."
"Why not? Why not Mexican? He is Mexican."
"Not as you are."
"How not as I am? He is Mexican."
"He seems to me to belong to the old, old Europe," she said.
"And he seems to me to belong to the old, old Mexico – and also to the new," he added quickly. (203)

Like the Holy Ghost, Ramon is the relation itself between opposites, and it is only in his spirit that they can be joined. As Lawrence says in *Mornings in Mexico*, written at the same time as *The Plumed Serpent*:

The acceptance of the great paradox of human consciousness is the first step to a new accomplishment.

The consciousness of one branch of humanity is the annihilation of the consciousness of another branch. That is, the life of the Indian, his stream of conscious being, is just death to the white man. And we can understand the consciousness of the Indian only in terms of the death of our consciousness.

... The only thing you can do is to have a little Ghost inside you which sees both ways, or even many ways. (55)

Each race has its characteristic way of seeing things – its own vision, its own eyes (Cipriano's are black, Kate's grey, and

Ramon's brown). European consciousness is centered in the head and eyes, which are keenly focused and myopic, like those of the German hotel manager: "a young man of about forty, with his blue eyes going opaque and stony behind his spectacles, though the centers were keen" (95). The natives, on the other hand, have "centreless dark eyes" (109); they "have no centre, no real *I*" (40). At the beginning Kate is repelled by the "bloody-eyed" natives, whose "middle is a raging black hole, like the middle of a maelstrom" (40). They "have never been able to win a soul for themselves, never been able to win themselves a nucleus, an individual integrity out of the chaos of passions and potencies and death" (135). Yet as she herself changes she is increasingly able to see something else in the natives' eyes. The change begins with her trip across the lake, when, after an encounter with the first of Quetzalcoatl's men, she looks at the boatman and "suddenly realized ... the central look in the native eyes" (91). "His face too had the abstracted transfigured look of a man perfectly suspended between the world's two strenuous wings of energy. A look of extraordinary, arresting beauty, the silent, vulnerable centre of all life's quivering, like the nucleus gleaming in tranquil suspense, within a cell" (92). "'You have the morning star in your eyes,'" she said to the man" (92). Kate comes to realize that she is imprisoned in her eyes and prays for deliverance:

"Let me close my eyes to him, and open only my soul. Let me close my prying *seeing* eyes, and sit in dark stillness along with these two men ... They have got rid of that itching of the eye, and the desire that works through the eye. The itching, prurient, *knowing*, imagining eye, I am cursed with it ... Oh, who will free me from the grappling of my eyes, from the impurity of sharp sight!" (184)

Kate wants to see with her soul, not her physical eyes. Hers is a poignant expression of what Coleridge calls "the tyranny of the eye." The physical eye, hooked on external surfaces, cannot penetrate to the sources of life because, as Coleridge says, "visible SURFACE and *power* of any kind, much more the *power* of life, are ideas which the very forms of the human understanding make it impossible to identify" ("Theory" 568). As Don Ramon says, we have to turn within, "We have to shut our eyes and sink down, sink away from the surface" (191). The inner eye perceives the causal, subtle world that is invisible to the physical eye. It is invisible because it is not contained in the Cartesian space of three dimensions; it is rather the container of space and is paradoxically found only within, in what Lawrence calls "the fourth dimension," the "heart of all the world" or "the quick" (252), the dimensionless point that is omnipresent. To arrive at this "inner mystery," man must reach

not into space, but into the other dimension of man's existence, where he finds himself in the infinite room that lies inside the axis of our wheeling space. Space, like the world, cannot but move. And like the world, there is an axis. And the axis of our worldly space, when you enter, is a vastness where even the trees come and go, and the soul is at home in its own dream, noble and unquestioned. (126)

It is only here "in the innermost far-off place of the human core, the ever-present" (126), that the subtle world exists, which is "the soul, the most ancient and everlasting soul of all men, where alone can the human family assemble in immediate contact" (126).

With great delicacy, Lawrence traces the opening of Kate's inner eye, which begins with her reading of a newspaper article about Ramon's revival of the ancient gods: "Yet, strangely, a different light than the common light seemed to gleam out of the words of even this newspaper paragraph ... A strange darkly-irridescent beam of wonder, of magic" (58). 8). "Ramon had lighted" "the light of her innermost soul" (307). Under the influence of Mexico, Cipriano, and Ramon, the strength of this inner light, "a different light than the common light" (58), gradually increases until it eclipses the everyday world, which "went hollow and dead" (307). The crisis comes just before her marriage, when "her eyes seemed to have gone dark" (306), and she suddenly "sees" Cipriano in a different way:

Almost she could *see* the black fume of power which he emitted, the dark, heavy vibration of his blood, which cast a spell over her ...

The mystery of the primeval world! She could feel it now in all its shadowy, furious magnificence. She knew now what was the black, glinting look in Cipriano's eyes. She could understand marrying him, now. In the shadowy world where men were visionless, and winds of fury rose up from the earth, Cipriano was still a power. Once you entered his mystery the scale of all things changed ... (310)

The "miracle" spoken of by Don Ramon has come to pass. The "little Ghost inside" enables Kate to see with the same "second sight" possessed by Cipriano's men:

When Cipriano was roused, his eyes flashed, and it was as if dark feathers, like pinions, were starting out of him, out of his shoulders and back, as if these dark pinions clashed and flashed like a roused eagle. His men seemed to see him, as by second sight, with the demonish clashing and dashing of wings, like an old god. (362)

"The black fume of power," "as if dark feathers ... were starting out of him," is strikingly similar to what David Tansley in his *The Subtle Body* describes as the subtle aura:

The light or radiance that fills man as he unites with the source of his being is depicted in religious paintings as the corona or halo around the head ... the plumes of the serpent, in the tradition of the Indians of Mexico, symbolize this same energy field or coronal discharge around the initiate or anointed one, and the magnificent feather headdresses of the North American chiefs, flowing from the crown of the head and down the back, indicate their spiritual status and wisdom. (11)

One of the most remarkable aspects of Lawrence's genius is his ability to convey this older way of seeing, in which man inhabits a vast "living cosmos" (316) of magical potencies and primeval gods. When for instance he sees "a small bird ... red as a drop of new blood, from the arteries of the air" (243), we sense the presence of a creative potency filling all space, just as for Boehme God's subtle body fills all space and God's blood flows through the invisible arteries of the air. When Lawrence describes the "great serpent" at "the heart of this earth ... in the midst of fire," we reexperience the primitive sense of participation:

At the heart of this earth sleeps a great serpent, in the midst of fire. Those that go down in mines feel the heat and the sweat of him, they feel him move. It is the living fire of the earth, for the earth is alive. The snake of the world is huge, and the rocks are his scales, trees grow between them. I tell you the earth you dig is alive as a snake that sleeps. So vast a serpent you walk on, this lake lies between his folds as a drop of rain in the folds of a sleeping rattlesnake. (196)

As Burckhardt notes, the "primordial symbol of the serpent or dragon" is "found in all parts of the world" and is "especially characteristic of those traditional arts, such as alchemy, which are concerned with the subtle world" (130). In alchemy, the dragon symbolizes *materia prima*, the subtle stuff out of which the world emerges. In yoga, another subtle art to which Lawrence has many affinities, the serpent power is the *kundalini*, which must enter us if we are to be more than we are now, and it is this entering that Ramon seeks and invokes in his ritual gestures: "snake that lives in the fire at the heart of the world, come! Come! Snake of the fire of the heart of the world, coil like gold round my ankles, and rise like life around my knee" (196). As the *kundalini* rises, the body is transmuted into a subtle body, which, in James Pryse's words, is "formed of etheric fire, and is in direct relation with, and is sustained by, the cosmic and divine forces" (215).

The transmutation of Kate's "subtlest plasm" results in her coming into direct relation with the cosmic serpent that is Mexico. At first Mexico's "reptile-like evil" (28) terrifies and repels her. She is Mexico's direct opposite, air and spirit to its earth and blood. "She felt like a bird round whose body a snake has coiled itself" (72). By the end of the novel, a very great change has taken place in her, which Lawrence delicately conveys by means of an encounter with a snake:

Suddenly before her she saw a long, dark soft rope, lying over a pale boulder. But her soul was softly alert, at once. It was a snake, with a subtle pattern along its soft dark back, lying there over a big stone, with its head sunk down to earth.

It felt her presence, too, for suddenly, with incredible soft quickness, it contracted itself down the boulder, and she saw it entering a little gap in the bottom of the wet wall. (424)

The snake looks at Kate for a moment and then disappears. Instead of the normal fear reaction, Kate "wondered over it" in a moment of pure apprehension. Now, having been resolved

back into a harmonious relationship with the lower forces, "she
felt a certain reconciliation between herself and it" (425). To
the eyes of the soul, the plumed serpent itself can be seen
stretching its wings across the gap in being:

> For I am Quetzalcoatl, the feathered snake,
> And I am not with you till my serpent has coiled his circle of
> rest in your belly.
> And I, Quetzalcoatl, the eagle of the air, am brushing your
> faces with vision.
> I am fanning your breasts with my breath.
> And building my nest of peace in your bones.
> I am Quetzalcoatl of the Two Ways.   (344–45)

It is Ramon-Quetzalcoatl's "great effort ... to bring the great
opposites into contact and into unison again" (418), and out of
the "fusion" or "marriage" is born "the new world of man"
(416). This new world comes to life in the final chapters, where
it is described in terms of a subtle new mood rather than
apocalyptic terrors. The rains come, transforming the waste-
land, harmoniously combining the opposites in the land itself,
the green of Malintzi-Kate softening the harsh red features of
Mexico-Cipriano. A lovely vignette shows some peasants trying
to load a "huge and spangled bull" onto a boat. The process is
awkward and difficult, even comic, but a deep peacefulness
envelops the episode, making it seem "near," yet "strange and
remote" – "the whole silhouette frieze motionless, against the
far water that was coloured brown like turtle doves" (431). The
men struggle against the reluctant bull but with patience and
gentleness – in complete contrast to the bullfight at the beginning. Their wills may be temporarily opposed but bull and
man are yet linked in a greater unity of purpose. Finally, the
bull is loaded: "Then quickly they hoisted the wide white sail.
The sail thrust up her horn and curved in a whorl to the wind.
The ship was going across the waters, with her massive, sky-
spangled cargo of life invisible" (433). Such beautiful moments
are the reason we read novels rather than treatises; they also
remind us that *The Plumed Serpent* – in spite of our necessarily
schematic reading – is a work of symbolic art, not an allegory.
Lawrence's wisdom is always poetic, whether expressed in the

form of nonfiction or fiction. The little black boat in the novel "with a red-painted roof and a tall mast" (431) is identical to the mythic "ship of Dionysos" mentioned in *The Symbolic Meaning*:

We wait for the miracle, for the new soft wind. Even the buds of iron break into soft little flames of issue. So will people change. So will the machine-parts open like buds and the great machines break into leaf. Even we can expect our iron ships to put forth vine and tendril and bunches of grapes, like the ship of Dionysos in full sail upon the ocean. (30)

"The miracle, the new, soft, creative wind" (30), comes to life in the novel: "The air seemed mysteriously alive, with a new Breath" (*Plumed* 431). This Breath is Quetzalcoatl, who is called "the wind, the breath of life" (58), the "supreme life-breath in the inner air" (109). Quetzalcoatl is also the Holy Ghost, and the final Hymn, following the loading of the bull, returns again to what we have called Lawrence's central and abiding symbol:

> My way is not thy way, and thine is not mine.
> But come, before we part
> Let us separately go to the Morning Star,
> And meet there.
>
> I do not point you to my road, nor yet
> Call: Oh come!
> But the Star is the same for both of us,
> Winsome.
>
> The good ghost of me goes down the distance
> To the Holy Ghost.
> Oh you, in the tent of the cloven flame
> Meet me, you I like most.
>
> Each man his own way forever, but towards
> The hoverer between;
> Who opens his flame like a tent-flap,
> As we slip in unseen.   (441)

The cloven flame recalls the Pentecostal descent of the Holy Ghost recorded in Acts, during which "there came a sound from heaven as of a rushing mighty wind ... And there appeared unto them cloven tongues like as of fire ... And they were all filled with the Holy Ghost" (2: 2–4).

THE RESURRECTION OF THE BODY

In one of his characteristically acute observations, W. H. Auden says that "Lawrence is best regarded as a Christian heretic" (483). From first to last his thinking defines itself in relation to and in opposition to Christianity. As Graham Hough says, "to trace Lawrence's relations to Christianity genetically ... would be to trace the whole course of his work ... from another and more specialized point of view" (240). One Christian doctrine in particular – the resurrection of the body – especially interested him. An early letter expresses the fervent belief that "Christianity should teach us now, that after our Crucifixion, and the darkness of the tomb, we shall rise again in the flesh, you, I, as we are today, resurrected in the bodies" (qtd. in Marcus, 213). At the end of his life he is saying the same thing: "And Church doctrine teaches the resurrection of the body; and if that doesn't mean the whole man, what does it mean?" (qtd. in Marcus, 223). In these statements Lawrence suggests that he is more Christian than the Church. He in fact does believe in the resurrection of the actual flesh-and-blood body, whereas the historical influence of Christianity has been to deny and to spiritualize the body.

The three major works of fiction of his later life are all concerned with the resurrection of the body and are intended at least in part as polemics against Christianity. *The Man Who Died* does not really die and emerges from the tomb to find physical fulfillment in sexual union with a woman. Lady Chatterley believes in "the resurrection of the body" and asserts that "even the true Christian creed insisted on it" (qtd. in Marcus, 231). Like Kate Leslie she is reborn into a new life in the body after her sexual union with the right man. Lawrence's polemical point in his quarrel with Christianity is easy enough to understand. It is less easy to understand exactly what the resurrection of the body means, either to Christianity or to Lawrence, as countless volumes of theology and numerous books and articles on Lawrence testify.

The debate within Christendom can be briefly summarized by distinguishing, as does G. R. S. Mead, between two schools

of thought, which could be called the literalist and the
spiritualist. The literalists, following the Latin Father Tertullian, take a "frankly materialistic view" that "the flesh, that
is the physical body, shall rise again in the case of every one –
the very same flesh in its absolute identity and in its absolute
integrity" (83). The "more spiritual view is chiefly connected
with the name of Origen" (83) and believes that we are
promised another body, a "spiritual and aetherial one" (85),
which can be described as "a garment of light" (92). This more
"spiritual" resurrection, however, was not "to be deferred to
post-mortem existence, though it had to be preceded by a mystical
death. It was a mystery wrought in the living body of a man"
(97–98). The Western Church has followed Tertullian and has
condemned Origen's views as heretical. Boehme and the
alchemists belong squarely with Origen; their subtle body is his
aetherial light body, and the subtle body (the transmuted
physical body), as Burckhardt makes clear, is identical with
"the 'glorious body' of the resurrected" (87). A superficial view
of Lawrence might be inclined to group him with the
materialists as opposed to the spiritualists, given his emphasis on
fulfillment in the flesh and his opposition to anything that
tended to spiritualize the body out of existence. Lawrence,
however, must be included with the heretics like Boehme, and
we can deepen our understanding of his thought by comparing
his views with theirs.

Boehme is entirely absorbed in the Bible; all of his reflections
begin and end with the Biblical account of man's origin and
destiny. This is one reason for the extraordinarily mythic and
organic quality of his thinking – even the most abstruse thought
is tied to a story. The entire structure of his thought can be seen
as a drawing-out of the implications of the first chapters of
Genesis. The first thing we learn when we turn to the Bible is
that Adam in Paradise indeed had a body – a twofold body
according to Boehme:

And out of the substance of the inward and outward world man was
created; out of and in the likeness of the birth of all substances. The
body is a limbus (an extract or a kind of seed, which containeth all that
which the thing from whence it is taken hath) of the earth, and also a

limbus of the heavenly substance; for the earth is breathed forth, outspoken, or created out of the dark and light world. (*Way* 95)

Adam is the union of earthly and heavenly substance. He was made of red earth, clay, into which was breathed the Spirit of God. The earth itself is a breathing forth, a speaking, created by God's holy *fiat*. Matter, which is real, was created to reflect the Spirit – man is created in the image of God. As long as Adam remained turned towards God he walked in the light of God. Adam partook of God's substance, which is light, and he himself possessed a body of light, a "lightbody" (*Way* 96). As the perfect image or reflection of God, his body was translucent. Adam lost this subtle body as a result of the Fall. For Boehme, however, the fall that occurred after the eating of the apple was not the first. The first fall occurred when Adam fell asleep, an act which signifies his turning away from God's countenance into himself. This gradually extinguished the light of reason which had enabled him to name the animals, to "see and know things through the light of God" (*Way* 66). Adam's body gradually turned opaque and he became "a dark coal in himself" (64).

It is essential to realize that Boehme has nothing against the body *per se*. God created earthly substance and declared it good. Christ's birth and death are ample testimony to the importance of the physical body. Christ became fully human, "entered into the human substance, and received it; not that part only of heavenly substantiality, which disappeared in Adam, but the whole human essence in soul and flesh" (*Way* 105). Substance is essential to the manifestation of divinity. Burckhardt's description of the alchemical point of view applies equally to Boehme: alchemy does not seek "the complete (spiritual) 'extinction' of the individual," as does "the Christian *unio mystica* or *deificatio*" (Burckhardt 73). Alchemy seeks the transmutation rather than the transcendence of the physical. Alchemy seeks to restore the "theomorphism" of Adam, which means the restoration of the subtle body of light. The "subtle power and virtue" hidden within the gross body "shall come again and live forever in a kind of transparent crystalline material property, in spiritual flesh and blood" (*Way* 151).

It is also essential to realize that it is not the body but rather the ego that is actually responsible for the fall – the "gross" body is the result, not the cause. Adam's turning away from God is an act of self-will, the sin of pride rather than lust. As Burckhardt puts it, the soul is "shut off from the outward psychic 'atmosphere' not so much by the body as by the conceptual ego-bound consciousness" (154). Boehme identifies this conceptual ego-bound consciousness with "*Vernunft*" (*Way* 57) and contrasts it with "*Verstand.*" The distinction between *Vernunft* and *Verstand* is identical to Coleridge's distinction between understanding and reason (although in one of the quirks of history the terms *Verstand* and *Vernunft* exchanged meanings with each other in the years between Boehme and Coleridge). It is the understanding that creates divisions; it is a "diabolical" faculty that can only separate, that fragments reality into logically incompatible opposites. Adam's falling asleep divided him from God and also created the split between spirit and matter. In fact, it is only with the appearance of the understanding that dead, inert, opaque matter is created – dead matter being precisely that which has been cut off from its living source. The reason, on the other hand, can maintain the living link; in Koyre's words, reason "sees that neither the spirit in itself nor the body in itself is real" (370) – they are the inner and outer of the same reality. Boehme seeks then not the elimination of one but the reconciliation of both. True reconciliation, however, means that each is in its place and that the inner rules the outer: "that original and universal power of the inward over the outward constituted the holy paradise" (*Way* 97).

Paradise still exists. Heaven is all around us, or rather within us, and it follows from what we have just said that it is the death of the ego, not the death of the body, that must occur if we are to be reborn into this heaven. The renewed body will have died "from the vanity and evil deeds" and "pride and insolence of the world" (*Way* 136). If man were to die to himself and turn again to God, the spark that still exists within him would grow until once again he possessed the body of light mentioned by Christ: "The light of the body is the eye: therefore when thine eye is single, thy whole body also is full of light; but when thine eye is evil, thy body also is full of darkness" (Luke 11 : 33). The death of the ego is in reality an opening to a wider world, a world of light surrounding the self, and is better thought of as an expansion than as an extinction.

Here is Boehme's description of the mystic death:

> When the ground of the will yieldeth itself up to God, then it sinketh down from itself beyond all ground and place, where God only is manifest, worketh and willeth, and then it becometh nothing to itself, as to its own willing, and so God worketh and willeth in it. Yea, God dwelleth in this resigned will by which means the soul is sanctified, and so cometh into divine rest ... the soul is thoroughly penetrated and saturated with the love of God, and throughly enlightened with the light of God; even as the fire thoroughly inflameth a red-hot iron, whereby it loseth its darkness. (*Way* 145)

With the yielding up of its separate existence (the ego or self will), the soul finds itself saturated with light like a red-hot iron. Compare Boehme's with Lawrence's description of the death of the separate self, a description we have already quoted:

> She trembled, and her limbs seemed to fuse like metal melting down. She fused into a molten unconsciousness, her will, her very self gone, leaving her lying in molten life, like a lake of still fire, unconscious of everything save the eternality of the fire in which she was gone. Gone as the burning bush was gone. Gone in the fadeless fire, which has no death. Only the fire can leave *us*, and we can die. (320)

I submit that there is no essential difference between these two visions. A superficial reading of the Lawrence passage would find in it only heightened Lawrencean rhetoric glorifying the sex act. In fact, however, physical love is often the occasion but not the essence nor even the necessary means of trans-mutation or regeneration. Lawrence is indeed concerned with sex, "but the greater, not the lesser sex" (*Plumed* 131). Don Ramon, for example, attains the same state without apparently going the sexual route. The process of rebirth envisioned by Lawrence is no more exclusively physical, no more a matter of physiological reactions like those measured by Masters and Johnson, than is Boehme's remarkably similar vision. After the

death of the ego or separate selfhood, there remains only what
Boehme calls God and what Lawrence calls "the eternality of
the fire" of the God who manifested to Moses in the burning
bush. The red-hot iron and the burning bush are both physical
objects yet at the same time more than physical. They are
transmuted by the divine influx, rendered transparent, made
into reflections or images of the power that created them.

The common misunderstanding of Lawrence, echoed by
Norman O. Brown in *Life Against Death*, is that the resurrection
of the body results simply from "genital intercourse – 'free' love
and the orgasm" (29). But this is not true even of *Lady
Chatterley's Lover*. Clearly the novel is a celebration of the saving
possibilities of sex, and its polemical intent is to counter the idea
associated with Christianity that all sex is bad, yet if we look
closely at the body in this novel we find what we have already
found in *The Plumed Serpent*. At the beginning of the novel,
Connie, lacking the "healthy human sensuality, that warms the
blood and freshens the whole being" (73), looks at herself in the
mirror and sees that "her body was going meaningless, going
dull and opaque, so much insignificant substance" (73). Her
body lacks meaning, which is another way of saying that it has
lost touch with the surrounding vital ambience and context that
alone is meaning. Even "the very air is half dead" (96). The
world has fallen, and it is the intellect that is responsible. In
Lawrence's myth the fall occurred not when Adam fell asleep
but when "Plato and Aristotle" "killed" the body (254):
"'while you *live* your life, you are in some way an organic whole
with all life. But once you start the mental life you pluck the
apple. You've severed the connection ... the organic connection'" (37). "There was no organic connection with the thought
and expression that had gone before" (15), and people have
"lost touch with the substantial and vital world" (18). The
world lacks both substance and meaning, and in some deep way
these are the same thing. Cut off from both a natural and a
historical paradise, where "once there had been deer, and
archers, and monks padding along on asses" (43), the inhab-
itants of Wragby hall find themselves living "always a dream or
a frenzy, inside an enclosure" (41). This enclosure is the

separate intellect or ego, Coleridge's Understanding. The dissolution of the ego will mean the return to the paradise that still exists all around us, that is preserved in the very "spirit of place," for "the place remembered, still remembered" (43).

Connie yearns for "the resurrection of the body!" but "didn't at all know what it meant" (78). She learns that it means that one must "smelt out the heaviest ore of the body into purity" (268), melt down into "one perfect concentric fluid of feeling," in which both "tissue and consciousness" (142) are dissolved. Making love with Mellors, "there awoke in her new strange thrills rippling inside her. Rippling, rippling, rippling, like a flapping overlapping of soft flames, soft as feathers, running to points of brilliance, exquisite, exquisite and melting her all molten inside" (141–42). This process continues until finally, "the quick of all her plasm was touched, she knew herself touched, the consummation was upon her, and she was gone. She was gone, she was not, and she was born: a woman" (187). What is "touched" here is much more than the epidermis – it is "herself," "the quick of all her plasm," and we have seen enough of Lawrence's special vocabulary to know that the "quick" and the "plasm" designate what we have been calling the subtle body. Where once her body had been "opaque" and "meaningless," now "her soul [is] washed transparent" (228). Having "risen from the tomb" (254), she perceives a world alive with subtle potency: "the trees in the park seemed bulging and surging at anchor on a tide, and the heave of the slope to the house was alive" (191). "The life of the body," Connie realizes, is indeed "a greater reality than the life of the mind," and when the body comes alive, "it will be a lovely, lovely life in the lovely universe, the life of the human body" (254).

Norman O. Brown's own quest in *Life Against Death* to recover the "polymorphously perverse" life of the body draws heavily on Boehme and, in Brown's last chapter, upon a dimly adumbrated idea of the "subtle body." But Lawrence is much closer to Boehme than Brown realizes and has a much better understanding of the subtle than does Brown at this point in his thinking. Lawrence already occupies the ground later discovered by Brown in his *Love's Body*, which moves beyond *Life*

Against Death into a profound exploration of the meaning of the resurrection of the body. Like Lawrence and Boehme, Brown identifies the fall with "the abstraction of the visual, obtained by putting to sleep the rest of the life of the body" (121). The eye-I exists in artificial abstraction, as does the purely physical world that it perceives, which is a world of opaque stone idols. This world must be burned up, consumed by fire, renewed, illuminated: "The true body is the body burnt up, the spiritual body. The unity is not organic-natural unity, but the unity of fire" (183). Brown quotes Boehme:

Our life is as a fire dampened, or as a fire shut up in stone. Dear children, it must blaze, and not remain smouldering, smothered ... it must be set on fire: the soul must break out of the reasoning of this world into the life of Christ, into Christ's flesh and blood; then it receives the fuel which makes it blaze. (214)

As the soul breaks out of "the reasoning of this world," it sees the deeper meaning of things intended by God (195); it discovers "symbolic consciousness" (217); it renews the creation because illumination is a repetition of "the original *fiat lux*" (211).

For Brown "the resurrection of the body" is "the awakening to the symbolical life of the body"; the body is raised "a spiritual or symbolical body" (191). This idea of a "symbolical body" is perhaps the best way to describe the body envisioned by both Lawrence and Boehme. They possess the same visionary "symbolic consciousness," the same capacity to "see" the "archetypal form" that is "the hidden life of things" (209). For Boehme the external "visible world [is] a manifestation of the inward spiritual world": "For the outward world with its substance is a cover to the spiritual world, as the body is to the soul" (*Way* 149). Body can either conceal or reveal the soul, just as the piece of iron can be dark and cold or red-hot. To the worldly minded, flesh is merely flesh, but to a visionary like Boehme, flesh is "the outward part of the soul" (*Way* 108). For Lawrence, too, bodies are "gestures from the soul" (*Plumed* 304). This is what is revealed to his characters in their moments of ultimate knowledge. Ursula in *Women in Love* "knew, with the clarity of ultimate knowledge, that the body is only one of the manifestations of the spirit" (192), and Kate has an identical moment as she looks at Don Ramon's prostrate and unconscious body: "And again Kate saw, vividly, how the body is the flame of the soul, leaping and sinking upon the invisible wick of the soul. And now the soul, like a wick, seemed spent, the body was a sinking, fading flame" (300). The body in Lawrence is always the body, but it is never merely what Boehme would call the "carnal" or "gross" body. It is the symbolic or subtle body in which are manifested the invisible forces "beneath" or "within" the surface that make the visible body what it is and without which there would be no body.

As we have seen repeatedly, to even begin to apprehend the union of soul and body, we must fight our way past the conceptual opposites created by the Understanding, and we can only do this in formulations that are contradictions to the Understanding. *The Plumed Serpent* repeatedly struggles to express a central paradox. The union is "the greater life of the soul" (265), as well as "a new body" (200). It is "not the physical woman herself" (321), yet it is "physical" as opposed to "mystical." It is physical, "only further" (370). It is "to be gone in the body beyond the individualism of the body" (131). It is "the sensual fulfillment of my soul" (273). Boehme struggles to express the same paradox when he says that "the new birth ... is not wrought in the mortal flesh, and yet is wrought truly and really in us, in flesh and blood" (*Way* 91).

Graham Hough contrasts Lawrence's view of the body with Christianity's view by saying that "For Christianity the life of the flesh receives its sanction and purpose from a life of the spirit which is eternal and transcendent. For Lawrence the life of the spirit has its justification in enriching and glorifying the life of the flesh of which it is in any case an epiphenomenon" (*Dark Sun* 253). If we have learned anything from the preceding chapters, we have learned that such easy divisions between spirit and flesh do not do justice to the comprehensiveness of Lawrence's vision and are precisely what Lawrence sought always to overcome. Hough then quotes in support of his case one of the most famous passages in all of Lawrence, the conclusion of *Apocalypse*:

What man most passionately wants is his living wholeness and his living unison, not his own isolate salvation of his "soul." Man wants his physical fulfilment first and foremost, since now, once and once only, he is in the flesh and potent. For man, the vast marvel is to be alive. For man, as for flower and beast and bird, the supreme triumph is to be most vividly, most perfectly alive. (149)

This is quintessential Lawrence, and it is for such passionate affirmations and for such language that we treasure him, yet the very categories in which we think make it almost inevitable that even as sensitive a critic as Hough will see as one-sided what is in fact a vision that transcends and encompasses the opposition spirit-flesh. Hough himself, after a discussion of Lawrence's last poems, is forced to conclude that in Lawrence "the flesh had never been the flesh in any common acceptance of the term, and that the frail soul had been there all the time" (260). For a more complete view of Lawrence we should place alongside the conclusion to *Apocalypse* the following fragment published for the first time in the Cambridge edition:

Man is essentially a soul. The soul is neither the body nor the spirit, but the central flame that burns between the two, as the flame of a lamp burns between the oil of the lamp and the oxygen of the air...

Body and spirit both must learn to obey the soul, since both are consummated in the soul. The soul is a flame that forever quivers between oil and air, between body and spirit, between substance and non-substance, between the senses and the mind. It is born of both and partakes of both and consummates both and surpasses both. But it is always midmost between the two. ("Man" 389)

CHAPTER 6

Conclusion: Romanticism and Christianity

For Lawrence the essential question was always: "How shall man put himself into relation to God, into a living relation" (*Phoenix* 726–27). Man is "related to the universe in some 'religious' way" (qtd. in Kalnins 19), but this way is constantly changing. Christianity once met the needs of man for a living contact with "this terrific and frightening and delighted potency I call Almighty God" (*Apocalypse* 155), but Lawrence in his youth found that Christianity in its present form was no longer able to meet his deepest needs, nor – he felt – the deepest needs of his civilization. He was preceded in this conviction by many of the Romantics, and it was to them that he turned after losing his faith. He followed the Romantics in his belief in art as another kind of religious experience:

And when our religious responses are dead, or inactive, we are really cut off from life, because the deepest part of our consciousness is not functioning. We try to take refuge in art. But to my mind, the essential feeling in all art is religious, and art is a form of religion without dogma. The *feeling* in art is religious, always. Whenever the soul is moved to a certain fullness of experience, that is religion. Every sincere and genuine feeling is a religious feeling. And the point of every work of art is that it achieves a state of feeling which becomes true experience, and so is religious. (*Apocalypse* 155)

The relation between Lawrence's Romanticism and Christianity has been one of the main themes of this study, and in this brief conclusion I propose to compare Lawrence's position with those of W. B. Yeats and T. S. Eliot, the two most important of Lawrence's English contemporaries. The comparison is fascinating because Yeats and Eliot are almost pure type and anti-type to Lawrence. Yeats held the Romantic belief that "whatever the great poets had affirmed in their finest moments was the nearest we could come to an authoritative religion" (*Autobiography* 60), while Eliot maintained that the only possible authoritative religion was Catholicism and that to think otherwise was heresy. Yeats and Eliot pose the issues with such stark clarity and conviction that they not only help us to better understand Lawrence's views but also force us to take a position concerning them.

The parallels between Yeats and Lawrence are extensive and striking. As a young man, Yeats also lost his Christianity and found a new faith in art: "I was unlike others of my generation in one thing only. I am very religious, and deprived by Huxley and Tyndall, whom I detested, of the simple-minded religion of my childhood, I had made a new religion, almost an infallible church of poetic tradition" (*Autobiography* 77). Graham Hough feels that Yeats and Lawrence are the only two recent English writers "to break into new spiritual territory outside the Christian boundaries" (*Dark Sun* i), and the territory explored is mostly the same for both men. At an early age, Yeats turned to Blake, Boehme, and Blavatsky, who became life-long objects of study. He also fell under the spell of "Nietzsche, that strong enchanter. I have read him so much that I have made my eyes bad again ... Nietzsche completes Blake and has the same roots" (*Letters*, 379). And *A Vision*, the entire system of which is based on polar opposites, is profoundly indebted to Heraclitus and Empedocles. There are many important differences between the two writers, but Yeats was correct to call Lawrence a "friend of his soul" (qtd. in Virginia Moore 416).

T. S. Eliot, the intransigent foe of all forms of Romanticism, devoted his considerable talents throughout his life to opposing the Romantic belief that, in Lawrence's words, "Art is a form of religion without dogma." Central to the Romantic enterprise is the belief that God constantly reveals Himself to man in new ways, that revelation is continuous, and that it is in the imagination of the artist that this revelation preeminently takes place. Again and again Eliot in opposition insisted that "poetry is not a substitute for philosophy or theology or religion" (*Selected* 118). "The decay of religion ... left dubious frontiers upon which the poet encroached," and the "poet" became the "priest" (*Use* 26). But "nothing in this world or the next is a substitute for anything else; and if you find that you must do without something, such as religious faith or philosophic belief, then you must just do without it" (*Use* 113). Romanticism cannot be religious because it is impossible to have a religion without a dogma and a theology. Revelation is the province of the Church, and it is a disaster for poets to take on that function.

Eliot knew the enemy well and realized that to effectively attack Romanticism he must attack the concept of the imagination. As we have seen, the Romantics thought of the imagination as the faculty that transcends the opposition of philosophy and poetry in a higher visionary synthesis. To destroy the validity of this idea is to destroy Romanticism's prophetic pretensions. Eliot therefore maintains repeatedly and insistently that philosophy and poetry are utterly distinct enterprises and should never be confused. "The poet makes poetry, the metaphysician makes metaphysics" (*Selected* 118).

I believe that for a poet to be also a philosopher he would have to be virtually two men; I cannot think of any example of this thorough schizophrenia, nor can I see anything to be gained by it: the work is better performed inside two skulls than one. Coleridge is the apparent example, but I believe that he was only able to exercise the one activity at the expense of the other. A poet may borrow a philosophy or he may do without one. It is when he philosophises upon his own *poetic* insight that he is apt to go wrong. (*Use* 98–99)

Unlike the Romantics who considered Shakespeare and Dante philosophers, Eliot maintains that "in truth, neither Shakespeare nor Dante did any real thinking" (*Selected* 116). "The poet who 'thinks' is merely the poet who can express the emotional equivalent of thought. But he is not necessarily interested in the thought itself" (*Selected* 115). Dante's poetry is unsurpassed because he had the great good fortune to be able to appropriate St. Thomas's philosophy for his poetry, but that does not mean that Dante necessarily believed or disbelieved the philosophy – "he merely made use of it" (*Selected* 118). The Romantics, however, do not use existing philosophies but make up their own. "A great change in the attitude towards poetry, in the expectations and demands made upon it, [came] towards the end of the eighteenth century" and reached its "highest point of exaggeration in Shelley's famous phrase, 'poets are the unacknowledged legislators of mankind'" (*Use* 25).

Eliot rejects Shelley's prophetic intentions and finds him guilty of an "abuse of poetry" by trying to make it the vehicle of abstract ideas that Eliot finds "abhorrent," "childish," and "feeble" (*Use* 89, 96). For Yeats, on the other hand, *Prometheus Unbound* is "a sacred book," a product of the "imagination," which "has some way of lighting on the truth that reason has not" (*Essays* 65). He rejects the idea that *Prometheus* is merely "Godwin's *Political Justice* put into rhyme." Shelley is not the "vague thinker" he is often taken to be but a "mystic" and visionary, who could have been "a metaphysician or a poet." Shelley's philosophical essays in fact "are instinct with the intensest spirit of poetry," just as the poetry is the form alone in which philosophy is made "permanent" (*Essays* 65–66).

Eliot and Yeats divide similarly on Blake, the other of Yeats's great heroes among the English Romantics. Eliot notes of Blake that "his philosophy ... was his own. And accordingly he was inclined to attach more importance to it than an artist should." Lacking Dante's ready-made philosophy, Blake "must needs create a philosophy as well as a poetry," a double task for which he did not know or see enough. Blake's philosophy is like "an ingenious piece of home-made furniture" that reflects a "certain meanness of culture." The result is "what we find in such a work as *Also Sprach Zarathustra*" – "confusion of thought, emotion, and vision" (*Selected* 275–80). Yeats by contrast finds in Blake one of the supreme revelations of the human imagination:

He had learned from Jacob Boehme and from old alchemist writers that imagination was the first emanation of divinity, "the body of God," "the Divine members," and he drew the deduction, which they did not draw, that the imaginative arts were therefore the greatest of Divine revelations ... (*Essays* 112)

Blake "announced the religion of art." Before his time

educated people believed that they amused themselves with books of imagination, but that they "made their souls" by listening to sermons and by doing or by not doing certain things ... In our time we are agreed that it is out of great works of art that we "make our souls" out of some one of the great poets of ancient times, or out of Shelley or Wordsworth ... (111)

Eliot everywhere separates what Yeats joins. He even pursues Romantic miscegenation as far back in history as the pre-Socratics:

The early philosophical poets, Parmenides and Empedocles, were apparently persons of an impure philosophical inspiration. Neither their predecessors nor their successors expressed themselves in verse; Parmenides and Empedocles were persons who mingled with genuine philosophical ability a good deal of the emotion of the founder of a second-rate religious system. They were not interested exclusively in philosophy, or religion, or poetry, but in something which was a mixture of all three; hence their reputation as poets is low and as philosophers should be considerably below Heraclitus, Zeno, Anaxagoras, or Democritus. (*Sacred* 160–61)

In his obsessive need to keep "poetry" "pure," Eliot commits the historical error of separating what was not yet separate in the pre-Socratics – poetry, philosophy, and religion. To say that Heraclitus is not poetic because he did not write in verse and that Parmenides is not philosophical because he did is surely to commit a number of errors in definition and logic, as well as to reveal an ignorance of the period.

Eliot's ideas were immensely influential in the first decades after Lawrence's death and constituted a formidable obstacle to understanding the nature and value of Lawrence's achievement. It is thus worth pursuing some of the many objections that have been raised to them. Edmund Wilson objects that Eliot's point of view is "absolutely unhistorical – an impossible attempt to make aesthetic values independent of all other values":

Who will agree with Eliot, for example, that a poet cannot be an original thinker and that it is not possible for a poet to be a completely successful artist and yet persuade us to accept his ideas at the same time? ... we cannot, in the case of Plato, discriminate so finely as to the

capacity of his philosophy for being "expanded into pure vision" that
we are able to put our finger on the point where the novelist or poet
stops and the scientist or metaphysician begins; nor, with Blake any
more than with Nietzsche and Emerson, distinguish the poet from the
aphorist. (119–20)

In *The Disinherited Mind* Erich Heller maintains that it is
impossible to distinguish between poetry and philosophy on the
basis of the difference between feeling and thought. "Rilke *as a
poet* is interested 'in the thought itself,' and Nietzsche *as a thinker*
also expressed 'the emotional equivalent of thought'" (149).
"To make poetry is to think. Of course, it is not *merely* thinking.
But there is no such activity as 'merely thinking,' unless we
confine the term to purely logical or mathematical operations"
(151). Furthermore, it is not "possible to 'use' thought without
thinking in the process of using it. For thought is not an object,
but an activity" (151). Eliot says that "we talk as if thought was
precise and emotion was vague. In reality there is precise
emotion and there is vague emotion. To express precise emotion
requires as great intellectual power as to express precise
thought" (*Selected* 115). Heller replies that "this is an important
point admirably put, although it would be difficult to find a
word other than 'thought' for the *intellectual* power required to
express precise emotion" (173).

Heller acutely remarks that Eliot is attempting to "clear up
a confusion by using tools of thought manufactured in the very
workshop that is responsible for the muddle" (149). In other
words, Eliot is himself a victim of the "dissociaton of sensibility"
that he did so much to popularize. In Eliot's view the relation
between thought and feeling has been hopelessly confused since
the seventeenth century, when "a dissociation of sensibility set
in, from which we have never recovered":

It is something which had happened to the mind of England between
the time of Donne or Lord Herbert of Cherbury and the time of
Tennyson and Browning; it is the difference between the intellectual
poet and the reflective poet. Tennyson and Browning are poets, and
they think; but they do not feel their thought as immediately as the
odour of a rose. A thought to Donne was an experience; it modified his
sensibility. (*Selected* 247)

Even in Donne, however, one can see the dire effects of the breakup in the Renaissance of the medieval Christian synthesis – "it seemed as if, [in Donne's time], the world was filled with broken fragments of systems" (118). Since the perfect marriage of poetry and philosophy in Dante, things have gone straight downhill at an increasing rate. The Romantics attempted to reunite thought and feeling, but Eliot asserts that "the sort of reassociation that was effected, in English verse, was inorganic"; "the poets thought and felt by fits, unbalanced" (qtd. in Lobb 40). Neither true poetry nor true philosophy is any longer possible, for both have been fatally infected by the plague of emotionalism, as Edward Lobb's summary of Eliot's unpublished lectures makes clear:

As a result of their divorce, feeling and thought enter each other's realms rather awkwardly; they corrupt rather than complete. Philosophy, which ought to be disinterested within its premises, takes on an emotional colouring in the work of Fichte, Schopenhauer, Hegel, James and Bradley, each of whom, Eliot suggests, passionately *wants* something to be true without being able to demonstrate it satisfactorily. Poetry, on the other hand, which should incarnate rather than analyse experience, becomes "philosophical," "corrupted by thought," in the work of Wordsworth and Shelley, Tennyson and Browning. (40–41)

Eliot of course did not discover the "dissociation of sensibility," he merely named it. The idea that a split occurred sometime around the time of Shakespeare is a commonplace among the Romantics, and Lawrence while still a schoolboy told Jessie Chambers, "'Shakespeare was the product of his age. Everything was somehow concentrated in him. Things are so split up now. There can never be another Shakespeare'" (59). Yeats too has his version:

When my generation denounced scientific humanitarian preoccupation, psychological curiosity, rhetoric, we had not found what ailed Victorian literature. The Elizabethans had all these things, especially rhetoric ... The mischief began at the end of the seventeenth century when man became passive before a mechanized nature; that lasted to our own day with the exception of a brief period between Smart's *Song of David* and the death of Byron, wherein imprisoned man beat upon the door. (*Oxford* xxvi–xxvii)

The brief period between Smart and Byron is of course the Romantic one.

According to Eliot, the consequences of the illegitimate union in Romanticism of religion, philosophy, and poetry can be seen most clearly by the end of the nineteenth century, in the "Humanism" of Matthew Arnold and after him in the "Aestheticism" of Pater. In his essay on "Arnold and Pater," Eliot says that for Arnold, "literature, or Culture, tended ... to usurp the place of Religion" (*Selected* 349). Arnold believes that "the emotions of Christianity can and must be preserved without the belief" (349), and "the effect of Arnold's campaign is to divorce Religion from thought" (349). But a religion cannot survive without "dogmatic essentials," without a theology and a creed. Since Arnold, like everyone else of whom Eliot disapproves, was "incapable of sustained reasoning," he "could not take philosophy or theology seriously" (354). "The total effect of Arnold's philosophy is ... to leave Religion to be laid waste by the anarchy of feeling" (351). "The degradation of philosophy and religion, skillfully initiated by Arnold, is competently continued by Pater" (352), in whom feeling further deteriorates into sensation. "'Art for art's sake' is the offspring of Arnold's Culture" (354), and we end finally with Pater's Marius the Epicurean, for whom Christianity is a matter of exquisite sensations.

In *After Strange Gods*: *A Primer of Modern Heresy*, Eliot continues his history of dissociation into the twentieth century. His two prime examples of modern heresy are Yeats and Lawrence, and he associates them with "the doctrine of Arnold, that Poetry can replace Religion." Yeats and Lawrence, both "restless seekers for myths," display the same "tendency to fabricate an *individual* religion" (48). Despite the strong similarities between Yeats and Lawrence, however, they receive very different treatment at Eliot's hands. Yeats is let off lightly for his sins, but Lawrence, "an almost perfect example of the heretic" (41), seems to become the culmination of the entire disastrous course of Western civilization in the last few centuries. He stands revealed in Eliot's pages as a virtual anti-Christ, an "instrument" of "daemonic powers" (65). Lawrence embodies all the errors of Romanticism, its tendency "for a writer of genius to conceive of himself as a messiah" (35), its emotionalism, its unbridled individualism, its cult of personality. Lawrence is "spiritually sick," sexually "morbid," a man whose "deplorable religious upbringing" gave him "a lust for intellectual independence": "The point is that Lawrence started life wholly free from any restriction of tradition or institution, that he had no guidance except the Inner Light, the most untrustworthy and deceitful guide that ever offered itself to wandering humanity" (66). Lacking "a trained mind like that of Mr. Joyce," Lawrence had "an incapacity for what we ordinarily call thinking," and hence could not distinguish between his good and evil impulses. Lacking a tradition of "Outside Authority" like Catholicism, he did not know that "the inner voice, which breathes the eternal message of vanity, fear, and lust" is the Devil's (*Selected* 16).

This is not the place to rebut Eliot's charges, which combine valid observations with snobbery, sexual hysteria, and ignorance. That job has already been well done by F. R. Leavis and others, and the preceding chapters of this book should have made it clear that if Lawrence could not think it is difficult to know what thinking is, and that if Lawrence was uneducated and lacking in tradition it is difficult to know what education and tradition are. Eliot's observations are nevertheless useful in highlighting the central issues raised by Lawrence's religion. And here we must note the tactical effectiveness of Eliot's associating Yeats and Lawrence with late nineteenth-century developments rather than the earlier high Romantic period. In doing so he subtly diminishes the achievement of Yeats and Lawrence, for there was indeed – and here Eliot is right – a marked deterioration in the course of the century. The deterioration is best represented by Ernst Renan, whose *Life of Jesus* was published in 1863 and sold more than sixty thousand copies in the first six months. Renan's Jesus is wrapped in a shroud of vague moralism and aestheticizing sentimentality.

His Jesus voices "the poetry of the soul – faith, liberty, virtue, devotion" (69); "his worship will constantly renew its youth, the tale of his life will cause endless tears, his sufferings will soften the best hearts" (199). It is only a short step from here to Arnold's *Literature and Dogma*, which defines religion as "morality touched by emotion" (27).

But it is the heretical Christianity of William Blake, not the pseudo-religion of Arnold, that stands behind Yeats and Lawrence. Not the "sweet reasonableness" of Arnold's Jesus, but the antinomian ferocity and intellectual strife of Blake's Jesus, who obeyed his impulses rather than moral rules and who broke each of the ten commandments (Blake 42). Blake's religion humanizes God because "All deities reside in the human breast" (37). "The worship of God is. Honouring his gifts in other men each according to his genius. and loving the greatest men best, those who envy or calumniate great men hate God, for there is no other God" (42). Eliot of course would have us identify Blake's and Arnold's humanisms, despite their very great differences. Eliot's objection to all humanisms is that the conflation of human and divine destroys the supernatural, and with the suppression of the "supernatural,"

the *dualism* of man and nature collapses at once. Man is man because he can recognize supernatural realities, not because he can invent them. Either everything in man can be traced as a development from below, or something must come from above. There is no avoiding the dilemma: you must be either a naturalist or a supernaturalist. If you remove from the word "human" all that the belief in the supernatural has given to man, you can view him finally as no more than an extremely clever, adaptable, and mischievous little animal. (*Selected* 396)

Here we have the opposition between Eliot and Romanticism in its starkest terms: for Eliot there is no possibility of the third position that we have been calling "ideal realism" or "natural supernaturalism," whereas for Romantics like Blake it is the essence of their belief.

We are really describing the eternal conflict between the orthodox and the heretic, a conflict unlikely to be resolved in these pages. The difference has been nicely formulated by

Henry B. Parkes in an essay on Emerson: "The core of heretical mysticism is the belief that the soul of man, not merely *like* God, as orthodox Christianity declares, is *of the same substance* as God; it is, therefore, untouched by original sin, has an innate knowledge of religious truth, and may attain to absolute union with the Godhead " (125). Parkes outlines a stream of European mysticism running into Emerson through Plotinus, Eckhart, Boehme, Swedenborg, Schelling, Coleridge, and Carlyle. The stream flowed on into Yeats and Lawrence.

In Eliot's view, the religion of Yeats and Lawrence is not only heretical – it is parochial and shallow as well. Eliot regrets that Yeats had to put together a philosophy out of "folklore, occultism, mythology and symbolism, crystal-gazing and her-metic writings" (*After* 48). It is unfortunate that such a fine poet as Yeats was not able to arrive "at a central and universal philosophy" like Catholicism (51). Yeats of course felt other-wise: "I have not found my tradition in the Catholic Church, which was not the Church of my childhood, but where the tradition is, as I believe, more universal and more ancient" (*Essays* 538). Yeats's tradition is, like Lawrence's and Blake's, what has been called the *philosophia perennis*. In the conviction that the truth, if it is truth, must be universal and timeless, Yeats and Lawrence turned to other religions and traditions for their inspiration.

Like Blake, Yeats and Lawrence believed that "All Religions are One" and that "The Religeons of all Nations are derived from each Nation's different reception of the Poetic Genius which is every where call'd ther Spirit of Prophecy" (Blake 2). It is thus for Yeats and Lawrence not a simple matter of Christian versus non-Christian, as it is for Eliot. Yeats and Lawrence could also consider themselves Christian in that they believed that the same truth that exists in other religions exists in Christianity as well. The Yeats who rejected Catholicism also said, on coming out of Sant'Ambrogio's in Milan, "That is my tradition, and I will let no priest rob me" (*Vision* 7). And Lawrence in a notebook fragment written shortly before his death, said: "There is no real battle between me and Christi-anity. Perhaps there is a certain battle between me and nonconformity, because, at the depth, my nature is catholic. But I believe in the all-overshadowing God. I believe that Jesus is one of the Sons of God" (*Apocalypse* 385). But, like Yeats, Nietzsche, Emerson, and Blavatsky, he did not believe that Jesus was the only Son of God: "So that the great Church of the future will know other saviours: men are saved variously, in various lands, in various climes, in various centuries... The great disaster of religion is that each religion tends to assert one exclusive saviour. One hates Christianity because it declares there is only one way to God" (*Apocalypse* 385).

Yeats and Lawrence were both strongly drawn to the early Church, which they distinguished sharply from post-Renaissance Christianity. Yeats found the "splendour" of the "Divine Being" in "the first four Christian centuries" (*Essays* 431), in the early Irish Church, and above all in Byzantium, where there still existed "Unity of Being," an undissociated oneness of "religious, aesthetic and practical life." He also found "the true Christ" depicted in the Byzantine mosaics: "stern, loving and 'supernatural'" (Moore 400). Yeats "drew a distinction between the true Christ of the Byzantine mosaics and the 'soft, domesticated Christ of the painters brush' and latterday Church" (Moore 421). We find the identical distinction in Lawrence. "The Jesus of the early Catholic Church," he says in *Apocalypse*, was the Cosmic Christ, "*Kosmokrator*," "the great Ruler of the Cosmos, and the Power of the Cosmos" (75). The early Church preserved "the magnificence of the Star-mover," "the whole great adventure of the human soul, as contrasted with the little petty personal adventure of modern Protestantism and Catholicism alike, cut off from the cosmos ... petty morality instead of cosmic splendour" (75).

Lawrence was fascinated by the idea of "a vast Cosmic lord," which he calls the "Zodiacal man," "standing among the seven eternal lamps of the archaic planets, sun and moon and five great stars around his feet" (*Apocalypse* 74). He first encountered the Zodiacal Man in the pages of Frederick Carter's *The Dragon of the Apocalypse*. In a review of Carter's book, he described the experience in which suddenly

a page, or a chapter ... would release my imagination and give me a whole great sky to move in. For the first time I strode forth into the grand fields of the sky ...

I have read books of astronomy which made me dizzy with the sense of illimitable space. But the heart melts and dies, it is the disembodied mind alone which follows on through this horrible hollow void of space, where lonely stars hang in awful isolation. And this is not a release. . .

In astronomical space, one can only *move*, one cannot *be*. In the astrological heavens, that is to say, the ancient zodiacal heavens, the whole man is set free, once the imagination crosses the border. The whole man, bodily and spiritual, walks in the magnificent fields of the stars, and the stars have names, and the feet tread splendidly upon – we know not what, but the heavens, instead of untreadable space ...

To enter the astrological sky of the zodiac and the living, roving planets is another experience, another *kind* of experience; it is truly imaginative, and to me, more valuable ... It is the entry into another world, another kind of world, measured by another dimension. And we find some prisoned self in us coming forth to live in this world. (46)

It is for Lawrence's remarkable ability to communicate this kind of experience that we value him. It is a religious experience, whether or not Eliot would accept it as one. Lawrence's description of the living heavens helps to restore in us "the sense of wonder" which is "the religious element inherent in all life" (*Phoenix* 2 599). This is "the essential poetic and vital act," the act of the living imagination, that "'discovers' a new world within the known world" (*Phoenix* 255). It is an apocalypse in the Romantic sense first defined by Coleridge, Wordsworth, Blake, Shelley, and Carlyle, an apocalypse that gives us a "new heaven and earth," not in the hereafter but in what Wordsworth called "the world / Of all of us, the place in which, in the end, / We find our happiness, or not at all."

Bibliography

Abrams, M. H. "Coleridge's 'A Light in Sound': Science, Meta-science, and Poetic Imagination." *The Correspondent Breeze: Essays on English Romanticism*. New York: Norton, 1984.
Natural Supernaturalism: Tradition and Revolution in Romantic Literature. New York: Norton, 1971.
Aiken, Henry David. "Introduction to *Zarathustra*." *Nietzsche: A Collection of Critical Essays*. Ed. Robert C. Solomon. University of Notre Dame Press, 1980.
Aristotle. *The Basic Works of Aristotle*. Ed. Richard McKeon. New York: Random House, 1941.
Arnold, Matthew. *Literature and Dogma*. New York: Frederick Ungar Publishing Co., 1970.
Auden, W. H. "Some Notes on D. H. Lawrence." *The Nation* (April 26, 1947): 482–84.
Barfield, Owen. "Matter, Imagination, and Spirit." *The Rediscovery of Meaning and Other Essays*. Middletown: Wesleyan University Press, 1985.
"Imagination and Inspiration." *The Rediscovery of Meaning and Other Essays*. Middletown: Wesleyan University Press, 1985.
Saving the Appearances: A Study in Idolatry. New York: Harcourt, Brace & World, n.d.
What Coleridge Thought. Middletown: Wesleyan University Press, 1971.
Barth, J. Robert. *Coleridge and Christian Doctrine*. New York: Fordham University Press, 1987.
Bate, W. Jackson. *Coleridge*. Cambridge, Mass.: Harvard University Press, 1987.
Bell, Michael. *D. H. Lawrence: Language and Being*. Cambridge University Press, 1991.
Berdyaev, Nicolas. Introduction. *Six Theosophic Points and Other Writings*. By Jacob Boehme. Ann Arbor: University of Michigan Press, 1958.

Bhagavad-Gita. Ed. R. C. Zaehner. New York: Oxford University Press, 1969.

Black, Michael. *D. H. Lawrence: The Early Fiction: A Commentary.* London: Macmillan, 1986.

   D. H. Lawrence: The Early Philosophical Works. London: Macmillan, 1991.

Blake, William. *The Poetry and Prose of William Blake.* Ed. David V. Erdman. Garden City: Doubleday, 1965.

Blavatsky, H. P. *Isis Unveiled: A Master-Key to the Mysteries of Ancient and Modern Science and Theology.* Pasadena: Theosophical University Press, 1972.

Bloom, Harold, ed. *Samuel Taylor Coleridge: Modern Critical Views.* New York: Chelsea House, 1986.

   Ed. *Thomas Carlyle: Modern Critical Views.* New York: Chelsea House, 1986.

Boehme, Jacob. *The Aurora.* London: John M. Watkins, 1960.

   Mysterium Magnum. 2 vols. London: John M. Watkins, 1965.

   The Signature of All Things. Cambridge: James Clarke & Co., 1969.

   The Way to Christ. New York: McGraw-Hill, 1965.

Bradley, A. C. "English Poetry and German Philosophy in the Age of Wordsworth." *A Miscellany.* New York: Books for Libraries Press, 1969. 105–38.

   "Wordsworth." *Oxford Lectures on Poetry.* Bloomington: Indiana University Press, 1961. 99–145.

Bridgewater, Patrick. *Nietzsche in Anglosaxony.* London: Leicester University Press, 1972.

Brinton, Howard H. *The Mystic Will: Based on a Study of the Philosophy of Jacob Boehme.* New York: Macmillan, 1930.

Brown, Norman O. *Life Against Death: The Psychoanalytic Meaning of History.* New York: Vintage Books, 1959.

   Love's Body. New York: Random House, 1966.

Brunsdale, Mitzi M. *The German Effect on D. H. Lawrence and His Works, 1885–1912.* Las Vegas: Peter Lang, 1978.

Burckhardt, Titus. *Alchemy: Science of the Cosmos, Science of the Soul.* Baltimore: Penguin Books, 1971.

Burnet, John. *Early Greek Philosophy.* New York: Meridian, 1957.

Burwell, Rose Marie. "A Catalogue of D. H. Lawrence's Reading from Early Childhood." *D. H. Lawrence Review* 3 (1970): iii–330.

   "A Checklist of Lawrence's Reading." *A D. H. Lawrence Handbook.* Ed. Keith Sagar. New York: Barnes and Noble, 1982.

Carlyle, Thomas. *The French Revolution.* New York: Dutton, 1906.

   The Life of John Sterling. Boston: Estes and Lauriat, n.d.

   On Heroes and Hero Worship. London: Dent, 1959.

Sartor Resartus. New York: The Odyssey Press, 1937.

Cassirer, Ernst. *An Essay on Man*. Garden City: Anchor-Doubleday, n.d.

Chambers, Jessie (E. T.). *D. H. Lawrence: A Personal Record*. London: Cass, 1965.

Clarke, Colin. *River of Dissolution*. New York: Barnes and Noble, 1969.

Coleridge, Samuel Taylor. *Aids to Reflection*. London: Bell, 1904.

    Biographia Literaria. Ed. James Engell and W. Jackson Bate. 2 vols. Princeton University Press, 1983.

    Collected Letters of Samuel Taylor Coleridge. Ed. E. L. Griggs. 6 vols. Oxford University Press, 1956–71.

    "Formation of a More Comprehensive Theory of Life." *Selected Poetry and Prose of Coleridge*. Ed. Donald A. Stauffer. New York: Modern Library, 1951. 558–606.

    The Friend. Ed. Barbara E. Rooke. 2 vols. Princeton University Press, 1969.

    Lectures 1808–1819: On Literature. Ed. R. A. Foakes. 2 vols. Princeton University Press, 1987.

    Marginalia 1: Abbt to Byfield. Ed. George Whalley. Princeton University Press, 1980.

    The Notebooks of Samuel Taylor Coleridge. Ed. Kathleen Coburn. 4 vols. Princeton University Press, 1957.

    "On Poesy or Art." *Biographia Literaria*. Ed. John Shawcross. 2 vols. Oxford University Press, 1907. Vol. 2: 253–63.

    Philosophical Lectures. Ed. Kathleen Coburn. New York: Philosophical Library, 1949.

    The Statesman's Manual in *Lay Sermons*. Ed. R. J. White. Princeton University Press, 1972.

Colmer, John. "Lawrence and Blake." *D. H. Lawrence and Tradition*. Ed. Jeffrey Meyers. Amherst: University of Massachusetts Press, 1985.

Cornford, F. M. *From Religion to Philosophy: A Study in the Origins of Western Speculation*. New York: Harper, 1957.

Cowan, James C. "Alchemy and *The Plumed Serpent*." *D. H. Lawrence and the Trembling Balance*. University Park: Penn State University Press, 1990.

Daleski, H. M. *The Forked Flame: A Study of D. H. Lawrence*. Evanston: Northwestern University Press, 1965.

Daniel, Glyn. *The Idea of Prehistory*. Baltimore: Penguin Books, 1962.

Danielou, Alain. *Yoga: The Method of Reintegration*. New York: University Books, 1955.

Darwin, Charles. *The Essential Darwin*. Ed. Kenneth Korey. Boston: Little, Brown, 1984.

Delany, Paul. *D. H. Lawrence's Nightmare: The Writer and His Circle in the Years of the Great War.* New York: Basic Books, 1978.

Delavenay, Emile. "Sur un Exemplaire de Schopenhauer Annoté par D. H. Lawrence." *Revue Anglo-Americaine* 13 (1936): 234–38.

Dewey, John. "Ralph Waldo Emerson." *Emerson: A Collection of Critical Essays.* Englewood Cliffs: Prentice-Hall, 1962. 24–30.

Draper, R. P., ed. *D. H. Lawrence: The Critical Heritage.* New York: Barnes and Noble, 1970.

Ebbatson, Roger. *The Evolutionary Self: Hardy, Forster, Lawrence.* New Jersey: Barnes and Noble, 1982.

Lawrence and the Nature Tradition: A Theme in English Fiction: 1859–1914. New Jersey: Humanities Press, 1980.

Eliade, Mircea. *The Two and the One.* University of Chicago Press, 1979.

Eliot, T. S. *After Strange Gods: A Primer of Modern Heresy.* New York: Harcourt, Brace and Co., 1934.

The Sacred Wood. London: Methuen and Co., 1950.

Selected Essays: 1917–1932. New York: Harcourt, Brace and Co., 1932.

The Use of Poetry and the Use of Criticism. London: Faber and Faber, 1933.

Emerson, Ralph Waldo. *Selected Writings.* Ed. William H. Gilman. New York: New American Library, 1965.

Nature. Boston: Beacon Press, 1985.

Ford, George H. *Double Measure: A Study of the Novels and Stories of D. H. Lawrence.* New York: Holt, 1965.

Forster, E. M. *Aspects of the Novel.* New York: Harcourt, 1954.

Foster, John Burt, Jr. *Heirs to Dionysus: A Nietzschean Current in Literary Modernism.* Princeton University Press, 1981.

Frankfort, Henri and Mrs. H. A. *Before Philosophy: The Intellectual Adventure of Ancient Man.* Baltimore: Penguin, 1949.

Freeman, Mary. *D. H. Lawrence: A Basic Study of His Ideas.* New York: Grosset and Dunlap, 1955.

Friedlander, Paul. *Plato: An Introduction.* New York: Harper, 1958.

Gardiner, Patrick. *Schopenhauer.* Baltimore: Penguin, 1963.

Ghose, Aurobindo. *Heraclitus.* Calcutta: Arya Publishing House, 1941.

Goodheart, Eugene. *The Utopian Vision of D. H. Lawrence.* University of Chicago Press, 1963.

Gray, Ronald. *The German Tradition in Literature 1871–1945.* Cambridge University Press, 1965.

Green, Eleanor H. "Schopenhauer and D. H. Lawrence on Sex and Love." *D. H. Lawrence Review* 8 (1975): 329–45.

Green, Martin. *The von Richtofen Sisters: The Triumphant and the Tragic Modes of Love.* New York: Basic Books, 1974.

Guenon, Rene. *Le Théosophisme: Histoire d'une Pseudo-Religion.* Paris: Editions Traditionnelles, 1969.

"*The Reign of Quantity*" *and* "*The Signs of the Times.*" Baltimore: Penguin, 1972.

Gutierrez, Donald. *Subject-Object Relations in Wordsworth and Lawrence.* Ann Arbor: UMI Research Press, 1987.

Haeckel, Ernst. *The Riddle of the Universe at the Close of the Nineteenth Century.* New York: Harper and Brothers, 1900.

Hartmann, Franz. *The Life and Doctrines of Jacob Boehme.* New York: Macoy Publishing Co., 1929.

Hayman, Ronald. *Nietzsche: A Critical Life.* New York: Penguin, 1982.

Heidegger, Martin. *Heraclitus Seminar 1966/67.* University of Alabama Press, 1979.

Heller, Erich. *The Disinherited Mind.* New York: Harcourt Brace Jovanovich, 1975.

The Ironic German: A Study of Thomas Mann. Boston: Little, Brown, 1958.

Heraclitus. *Heraclitus.* Ed. and Trans. Philip Wheelwright. New York: Atheneum, 1971.

Hirsch, E. D. *Wordsworth and Schelling: A Typological Study of Romanticism.* New Haven: Yale University Press, 1960.

Hollingdale, R. J. *Nietzsche.* London: Routledge, 1973.

Hough, Graham. *The Dark Sun: A Study of D. H. Lawrence.* New York: Capricorn, 1956.

The Last Romantics. New York: Barnes and Noble, 1961.

Houghton, Walter E. *The Victorian Frame of Mind 1830–1870.* New Haven: Yale University Press, 1957.

Huxley, Aldous. "D. H. Lawrence." *Collected Essays.* New York: Bantam, 1960. 115–29.

James, William. *Pragmatism.* New York: Meridian, 1955.

Jaspers, Karl. *Nietzsche: An Introduction to the Understanding of His Philosophical Activity.* Lanham: University Press of America, 1965.

Kahn, Charles H. *The Art and Thought of Heraclitus.* New York: Cambridge University Press, 1979.

Kalnins, Mara. "Introduction." *Apocalypse and the Writings on Revelation.* Ed. Mara Kalnins. Cambridge University Press, 1980. 1–38.

Kaufmann, Walter. *Nietzsche: Philosopher, Psychologist, Anti-Christ.* Princeton University Press, 1974.

Keats, John. *Letters of John Keats.* Ed. Robert Gittings. New York: Oxford University Press, 1970.

Klossowski de Rola, Stanislas. *Alchemy: The Secret Art.* London: Thames and Hudson, 1973.

Knight, G. Wilson. *The Mutual Flame*. New York: Barnes and Noble, 1973.

Koyre, Alexandre. *La Philosophie de Jacob Boehme*. Paris: Librarie Philosophique, 1929.

Kuczkowski, Richard J. *Lawrence's "Esoteric" Psychology*. Ann Arbor: University Microfilms, 1974.

Lawrence, D. H. *Apocalypse and the Writings on Revelation*. Ed. Mara Kalnins. Cambridge University Press, 1980.

"Books." *Phoenix: The Posthumous Papers of D. H. Lawrence*. Ed. Edward D. McDonald. New York: Viking, 1968. 731- 34.

The Complete Poems of D. H. Lawrence. Ed. Vivian de Sola Pinto and F. Warren Roberts. New York: Viking, 1964.

"The Crown." *Phoenix 2: Uncollected, Unpublished, and Other Prose Works*. Ed. Warren Roberts and Harry T. Moore. New York: Viking, 1959.

Fantasia of the Unconscious. New York: Viking, 1960.

The First Lady Chatterley. London: Heinemann, 1972.

"Foreword to *Sons and Lovers*." *Sons and Lovers*. Ed. Helen and Carl Baron. Cambridge University Press, 1992.

"The Future of the Novel." *Study of Thomas Hardy and Other Essays*. Ed. Bruce Steele. Cambridge University Press, 1985. 151–55.

"Introduction to These Paintings." *Phoenix: The Posthumous Papers of D. H. Lawrence*. Ed. Edward D. McDonald. New York: Viking, 1968. 551–86.

Lady Chatterley's Lover. New York: Bantam, 1968.

The Letters of D. H. Lawrence. Gen. Ed. James T. Boulton. 5 vols. to date. Cambridge University Press, 1979–.

The Letters of D. H. Lawrence. Ed. Aldous Huxley. London: Heinemann, 1932.

"Man is Essentially a Soul ... " *Reflections on the Death of a Porcupine and Other Essays*. Ed. Michael Herbert. Cambridge University Press, 1988.

"A Modern Lover." *The Complete Short Stories of D. H. Lawrence*, vol. 1. New York: Viking, 1961. 1–22.

Mornings in Mexico. Harmondsworth: Penguin, 1960.

Phoenix. Ed. Edward D. McDonald. New York: The Viking Press, 1936.

The Plumed Serpent. Ed. L. D. Clark. Cambridge University Press, 1987.

Psychoanalysis and the Unconscious. New York: Viking, 1960.

"The Reality of Peace." *Phoenix*. Ed. Edward D. McDonald. New York: The Viking Press, 1936. 669–94.

Study of Thomas Hardy and Other Essays. Ed. Bruce Steele. Cambridge University Press, 1985.

The Symbolic Meaning. Ed. Armin Arnold. New York: Viking, 1964.

Twilight in Italy. New York: The Viking Press, 1958.

The White Peacock. Carbondale: Southern Illinois University Press, 1966.

Women in Love. Ed. David Farmer, Lindeth Vasey, and John Worthen. Cambridge University Press, 1987.

Leavis, F. R. *D. H. Lawrence: Novelist*. University of Chicago Press, 1955.

Thought, Words and Creativity: Art and Thought in Lawrence. New York: Oxford University Press, 1976.

Lester, John. *Journey Through Despair 1880–1914: Transformations in British Literary Culture*. Princeton University Press, 1968.

Levy-Bruhl, Lucien. *How Natives Think*. Princeton University Press, 1985.

Lobb, Edward. *T. S. Eliot and the Romantic Critical Tradition*. London: Routledge & Kegan Paul, 1981.

Lovejoy, Arthur O. *The Great Chain of Being*. Cambridge, Mass.: Harvard University Press, 1964.

Marcus, Phillip L. "Lawrence, Yeats, and 'the Resurrection of the Body.'" *D. H. Lawrence: A Centenary Consideration*. Ed. Peter Balbert and Phillip L. Marcus. Ithaca: Cornell University Press, 1985.

Mead, G. R. S. *The Doctrine of the Subtle Body in Western Tradition*. London: Stuart & Watkins, 1967.

Michaels-Tonks, Jennifer. *D. H. Lawrence: The Polarity of North and South; Germany and Italy in His Prose Works*. Bonn: Bouvier, 1976.

Miko, Stephen. *Toward Women in Love: The Emergence of a Lawrentian Aesthetic*. New Haven: Yale University Press, 1971.

Milosz, Czeslaw. *The Land of Ulro*. New York: Farrar, Strauss and Giroux, 1981.

Milton, Colin. *Lawrence and Nietzsche: A Study in Influence*. Aberdeen University Press, 1987.

Moore, Harry T. *The Intelligent Heart: The Story of D. H. Lawrence*. New York: Farrar, Strauss and Young, 1954.

Moore, Virginia. *The Unicorn: William Butler Yeats' Search for Reality*. New York: Macmillan, 1954.

Moynahan, Julian. *The Deed of Life: The Novels and Tales of D. H. Lawrence*. Princeton University Press, 1963.

Murry, John Middleton. *Son of Woman: The Story of D. H. Lawrence*. New York: Jonathan Cape, 1931.

Nehls, Edward, ed. *D. H. Lawrence: A Composite Biography*. 3 vols. Madison: University of Wisconsin Press, 1957–9.

Nietzsche, Friedrich. *Beyond Good and Evil: Prelude to a Philosophy of the Future*. Trans. Walter Kaufmann. New York: Vintage, 1966.

" *The Birth of Tragedy*" and " *The Case of Wagner*". Trans. Walter Kaufmann. New York: Vintage, 1967.

"David Strauss, the Confessor and the Writer." *Untimely Meditations*. Trans. R. J. Hollingdale. Cambridge University Press, 1983.

Human, All-Too-Human. Trans. Marion Faber. Lincoln: University of Nebraska Press, 1984.

" *On the Genealogy of Morals*" and " *Ecce Homo*". Trans. Walter Kaufmann and R. J. Hollingdale. New York: Vintage, 1969.

Philosophy in the Tragic Age of the Greeks. Chicago: Regnery, 1962.

The Portable Nietzsche. Trans. Walter Kaufmann. New York: Viking, 1954.

Schopenhauer as Educator. South Bend: Gateway, 1965.

Thus Spoke Zarathustra. Trans. Walter Kaufmann. New York: Viking, 1966.

The Use and Abuse of History. New York: The Liberal Arts Press, 1957.

The Will to Power. Trans. Walter Kaufmann and R. J. Hollingdale. New York: Vintage, 1968.

Oates, Joyce Carol. *New Heaven, New Earth: The Visionary Experience in Literature*. New York: Fawcett Crest, 1974.

O'Keefe, Daniel Lawrence. *Stolen Lightning: The Social Theory of Magic*. New York: Continuum, 1982.

Orage, A. R. *Selected Essays and Critical Writings*. Ed. Herbert Read and Denis Saurat. London: Stanley Nott, 1935.

Osborn, Henry Fairfield. *From the Greeks to Darwin: The Development of the Evolution Idea Through Twenty-Four Centuries*. New York: Scribner's, 1929.

Panichas, George A. "Lawrence and the Ancient Greeks." *The Reverent Discipline: Essays in Criticism and Culture*. Knoxville: University of Tennessee Press, 1974.

Parkes, Henry B. "Emerson." *Emerson: A Collection of Critical Essays*. Ed. Milton Konvitz and Stephen Whicher. Englewood Cliffs: Prentice-Hall, 1962. 121–35.

Peckham, Morse. "Toward a Theory of Romanticism." *PMLA* 66 (1951): 3–23.

Pryse, James M. *The Apocalypse Unsealed*. North Hollywood: Symbols and Signs, 1972.

Putz, Peter. "Nietzsche: Art and Intellectual Inquiry." *Nietzsche: Imagery and Thought: A Collection of Essays*. Ed. Malcolm Pasley. Berkeley: University of California Press, 1978. 1–32.

Ragussis, Michael. *The Subterfuge of Art: Language and the Romantic Tradition*. Baltimore: Johns Hopkins University Press, 1978.

Renan, Ernest. *The Life of Jesus.* New York: Modern Library, 1927.

Schneider, Daniel J. *The Consciousness of D. H. Lawrence: An Intellectual Biography.* Lawrence: University Press of Kansas, 1986.

D. H. Lawrence: The Artist as Psychologist. Lawrence: University Press of Kansas, 1984.

Schopenhauer, Arthur. "Epiphilosophy." *Schopenhauer: Selections.* Ed. DeWitt H. Parker. New York: Scribner's, 1928.

Essays and Aphorisms. Trans. R. J. Hollingdale. Baltimore: Penguin, 1970.

"The Metaphysics of the Love of the Sexes." *Schopenhauer: Selections.* Ed. DeWitt H. Parker. New York: Scribner's, 1928.

The World as Will and Idea. Trans. R. B. Haldane and J. Kemp. Garden City: Doubleday, 1961.

Shelley, Percy Bysshe. *A Defense of Poetry. Selected Poetry.* Ed. Harold Bloom. New York: New American Library, 1966. 415–48.

Sigman, Joseph. "'Diabolico-angelical Indifference': The Imagery of Polarity in *Sartor Resartus.*" *Southern Review* (Australia) 5 (1972): 207–24.

Spencer, Herbert. *First Principles.* New York: De Witt Revolving Fund, 1958.

Spilka, Mark. *The Love Ethic of D. H. Lawrence.* Bloomington: Indiana University Press, 1955.

Steinhauer, Harry. "Eros and Psyche: a Nietzschean motif in Anglo-American Literature." *Modern Language Notes* 64 (1949): 217–228.

Stern, J. P. "Nietzsche and the Idea of Metaphor." *Nietzsche: Imagery and Thought: A Collection of Essays.* Ed. Malcolm Pasley. Berkeley, University of California Press, 1978. 64–82.

A Study of Nietzsche. Cambridge University Press, 1979.

Tansley, David V. *The Subtle Body: Essence and Shadow.* Netherlands: Thames and Hudson, 1977.

Thatcher, David S. *Nietzsche in England 1890–1914: The Growth of a Reputation.* University of Toronto Press, 1970.

Tindall, William York. *D. H. Lawrence and Susan His Cow.* New York: Columbia University Press, 1939.

Vivas, Eliseo. *D. H. Lawrence: The Failure and the Triumph of Love.* Bloomington: Indiana University Press, 1960.

Watts, Alan. *The Two Hands of God: The Myths of Polarity.* New York: Braziller, 1963.

Wellek, Rene. "Emerson and German Philosophy." *Confrontations: Studies in the Intellectual and Literary Relations Between Germany, England, and the United States During the Nineteenth Century.* Princeton University Press, 1965. 187–212.

Wheelwright, Philip. *The Burning Fountain: A Study in the Language of Symbolism*. Bloomington: Indiana University Press, 1968.

    Heraclitus. New York: Atheneum, 1971.

    Metaphor and Reality. Bloomington: Indiana University Press, 1968.

Whelan, P. T. *D. H. Lawrence: Myth and Metaphysic in " The Rainbow" and " Women in Love"*. Ann Arbor: UMI Research Press, 1988.

Whyte, Lancelot Law. *The Unconscious Before Freud*. Garden City: Anchor, 1962.

Widmer, Kingsley. "Lawrence and the Nietzschean Matrix." *D. H. Lawrence and Tradition*. Ed. Jeffrey Meyers. Amherst: University of Massachusetts Press, 1985. 115–31.

Wilson, Edmund. *Axel's Castle: A Study in the Imaginative Literature of 1870–1930*. New York: Norton, 1984.

Wordsworth, William. *Poetical Works*. London: Oxford University Press, 1936.

    The Prelude. Ed. Ernest de Selincourt. London: Oxford University Press: 1960.

Worthen, John. *D. H. Lawrence: The Early Years: 1885–1912*. Cambridge University Press, 1991.

Yeats, William Butler. *The Autobiography of William Butler Yeats*. New York: Collier Books, 1965.

    Essays and Introductions. New York: Collier Books, 1961.

    The Letters of W. B. Yeats. London: Macmillan, 1954.

    Ed. *Oxford Book of Modern Verse 1892–1935*. Oxford: Clarendon Press, 1936.

    A Vision. New York: Macmillan, 1961.

Zoll, Allan R. "Vitalism and the Metaphysics of Love: D. H. Lawrence and Schopenhauer." *D. H. Lawrence Review* 11 (1978): 1–20.

Zytaruk, George J. "The Doctrine of Individuality: D. H. Lawrence's 'Metaphysic.'" *D. H. Lawrence: A Centenary Consideration*. Ed. Peter Balbert and Phillip L. Marcus. Ithaca: Cornell University Press, 1985.

Index

Abrams, M. H., 9, 10, 17–18, 184
Abstract *vs.* concrete distinction, 141–42, 144–47
Aeschylus, 76, 77
Aiken, H. D., 112
Alchemy, 191–207
America, and Spirit of Place, 197–99
American Indians, 150, 151, 198–200
Anaximander, 138–39
Aristotle, 3, 4, 6, 24, 104, 142–43
Arnold, Matthew, 225, 226, 227
Art–philosophy opposition, 106–11. *See also* Philosopher–poets; Philosophy; *specific schools of philosophical thought*
Ascetic saints, 67
Asquith, Cynthia, 147
Astrology, 180–83
Athanor, 195
Auden, W. H., 50, 208
Ayer, A. J., 6

Barfield, O., 21, 22, 23, 24, 25, 26, 37, 71–2, 181–82, 184, 189–200
Beauty, 54, 99
Bell, M., 40, 148
Berdyaev, N., 39, 173
Bergson, Henri, 175, 176
Bhagavad-Gita, 85
Black, M., 16–17, 20, 40, 69–70, 86–87, 160
Blake, William, 7, 8, 19, 85, 126
  Eliot's view of, 221–22
  religion and, 227
  Yeats and, 219
Blavatsky, H. P., 35–36, 168–69, 171–72, 219
Blood *vs.* intellect, 60–72, 151. *See also* Flesh *vs.* Word; Will *vs.* idea

Bloom, H., 21
Body. *See also* Love, physical; Nature; Subtle body
  achievement of unity of mind with, 117–25
  alchemy and, 210, 214–17
  consciousness and, 101, 211–13
  Nietzsche's will to power and, 100
  resurrection of the, 208–17
  Schopenhauer and, 50–51, 62, 70
  symbolical, 215–16
Boehme, Jacob, 40, 42
  alchemical transmutation and, 191, 192, 193, 194–96
  Coleridge and, 41, 170, 185–86
  consciousness and, 68
  fire symbolism in, 171–74, 176
  Lawrence and, 35–36, 170–71
  nature in, 68
  polarity in, 71, 187–89
  subtle body and, 215–16
  theosophy and, 170, 171–75, 180
  Vernunft and *Verstand* and, 211–13
  Yeats and, 219
Bradley, A. C., 21, 40
Bridgewater, P., 74
Brinton, H. H., 175, 185
Brown, N. O., 213–15
Brunsdale, M. M., 46
Burckhardt, T., 192, 205
Burnet, J., 34, 39, 140–41, 147
Burwell, R. M., 45, 74

Campbell, J. R., 28
Carlyle, Thomas, 7, 8, 11
  Sartor Resartus, 11–12, 18, 30–31
Carter, Frederick, 169, 229
Cartesian dualism. *See* Dualism